Everton

EVERTON
THE OFFICIAL GUIDE
2008

Sport Media
A Trinity Mirror Business

HONOURS

DIVISION ONE CHAMPIONS
1890/91, 1914/15, 1927/28, 1931/32, 1938/39, 1962/63, 1969/70, 1984/85, 1986/87

DIVISION ONE RUNNERS-UP
1889/90, 1894/95, 1901/02, 1904/05, 1908/09, 1911/12, 1985/86

DIVISION TWO CHAMPIONS
1930/31

DIVISION TWO RUNNERS-UP
1953/54

FA CUP WINNERS
1906, 1933, 1966, 1984, 1995

FA CUP RUNNERS-UP
1893, 1897, 1907, 1968, 1985, 1986, 1989

LEAGUE CUP RUNNERS-UP
1976/77, 1983/84

FA CHARITY SHIELD WINNERS
(FA COMMUNITY SHIELD)
1928, 1932, 1963, 1970, 1984, 1985, 1987, 1995

FA CHARITY SHIELD SHARED
(FA COMMUNITY SHIELD)
1986

EUROPEAN CUP WINNERS' CUP WINNERS
1984/85

SCREEN SPORT SUPER CUP RUNNERS-UP
1985/86

SIMOD CUP RUNNERS-UP
1988/89

ZENITH DATA SYSTEMS CUP RUNNERS-UP
1990/91

FA YOUTH CUP WINNERS
1964/65, 1983/84, 1997/98

INTRODUCTION

Welcome to the first edition of Everton : The Official Guide 2008, a publication which is sure to become a regular fixture for Evertonians young and old. With information on every aspect of the club's off-field activites together with the most accurate facts, statistics and pictures featuring the Blues on the field, it is a fitting representation of one of England's finest clubs.

To achieve statistical accuracy and maintain the high quality of this product, we have utilised the services of official club statistician Gavin Buckland, who has written and contributed to numerous books about the club and who retains a keen eye for detail involving the current side.

The Guide aims to carry regular features, which will include: 'The Players', up-to-date statistics about the current Everton squad; 'The Boss', an analysis of the current man in charge and 'EFC Records', which aims to maintain the most accurate statistics regarding club appearances, goals and other relevant landmarks.

We also plan to mark landmarks and happenings of the previous 12 months. In this Guide we celebrate the life of Alan Ball, whose untimely death in April touched all Evertonians. We look at the club's full European record, and celebrate the 1984/85 European Cup Winners' Cup run. There's also a chance to recognise Everton ever-presents in the wake of Joseph Yobo playing every minute of the 2006/07 Premiership campaign.

Of course, the full list of 2006/07 statistics are recorded here, and the ultimate aim of the publication will be to act as a permanent record, a point of reference which can solve numerous pub quiz questions. We hope you enjoy what is on offer.

WRITERS

Club statistician Gavin Buckland has provided major statistical support and ideas.
James Cleary has also played a major role in writing, researching and editing key information.

Sport Media
A Trinity Mirror Business

Executive Editor: KEN ROGERS Editor: STEVE HANRAHAN
Art Editor: RICK COOKE Production Editor: PAUL DOVE
Sub Editor: ROY GILFOYLE
Editorial Assistant: JAMES CLEARY
Sales and Marketing Manager: ELIZABETH MORGAN
Design Team: BARRY PARKER, COLIN SUMPTER, GLEN HIND, LEE ASHUN, ALISON GILLILAND, JAMIE DUNMORE, JAMES KENYON
Everton Writers: WILLIAM HUGHES, ALAN JEWELL

ISBN 9781905266432: Printed and finished by Scotprint, Haddington, Scotland

CLUB TELEPHONE NUMBERS

General Enquiries	0870 442 1878
Feedback	0870 442 1878
Box Office	0870 442 1878
Dial-A-Seat	0870 442 1878
Events and Hospitality	0151 330 2499
Marketing Department	0870 442 1878
Corporate Hospitality	0870 442 1878
Graeme Sharp (Fans Liaison Officer)	0870 442 1878
Communications Department	0870 442 1878
Everton Megastore	0870 005 2300/0870 005 2022
Evertonia	0870 442 1878
Everton in the Community	0870 442 1878/0151 330 2307
Everton Against Racism	0870 442 1878
Everton Former Players' Foundation	0151 520 2362
Everton Disabled Supporters' Association	0151 286 9666/0151 330 2217
Lotteries Department	0151 330 2266
International Department	0151 286 6866
Website Enquiries (General)	0870 442 1878
Everton Academy	0870 442 1878
Everton Mastercard	0870 600 5127
Everton Phonestore	0800 049 6055

SUBSCRIBE TO THE OFFICIAL EFC PROGRAMME AND MONTHLY EVERTONIAN MAGAZINE
To take out a subscription please call: 0845 1430001

CLUB WHO'S WHO

Chairman	Bill Kenwright CBE
Deputy Chairman	Jon Woods
Chief Executive & Director	Keith Wyness
Director	Robert Earl
Team Manager	David Moyes
Life President	Sir Philip Carter OBE
Vice-Life President	Keith Tamlin

CONTENTS

THE BOSS

A full analysis of David Moyes' Everton record plus the full statistical record of every Blues boss – from Theo Kelly onwards.

THE PLAYERS 07/08

The Everton playing squad taking into account any changes made by August 31, including statistics and honours won. This section also highlights statistics for the Reserves, Academy and Ladies team, including fixture lists for the season.

TOP 10 MOMENTS 2006/07

A pictorial reminder of the occasions that stood out during last season.

BLUES IN EUROPE

A full account of the club's European results and records plus a look back at the 1984/85 season in European competition.

THE 2006/07 SEASON

A look back at the campaign, documenting results, league progress, new landmarks and quotes of the month including the words of David Moyes.

THE PREMIERSHIP

Full record of Everton in the Premier League, including record appearance holders and goalscorers since 1992/93, plus other fascinating facts and statistics.

THE CUPS

Comprehensive list of Everton's FA Cup and League Cup games, plus other domestic competitions the Blues have participated in.

THE EFC RECORD

Selected information and statistics looking at playing records through Everton history.

PREMIERSHIP OPPONENTS

A look at each top-flight club the Blues will be facing in 2007/08, with useful information related to each club including travel guides, Everton's recent record against each team and other information.

CLUB ESSENTIALS

Everything from ticket information and joining Evertonia to the work of Everton in the Community and Blues legends in the media, this section includes essential information on the club.

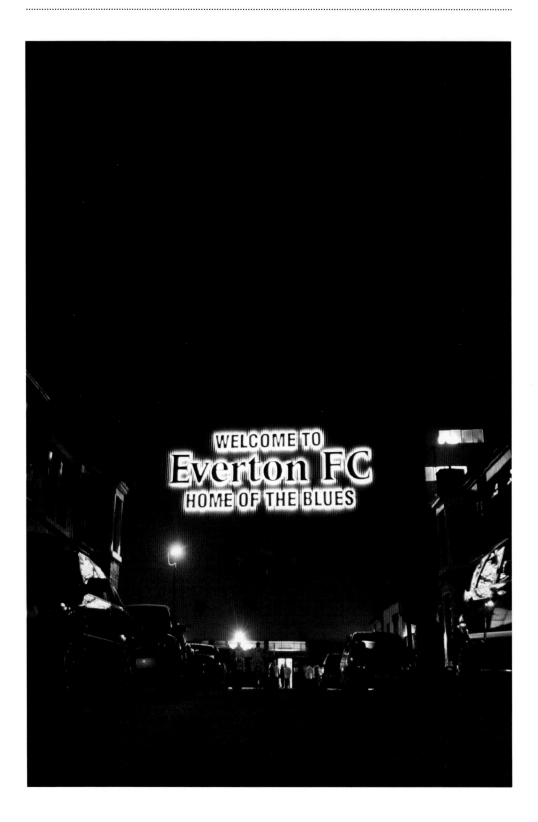

FOREWORD

Welcome to the first edition of Everton : The Official Guide.

After the success of European qualification last season, we are now into our stride in what is sure to be a fascinating new campaign, having further strengthened our squad in the summer to give us the best possible chance of driving forward.

The aim of the Guide is to highlight the rich history and heritage of the People's Club, to ensure a permanent club record of the time and highlight the achievements of the current team.

We work tremendously hard to keep you informed across a range of mediums.

* Our website – evertonfc.tv – remains one of the most popular in the country, and is one of the most established platforms reflecting everything going on at the club.
* *The Evertonian* is the club's official monthly magazine and includes exclusive news, views and interviews with players past and present.
* The *EFC* Programme is bigger than ever for 2007/08 and includes everything you need to enhance the Goodison experience.
* evertonTV is an exclusive service to Evertonians, which continues to grow. It features match action, interviews, archive material and much more.
* BLUES is our bi-monthly magazine aimed at younger Evertonians packed with skills tips, cartoons, Everton news and posters.

Everton : The Official Guide 2008 will tell you everything you need to know about the club, with the aim of becoming a collectable, must-have publication for Evertonians every year. The Guide is the definitive information package for Blues everywhere and is sure to provide you with everything from a club phone number to the answer to any number of teasing statistical queries.

Thanks for your magnificent support of the People's Club.

KEY DATES 2007/2008

(Dates are subject to change)

August 2007

11	Barclays Premier League kick-off
31	UEFA Cup first-round draw
31	Transfer window closes

September 2007

20	UEFA Cup first round, first leg
24 (w/c)	Carling Cup third round

October 2007

4	UEFA Cup first round, second leg
9	UEFA Cup group stage draw (11am)
25	UEFA Cup group stage matchday 1
29 (w/c)	Carling Cup fourth round

November 2007

8	UEFA Cup group stage matchday 2
29	UEFA Cup group stage matchday 3

December 2007

2	European Championship finals draw
3 (w/c)	Carling Cup quarter-finals
5/6	UEFA Cup group stage matchday 4
19/20	UEFA Cup group stage matchday 5
21	UEFA Cup round of 32 & round of 16 draw (12pm)
31	Transfer window re-opens

January 2008

5	FA Cup third round
7 (w/c)	Carling Cup semi-final 1st leg
21 (w/c)	Carling Cup semi-final 2nd leg
26	FA Cup fourth round
31	Transfer window closes (5pm)

KEY DATES 2007/2008

(Dates are subject to change)

February 2008

13/14	UEFA Cup round of 32, first leg
16	FA Cup fifth round
21	UEFA Cup round of 32, second leg
24	Carling Cup final (Wembley Stadium, London)

March 2008

6	UEFA Cup round of 16, first leg
8	FA Cup quarter-finals
12/13	UEFA Cup round of 16, second leg
14	UEFA Cup quarter-finals & semi-finals draw (12pm)

April 2008

3	UEFA Cup quarter-finals, first leg
5	FA Cup semi-finals
10	UEFA Cup quarter-finals, second leg
24	UEFA Cup semi-finals, first leg

May 2008

1	UEFA Cup semi-finals, second leg
11	Barclays Premier League final day
14	UEFA Cup final (City of Manchester Stadium, Manchester, England)
17	FA Cup final (Wembley Stadium, London)

June 2008

7	European Championship finals begin (St. Jakob-Park, Basle)

FIXTURE LIST 2007/2008

August

11	Wigan Athletic	(H)	-	3pm
14	Tottenham Hotspur	(A)	-	8pm
18	Reading	(A)	-	3pm
25	Blackburn Rovers	(H)	-	5.15pm

September

1	Bolton Wanderers	(A)	-	3pm
15	Manchester United	(H)	-	12pm
20	Metalist Kharkiv UEFA CUP	(H)	-	8pm
23	Aston Villa	(A)	-	2pm
26	Sheffield Wednesday C. CUP	(A)	-	7.45pm
30	Middlesbrough	(H)	-	4pm

October

4	Metalist Kharkiv UEFA CUP	(A)	-	TBC
7	Newcastle United	(A)	-	3pm
20	Liverpool	(H)	-	12.45pm
25	UEFA CUP GROUP STAGE MATCHDAY 1			
27*	Derby County	(A)	-	3pm
30/31	CARLING CUP FOURTH ROUND			

November

3	Birmingham City	(H)	-	3pm
8	UEFA CUP GROUP STAGE MATCHDAY 2			
10*	Chelsea	(A)	-	3pm
24	Sunderland	(H)	-	3pm
29	UEFA CUP GROUP STAGE MATCHDAY 3			

December

1*	Portsmouth	(A)	-	3pm
4/5*	CARLING CUP QUARTER-FINALS			
6	UEFA CUP GROUP STAGE MATCHDAY 4			
8*	Fulham	(H)	-	3pm
15	West Ham United	(A)	-	3pm
19/20	UEFA CUP GROUP STAGE MATCHDAY 5			
22*	Manchester United	(A)	-	3pm
26	Bolton Wanderers	(H)	-	3pm
29	Arsenal	(H)	-	3pm

January 2008

1	Middlesbrough	(A)	-	3pm
5	FA CUP THIRD ROUND			
8/9	CARLING CUP SEMI-FINALS, FIRST LEG			
12	Manchester City	(H)	-	3pm
19	Wigan Athletic	(A)	-	3pm

FIXTURE LIST 2007/2008

January 2008

22/23	CARLING CUP SEMI-FINALS, SECOND LEG			
26	FA CUP FOURTH ROUND			
30	Tottenham Hotspur	(H)	-	7.45pm

February

2	Blackburn Rovers	(A)	-	3pm
9	Reading	(H)	-	3pm
13/14	UEFA CUP ROUND OF 32, FIRST LEG			
16*	FA CUP FIFTH ROUND			
21	UEFA CUP ROUND OF 32, SECOND LEG			
23*	Manchester City	(A)	-	3pm
24	CARLING CUP FINAL			

March

1	Portsmouth	(H)	-	3pm
6	UEFA CUP ROUND OF 16, FIRST LEG			
8*	Sunderland	(A)	-	3pm
8*	FA CUP QUARTER-FINALS			
12/13	UEFA CUP ROUND OF 16, SECOND LEG			
15	Fulham	(A)	-	3pm
22	West Ham United	(H)	-	3pm
29	Liverpool	(A)	-	3pm

April

3	UEFA CUP QUARTER-FINALS, FIRST LEG			
5*	FA CUP SEMI-FINALS			
6*	Derby County	(H)	-	3pm
10	UEFA CUP QUARTER-FINALS, SECOND LEG			
12*	Birmingham City	(A)	-	3pm
19	Chelsea	(H)	-	3pm
24	UEFA CUP SEMI-FINALS, FIRST LEG			
26*	Aston Villa	(H)	-	3pm

May

1	UEFA CUP SEMI-FINALS, SECOND LEG			
3*	Arsenal	(A)	-	3pm
11	Newcastle United	(H)	-	3pm
14	UEFA CUP FINAL			
17	FA CUP FINAL			

- Please note all fixtures, kick-off times and dates are subject to change
* Date could change should UEFA Cup progress be made.

GOODISON PARK PAST AND PRESENT

Current Capacity - 40,216

GWLADYS STREET

Like the Bullens Road, originally designed by Archibald Leitch in 1938 (at a cost of £50,000) and also a two-tier structure divided into the Upper and Lower Gwladys Street End. The lower area contains the most vociferous Evertonians, with the home side regularly choosing to kick towards there in the second half. Apart from the lower area being made all-seated in 1991, the only other change in recent times was the structure of a new roof being erected in 1987.

MAIN STAND

Completed in 1971 at a cost of £1m, this structure was the first three-tier development in England when it was constructed, and was the largest in Britain at the time. Consisting of a Family Enclosure, Main Stand and Top Balcony (the latter being reached by escalator), the area also houses corporate boxes. The stand replaced another Archibald Leitch design, built in 1909 at a cost of £28,000, and also incorporates the tunnel onto the pitch leading from the changing rooms. When it was built the floodlight pylons were removed and lamps but on gantries along the roof.

BULLENS ROAD

Two-tier structure designed by Archibald Leitch in 1926, which still incorporates his trademark criss-cross finishing. The area is divided into three sections – Upper and Lower Bullens, plus the Paddock, while the south end of the stand, nearest the Park End, houses away fans. The old-fashioned original roof was replaced in the early 1970s and replaced by a much flatter modern structure and like the Main Stand, gantries incorporating floodlights were installed.

PARK END

Single cantilever stand, built in 1994 to replace the previous two-tier structure that housed away fans, the original being built in 1907 at a cost of £13,000.

NOTES ABOUT THE STADIUM

* The ground staged five games during the 1966 World Cup, including a semi-final (it was due to stage England's last-four tie with Portugal before being switched to Wembley).
* It hosted the 1894 FA Cup final between Notts County and Bolton Wanderers and the FA Cup final replay of 1910 between Newcastle United and Barnsley.
* In 1938, with the development of the Gwladys Street End, it became the first ground in Britain to have four double-decker stands.
* Everton have hosted more international matches than any other English club.
* The first covered dugouts in England were constructed at Goodison Park in 1931, following Everton's visit to Pittodrie to play Aberdeen in a friendly, where such dugouts had been constructed by Dons' trainer Donald Coleman.
* Floodlights came to both Everton and Liverpool in October 1957 – being switched on at Goodison Park for a friendly between the two sides to celebrate the 75th anniversary of Liverpool County FA.
* Undersoil heating was first introduced in 1958.

RECORD GOODISON PARK ATTENDANCES (Highs)

Overall:	78,299 v Liverpool, 18/9/1948
Pre-War:	68,158 v Sunderland, 22/1/1938
League:	78,299 v Liverpool, 18/9/1948
Pre-War:	65,729 v Liverpool, 15/10/1927
FA Cup:	77,920 v Manchester United, 14/2/1953
Pre-War:	68,158 v Sunderland, 22/1/1938
League Cup:	54,032 v Bolton Wanderers, 18/1/1977
Europe:	62,408 v Inter Milan, 18/9/1963

RECORD GOODISON PARK ATTENDANCES (Lows)

Overall:	2,079 v West Bromwich Albion, 23/2/1889
Post-War:	3,703 v Millwall (Simod Cup), 20/12/1988
League Post-War:	10,829 v Fulham, 25/3/1953
FA Cup:	3,000 v Jarrow, 28/1/1899
Post-War:	15,293 v Wimbledon, 12/1/1993
League Cup:	7,415 v Wrexham, 9/10/1990
Europe:	16,277 v UCD, 2/10/1984

EVERTON FUTURE

The year 2007 saw the club confirm plans to move to a new 50,000-seater stadium in Kirkby, four miles from the club's present home, which could open as early as 2010. Season-ticket holders from the past three years, adult Evertonia members and shareholders were all given a vote as to whether the club should leave Goodison Park, and nearly 60% of people who voted were in favour of a move in August 2007.

Chief executive Keith Wyness described the proposed stadium move as the deal of the century, and he has since revealed the following:

On the opportunity to move:
"We're very lucky to have this opportunity; it's a wonderful deal because we'll end up with a stadium with a very low level of debt added to the club."

On stadium design:
"The stadium is four stands. In the discussions we've had with the fans, most of them have said they don't want a bowl. I think, for fans, a sense of place is important – historically, you always had an end. Four stands is definitely a nod to that tradition and it's different from a lot of new stadiums. Along with that, we already know the Cologne stadium is felt to have the best atmosphere of the new stadiums built in Europe. We've incorporated a lot of the design from that stadium to help us improve the atmosphere. We have worked on atmosphere and tradition. It also leaves us scope to expand in the future if we need to."

On moving outside the traditional Liverpool boundary:
"Part of this whole decision must be based on the future. Right now the plans are working towards a city region, which would include Sefton, Knowsley, Liverpool, St Helens and Halton. That would become Greater Liverpool. I think that's what you must look at – that's what our children will grow up with. I find it very hard to accept the argument that Kirkby is not part of Liverpool. It's like saying Bootle is not part of Liverpool. Kirkby is an 'L' postcode. It's a random administrative boundary that was drawn up. This is Liverpool as far as I'm concerned."

On voting on the decision:
"Yes, it's true, most clubs have not, they just decided to go ahead and impose it. I think we have a certain different culture at Everton and I hope the fans respected that we tried our best to do a very inclusive ballot. We initially thought it was going to be 30,000 fans eligible to vote, but it was closer to 40,000. That is a very big representation of the Everton fan base. I think that says a lot about the football club, and how fair we are and how transparent we are. We have been very open through this whole process about all the questions and answers that fans have got."

On the importance of the decision to move to a new stadium:
"I think it is. I can't see anything that could be bigger than actually moving the spiritual home of the club. I don't underestimate in any way, shape or form how serious this decision is. But we have to understand that options like this, the one we have on the table right now, do not come along that often either. It's something I believe we should grab with both hands."

Stadium plans: The views from outside and inside the proposed new stadium

FROM BELLEFIELD TO FINCH FARM

The 2007/08 season sees the club move to Finch Farm, a new state-of-the-art training ground in the south of Liverpool, leaving Bellefield, their traditional training headquarters, after well over half a century.
Although first used by Everton in 1946, it wasn't until the mid 1960s that the club bought the grounds from builder William Tyson for an estimated £25,000.
It was developed for the World Cup in England in 1966, although Brazil, who were originally supposed to use the facility, stayed elsewhere in the region.
A frequent visitor during the period would be Liverpool manager Bill Shankly, who lived on Bellefield Road and was always made welcome by the Everton staff including Doug Rose, who was on the Everton groundstaff for half a century. Doug lived in a house within the grounds from 1966 until 2005.

The new facility at Finch Farm in Halewood will be home to the senior squad and the Everton Academy, and will boast some of the finest training facilities in the world. The new complex boasts 10 full-size pitches, one of which will be floodlit along with an additional floodlit synthetic pitch and specialist training areas for fitness work and goalkeepers. The complex will also include a gym, synthetic indoor training pitch, hydrotherapy pools, spa, sauna, physiotherapy rooms, media centre and video lounges, including a video editing suite.

The address for the new site is:
Finch Lane
Halewood
Knowsley
Liverpool
L26 3UE

A new scene: Artist impressions of the new facility from Finch Lane

Bellefield scenes: Pre-season training, July 1971 (above) and Bellefield plaques

EVERTON'S MANAGERS

The 2007/08 campaign marks the beginning of David Moyes' 6th full season in charge at Goodison, a period which should see him become the longest-serving manager (in one spell) since Harry Catterick.

Moyes is Everton's 13th full-time boss, and in terms of results one of the most successful despite the lack of silverware claimed in arguably the most difficult of footballing environments.

Everton were one of the last clubs to be led by one man, thus it was 1939 before then club secretary Theo Kelly was appointed, bringing an end to team selection via a committee of club officials.

For the record Howard Kendall remains the club's most successful manager. Like Harry Catterick, he led the Blues to the title twice and also won the FA Cup, but unlike "The Cat", Kendall led his side to European success in 1985.

DAVID MOYES	**March 2002-Present**
WALTER SMITH	July 1998-March 2002
HOWARD KENDALL	June 1997-June 1998
DAVE WATSON (caretaker)	April 1997-May 1997
JOE ROYLE	November 1994-March 1997
MIKE WALKER	January 1994-November 1994
JIMMY GABRIEL (caretaker)	December 1993-January 1994
HOWARD KENDALL	November 1990-December 1993
JIMMY GABRIEL (caretaker)	November 1990
COLIN HARVEY	June 1987-October 1990
HOWARD KENDALL	May 1981-June 1987
GORDON LEE	January 1977-May 1981
STEVE BURTENSHAW (caretaker)	January 1977
BILLY BINGHAM	May 1973-January 1977
TOM EGGLESTON (caretaker)	April 1973-May 1973
HARRY CATTERICK	April 1961-April 1973
JOHNNY CAREY	October 1958-April 1961
IAN BUCHAN	August 1956-September 1958
CLIFF BRITTON	September 1948-February 1956
THEO KELLY	June 1939-September 1948

DAVID MOYES'S RECORD

Now part of Goodison folklore, David Moyes' proclamations that Everton are the "People's Club" upon his appointment in March 2002 struck a chord with supporters who were at a low ebb.

The dismissal of Walter Smith on the back of a live televised FA Cup quarter-final debacle at Middlesbrough, coupled with week-to-week Premiership struggles highlighted the need for a new broom, stability and progress. And looking back on that time over five years later, it is fair to say that despite a failure to land silverware and underachievement in the cup competitions, the Scot has proved a canny operator both tactically and in the transfer market.

His achievements on a limited budget compared to many in the top flight have included European qualification twice (including Champions League qualifier participation) and steady squad and result improvement. Recognition has included twice being named LMA Manager of the Year in 2003 and 2005, performances achieved after massively exceeding expectations following relatively poor seasons the previous year.

The following statistics are a breakdown of Moyes' fifth full season at the helm, and his overall record in charge.

2006/2007 SEASON

	Pld	W	HOME D	L	F	A	W	AWAY D	L	F	A	GD	Pts
LEAGUE	38	11	4	4	33	17	4	9	6	19	19	+16	58
FA CUP	1	0	0	1	1	4	0	0	0	0	0	-	-
LEAGUE CUP	3	1	0	1	4	1	1	0	0	2	1	-	-
TOTAL	42	12	4	6	38	22	5	9	6	21	20	-	-

Pld	W	D	L	F	A
42	17	13	12	59	42

OVERALL MOYES RECORD

	Pld	W	D	L	F	A	Pts
LEAGUE	199	77	49	73	242	259	279
FA CUP	12	4	3	5	17	19	-
LEAGUE CUP	13	6	3	4	22	15	-
CHAMPIONS LEAGUE	2	0	0	2	2	4	-
UEFA CUP	2	1	0	1	2	5	-
TOTAL	228	88	55	85	285	302	-

(*PENALTY SHOOT-OUTS COUNTED AS DRAWS)

Correct at 10th August 2007

KELLY TO MOYES - THE EVERTON MANAGERS

Theo Kelly

First game: Preston North End (a – FA Cup), 5/1/1946
Last game: Liverpool (h), 18/9/1948

	P	W	D	L	F	A
League	93	35	17	41	120	160
FA Cup	9	3	3	3	17	14
Total	102	38	20	44	137	174

Everton were one of the last clubs to hand the managerial reigns over to one man, and when Theo Kelly was appointed in 1939 it brought an end to team selection by committee or by club officials. The then club secretary was the first of the Toffees' 13 permanent first-team managers.

Kelly's first seven years saw Everton engaged in regional matches following the outbreak of World War Two. The resumption of League football saw Everton minus the services of Tommy Lawton and Joe Mercer, who had moved to Chelsea and Arsenal respectively. The club never recovered from the sale of those players and Kelly was relieved of his duties in 1948.

Cliff Britton

First game: Preston North End (h), 25/9/1948
Last game: Arsenal (a), 21/2/1956

	P	W	D	L	F	A
League	316	110	90	116	459	496
FA Cup	23	15	1	7	38	31
Total	339	125	91	123	497	527

Bristol-born Cliff Britton was one of the finest players to appear for the club in the pre-World War Two era. A wing-half of class and vision, he played in both the 1932 League and 1933 FA Cup-winning sides.

Britton came to Goodison in September 1948 and although he took Everton to an FA Cup semi-final two years later, the former Burnley manager watched over as the Toffees were relegated for only the second time in their history in 1951. Although Everton bounced back three years later, in 1956 Britton resigned following a disagreement with the Board.

Ian Buchan

First game: Leeds United (a), 18/8/1956
Last game: Leeds (h), 20/9/1958

	P	W	D	L	F	A
League	93	29	21	43	137	179
FA Cup	6	3	1	2	9	7
Total	99	32	22	45	146	186

The Scot's appointment as successor to Britton was – and still is now – regarded as a strange choice. A coach, rather than a manager, Buchan failed to ignite the side in his two-year stay.

KELLY TO MOYES - THE EVERTON MANAGERS

Johnny Carey

First game: Blackpool (a), 25/10/1958
Last game: Newcastle United (a), 8/4/1961

	P	W	D	L	F	A
League	110	44	21	45	196	191
FA Cup	6	2	1	3	11	11
League Cup	5	4	0	1	14	5
Total	121	50	22	49	222	208

One of the most influential players of the immediate post-War years, the former Manchester United captain was charged with overseeing John Moores'-funded Goodison revolution. Although Carey enjoyed relative success compared with his predecessors – he was primarily responsible for a fifth-place league finish in 1960/61, the club's highest in the post-War era – his managerial style was not to Moores' liking and in April 1961 this likeable and honourable man was famously relieved of his duties in the back of a London taxi. His successor, though, would set the standards for all subsequent Everton managers.

Harry Catterick

First game: Sheffield Wednesday (a), 22/4/1961
Last game: Coventry City (h), 7/4/1973

	P	W	D	L	F	A
League	500	225	137	138	795	586
FA Cup	53	32	9	12	93	46
League Cup	12	5	2	5	19	10
Europe	24	11	8	5	37	24
Other	5	3	1	1	10	4
Total	594	276	157	162	954	670

Harry Catterick's brand of management was ruthless and shrewd but was exactly what John Moores required. Arriving from Goodison after success at Sheffield Wednesday, the former Everton centre-forward was wise enough to realise that Carey's legacy – Alex Parker, Brian Labone, Jimmy Gabriel, Billy Bingham, Roy Vernon and Alex Young – was a sound base for mounting a Championship-winning campaign. So rather than make wholesale changes, Catterick reinforced the team with a limited number of signings – Gordon West, Johnny Morrissey and Dennis Stevens – and that strategy enabled the Toffees to romp to the title with a club record 61 points in 1962/63.

For the rest of the decade Catterick enhanced his reputation as a manager who respected the best traditions of the *School of Science*. The FA Cup was won for a third time in 1966 – the only season Everton finished outside the top six during the decade. After signing Alan Ball that summer, Catterick built a second great side that was good enough to win a seventh league title in 1970.

A combination of several factors contributed to the team's demise and with Catterick losing his Midas touch in the transfer market, Everton's first great manager accepted a move upstairs in 1973.

KELLY TO MOYES - THE EVERTON MANAGERS

Billy Bingham

First game: Leeds United (a), 25/8/1973
Last game: Stoke City (h – FA Cup), 8/1/1977

	P	W	D	L	F	A
League	146	53	48	45	197	194
FA Cup	9	4	2	3	13	7
League Cup	13	7	3	3	19	11
Europe	2	0	1	1	0	1
Other	2	0	1	1	0	1
Total	172	64	55	53	229	214

The former Everton winger had established a sound reputation as a manager after leaving Goodison in 1963, and the Irishman was unfortunate in 1974/75 not to lead Everton to another league title victory. With Martin Dobson and Bob Latchford now established in the side, Everton spent the season as favourites for the crown, but disastrous defeats in the home straight to relegated Luton Town and Carlisle United gifted the title to Derby County.

The side did not really recover; following a patchy and inconsistent 18 months Bingham left the club in January 1977. But his greatest managerial days lay ahead and he memorably took Northern Ireland to two World Cup finals in 1982 and 1986.

Gordon Lee

First game: Swindon Town (h – FA Cup), 30/1/1977
Last game: Wolverhampton Wanderers (a), 4/5/1981

	P	W	D	L	F	A
League	188	69	63	56	256	215
FA Cup	20	11	4	5	39	26
League Cup	20	9	5	6	39	23
Europe	6	3	0	3	12	4
Total	234	92	72	70	346	268

The former Aston Villa defender moved from Newcastle United to replace Bingham. The Toffees were still in both Cup competitions and within two months Lee led Everton out at Wembley in the League Cup final. An unlucky defeat to Aston Villa in a second replay was typical of his four-year spell as manager, when luck deserted the side at key moments.

The following season his Everton team – inspired by Latchford's 30 League goals – were top-scorers in the First Division and went 22 matches without defeat. The 1978/79 season saw a record-breaking 19-match unbeaten start to the League campaign, but two disappointing seasons followed and Lee left in May 1981.

Clockwise from top left: Former managers Harry Catterick, Billy Bingham, Colin Harvey and Howard Kendall, plus Gordon Lee

KELLY TO MOYES - THE EVERTON MANAGERS

Howard Kendall

First game: Birmingham City (h), 29/8/1981
Last game: Tottenham Hotspur (h), 11/5/1987

	P	W	D	L	F	A
League	252	131	59	62	422	255
FA Cup	31	21	5	5	49	23
League Cup	33	17	9	7	58	33
Europe	9	7	2	0	16	2
Other	13	7	3	3	22	16
Total	338	183	78	77	567	329

A great midfield player in the 1970 Championship-winning side, Everton's most successful-ever manager survived a notoriously rocky patch in the second half of 1983 to emerge triumphant with the FA Cup to end a barren spell of 14 years without a trophy. The 1984/85 season was quite magnificent, as the side chased a unique treble, with the reward being a dominant League Championship triumph and a glorious victory in Rotterdam in the Cup Winners' Cup final.

The following season saw a double disappointment at the hands of Liverpool but Kendall's side regrouped doggedly and the Toffees regained the title in 1987 despite a lengthy injury list. The double-title winner left Goodison in the summer for a new challenge in Spain with Athletic Bilbao, although he would return for two further spells.

Colin Harvey

First game: Coventry City (Wembley – FA Charity Shield), 1/8/1987
Last game: Sheffield United (a – League Cup), 30/10/1990

	P	W	D	L	F	A
League	126	51	37	38	173	135
FA Cup	23	9	11	3	33	20
League Cup	19	10	4	5	37	18
Other	7	5	0	2	13	8
Total	175	75	52	48	256	181

As a magnificent Toffees midfield player in his own right and as one half of a hugely successful managerial duo, the hugely respected and gifted first-team coach was the natural successor for Kendall when he left Goodison. On face value, three finishes in the top eight in his three full seasons – plus Simod Cup and FA Cup final appearances in 1989 – were highly creditable, but the standards of the proceeding years were a benchmark.

The defence had become increasingly impregnable – in his first season a club-record low of 27 goals was conceded – but the European ban led indirectly to the departure of Gary Stevens and Trevor Steven. Home form was formidable, with 38 league wins and just six defeats at Goodison in three seasons, but on their travels the side failed to match that standard. With injuries to key players and the failure of new signings to settle, Harvey's task was becoming increasingly more difficult and he departed in October 1990. But one of Everton's greatest servants was back sooner than expected...

KELLY TO MOYES - THE EVERTON MANAGERS

Howard Kendall

First game: Sheffield United (a), 10/11/1990
Last game: Southampton (h), 4/12/1993

	P	W	D	L	F	A
League	129	46	33	50	159	158
FA Cup	10	4	3	3	11	10
League Cup	15	8	3	4	28	20
Other	8	5	1	2	20	14
Total	162	63	40	59	218	202

"Manchester City was a like a love affair while Everton is like a marriage," proclaimed the former Everton boss as he left Maine Road and returned to Goodison nine years after taking his first bow in 1981. With Colin Harvey back as well supporters hoped that the magic of the mid-1980s could return, but the footballing landscape had changed and although his second spell was not a disaster, the team failed to progress and Kendall resigned midway through the 1993/94 campaign.

Mike Walker

First game: Bolton Wanderers (h – FA Cup), 8/1/1994
Last game: Norwich City (a), 5/11/1994

	P	W	D	L	F	A
League	31	6	9	16	29	52
FA Cup	2	0	1	1	3	4
League Cup	2	0	1	1	3	4
Total	35	6	11	18	35	60

Eighteen months of success at Carrow Road, incorporating a third-place finish in the Premiership and a memorable UEFA Cup run, was enough evidence to convince the Goodison hierarchy and other observers that the former Watford and Colchester goalkeeper was the right man for the manager's job. But after a final-day escape in May 1994 against Wimbledon, a poor start to the 1994/95 campaign heralded his exit and the arrival of a former player whose appointment as Everton boss was considered long overdue.

Joe Royle

First game: Liverpool (h), 21/11/1994
Last game: Manchester United (h), 22/3/1997

	P	W	D	L	F	A
League	97	36	31	30	136	116
FA Cup	12	8	2	2	26	12
League Cup	4	0	2	2	5	8
Europe	4	2	1	1	6	4
Other	1	1	0	0	1	0
Total	118	47	36	35	174	140

A derby victory was a hugely significant way to start a managerial career at Goodison and after securing Everton's Premiership safety, one of the club's finest centre-forwards led the Toffees to a hugely deserved FA Cup final triumph at Wembley against Manchester United at the end of 1994/95.

With Andrei Kanchelskis providing pace and goals from the right flank, a strong finish to the 1995/96 season brought a club Premiership record 61 points and 64 goals. But with hopes high at the start of the 1996/97 season, a crippling injury list hit the club hard after Christmas. Royle left in March 1997 having set one notable record: the only Everton manager not to lose a derby game.

KELLY TO MOYES - THE EVERTON MANAGERS

Howard Kendall

First game: Crystal Palace (h), 9/8/1997
Last game: Coventry City (h), 10/5/1998

	P	W	D	L	F	A
League	38	9	13	16	41	56
FA Cup	1	0	0	1	0	1
League Cup	3	2	0	1	7	4
Total	42	11	13	18	48	61

After Dave Watson had safely steered Everton away from the relegation zone in the spring of 1997, Kendall returned to Goodison to hopefully provide some much-needed stability. The club's top-flight status was maintained, but only after a heart-stopping draw on the final day against Coventry City.

Walter Smith

First game: Aston Villa (h), 15/8/1998
Last game: Middlesbrough (a – FA Cup), 10/3/2002

	P	W	D	L	F	A
League	143	41	42	60	173	190
FA Cup	16	10	2	4	21	16
League Cup	9	2	6	1	11	10
Total	168	53	50	65	205	216

Following success with Glasgow Rangers, Walter Smith headed south of the border in 1998 and he was poached as Everton boss from under the noses of Sheffield Wednesday. But with stability on the pitch threatened by uncertainty off it – only ended when Bill Kenwright's consortium took over the club at the end of 1999 – the former Rangers' manager was unable to bring the success the club and fans craved.

David Moyes

First game: Fulham (h), 16/3/2002

	P	W	D	L	F	A
League	199	77	49	73	242	259
FA Cup	12	4	3	5	17	19
League Cup	13	6	3	4	22	15
Europe	4	1	0	3	4	9
Total	228	88	55	85	285	302

One of the most promising young managers in the country spent little time in announcing his arrival at Goodison – 32 seconds in fact, or the time it took David Unsworth to score the Toffees' first goal in the former Preston North End manager's first game in charge.

After four wins in nine matches secured the club's safety in 2001/02, Moyes' next season saw a sustained challenge for Europe, one that was scuppered by a final-day defeat by Manchester United. Although the following season saw a drop down the table, in 2004/05 the Toffees finished fourth – the best for 17 years – and qualified for the Champions' League after memorable Goodison wins over Liverpool and United.

A mid-table position followed but in 2006/07 Everton – fortified by new-boys Tim Howard, Joleon Lescott and Andy Johnson – arguably enjoyed their most consistent season for nearly 20 years, losing only 10 matches and conceding just 36 goals. In only two games – Manchester United and Portsmouth away – were Everton out of the game going into the final 10 minutes. Highlights were many, but the ending of the White Hart Lane hoodoo and a tumultuous derby win in successive games in the late summer sunshine took some beating.

MOYES' 200 UP

The opening game of the 2007/08 season saw David Moyes become only the fourth manager to take charge of Everton in 200 league matches. Here's how his record compares to other Everton managers in league games (correct at end of 2006/07 campaign).

Manager	Games	W	D	L	PTS	Pts per game
Harry Catterick	500	225	137	138	812	1.62
Cliff Britton	316	110	90	116	420	1.33
Howard Kendall (81-87)	252	131	59	62	452	1.79
David Moyes	199	77	49	73	280	1.41
Gordon Lee	188	69	63	56	270	1.44
Billy Bingham	146	53	48	45	207	1.42
Walter Smith	143	41	42	60	165	1.15
Howard Kendall (90-91)	129	46	33	50	171	1.33
Colin Harvey	126	51	37	38	190	1.51
Johnny Carey	110	44	21	45	153	1.39
Joe Royle	97	36	31	30	139	1.43
Theo Kelly	93	35	17	41	122	1.31
Ian Buchan	93	29	21	43	108	1.16
Howard Kendall (97-98)	38	9	13	16	40	1.05
Mike Walker	31	6	9	16	27	0.87
Howard Kendall (Overall)	419	186	105	128	663	1.58

THE SQUAD 2007/08

Tim Howard

Position	Goalkeeper
Born	North Brunswick, New Jersey, USA
Age (at start of 07/08)	28
Birth date	06/03/79
Height	6ft 3ins
Other clubs	New Jersey Imperials, MetroStars, Man Utd
Honours	2003 FA Comm. Shield, 2004 FA Cup, 2006 League Cup
Everton debut	19/08/06 v Watford
Everton appearances	38 + 0 as substitute
Everton goals	0
International caps	23 (0 goals)
International honours	2007 Gold Cup

John Ruddy

Position	Goalkeeper
Born	St Ives, Cambridgeshire
Age (at start of 07/08)	20
Birth date	24/10/86
Height	6ft 4ins
Other clubs	Cambridge U, Walsall, Rushden, Chester City, Stockport C, Wrexham, Bristol City
Honours	-
Everton debut	11/02/06 v Blackburn R
Everton appearances	0 + 1 as substitute
Everton goals	0

Iain Turner

Position	Goalkeeper
Born	Stirling, Scotland
Age (at start of 07/08)	23
Birth date	26/01/84
Height	6ft 4ins
Other clubs	Stirling, Chester City, Doncaster, Wycombe, Crystal Palace, Sheff Wed
Honours	2004 Conference
Everton debut	08/02/06 v Chelsea
Everton appearances	5 + 1 as substitute
Everton goals	0

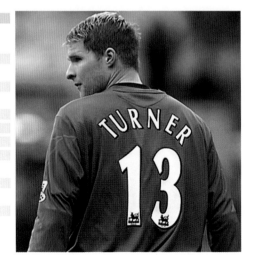

Stefan Wessels

Position	Goalkeeper
Born	Rahden, Germany
Age (at start of 07/08)	28
Birth date	28/02/79
Height	6ft 3ins
Other clubs	Bayern Munich, FC Cologne
Honours	1999, 2000 German League Cup, 2000, 2001, 2003 German League, 2000, 2003 German Cup, 2001 Champions League, 2001 Intercontinental Cup, 2005 German Second Division
Everton debut	-
Everton appearances	-
Everton goals	-

Leighton Baines

Position	Left-back
Born	Liverpool
Age (at start of 07/08)	22
Birth date	11/12/84
Height	5ft 8ins
Other club	Wigan Athletic
Honours	-
Everton debut	-
Everton appearances	0
Everton goals	0

Patrick Boyle

Position	Left-back
Born	Glasgow, Scotland
Age (at start of 07/08)	20
Birth date	20/03/87
Height	5ft 10ins
Other club	Norwich City
Honours	-
Everton debut	-
Everton appearances	0
Everton goals	0

Tony Hibbert

Position	Right-back
Born	Liverpool
Age (at start of 07/08)	26
Birth date	20/02/81
Height	5ft 8ins
Other clubs	-
Honours (Youth)	1998 FA Youth Cup
Everton debut	31/03/01 v West Ham
Everton appearances	152 + 10 as substitute
Everton goals	0

Joleon Lescott

Position	Left/Central Defence
Born	Birmingham
Age (at start of 07/08)	24
Birth date	16/08/82
Height	6ft 2ins
Other clubs	Wolverhampton W.
Honours	2003 Championship Play-Off Winner
Everton debut	19/08/06 v Watford
Everton appearances	40 + 2 as substitute
Everton goals	2

Phil Neville

Position	Right/Central Defence or Midfield
Born	Bury
Age (at start of 07/08)	30
Birth date	21/01/77
Height	5ft 11ins
Other club	Manchester United
Honours	1996, 1997, 1999, 2000, 2001, 2003 League, 1996, 1999, 2004 FA Cup, 1997, 2003 FA Community Shield, 1999 Ch. Lge,
Everton debut	09/08/05 v Villarreal
Everton appearances	81 + 0 as substitute
Everton goals	1
International caps	56 (0 goals)

Alan Stubbs

Position	Central Defence
Born	Kirkby, Merseyside
Age (at start of 07/08)	35
Birth date	06/10/71
Height	6ft 2ins
Other clubs	Bolton W, Celtic, Everton, Sunderland
Honours	1995 C'ship Play-Off Winner,1998, 2001 Scottish League, 2001 Scottish Cup, 1998, 2000 Scottish League Cup
Everton debuts	18/08/01 v Charlton, 21/01/06 v Arsenal
Everton appearances	170 + 10 as substitute
Everton goals	6

Nuno Valente

Position	Left-back
Born	Lisbon, Portugal
Age (at start of 07/08)	32
Birth date	12/09/74
Height	5ft 11ins
Other clubs	Portimonense, S. Lisbon, Maritimo, U. Leiria, FC Porto
Honours	1995 Portuguese Cup, 2003, 2004 Portuguese Lge, 2003 UEFA Cup, 2004 Champions Lge, 2004 World Club C'ship
Everton debut	10/09/05 v Portsmouth
Everton appearances	39 + 4 as substitute
Everton goals	0
International caps	33 (1 goal)

Joseph Yobo

Position	Central Defence
Born	Kano, Nigeria
Age (at start of 07/08)	26
Birth date	06/09/80
Height	6ft 0ins
Other clubs	Standard Liege, Marseille, Tenerife
Honours	-
Everton debut	28/09/02 v Fulham
Everton appearances	152 + 12 as substitute
Everton goals	6
International caps	48 (2 goals)

Mikel Arteta

Position	Left/Centre/Right Midfield
Born	San Sebastian, Spain
Age (at start of 07/08)	25
Birth date	26/03/82
Height	5ft 9ins
Other clubs	Barcelona, Paris SG, Rangers, Real Sociedad
Honours	2003 Scottish League, 2003 Scottish Cup, 2003 Scottish Lge Cup
Everton debut	06/02/05 v Southampton
Everton appearances	84 + 5 substitute
Everton goals	13

Tim Cahill

Position	Central Midfield
Born	Sydney, Australia
Age (at start of 07/08)	27
Birth date	06/12/79
Height	5ft 10ins
Other clubs	Sydney United, Millwall
Honours	-
Everton debut	30/08/04 v Man Utd
Everton appearances	94 + 4 as substitute
Everton goals	27
International caps	27 (12 goals)

Lee Carsley

Position	Central Midfield
Born	Birmingham
Age (at start of 07/08)	33
Birth date	28/02/74
Height	5ft 11ins
Other clubs	Derby County, Blackburn Rovers, Coventry City
Honours	-
Everton debut	10/02/02 v Arsenal
Everton appearances	136 + 13 substitute
Everton goals	12
International caps (Eire)	34 (0 goals)

Thomas Gravesen (on loan from Celtic)

Position	Midfield
Born	Vejle, Denmark
Age (at start of 07/08)	31
Birth date	11/03/76
Height	5ft 10ins
Other clubs	Vejle Boldklub, Hamburg, Everton, Real Madrid, Celtic
Honours	2007 Scottish League
Everton debut (1st spell)	23/08/00 v Charlton Athletic
Everton appearances	143 + 12 as substitute
Everton goals	12
International caps	66 (5 goals)

Phil Jagielka

Position	Right/Central Defence or Midfield
Born	Sale
Age (at start of 07/08)	24
Birth date	17/08/82
Height	5ft 11ins
Other club	Sheffield United
Honours	-
Everton debut	-
Everton appearances	-
Everton goals	-

Leon Osman

Position	Midfield
Born	Billinge
Age (at start of 07/08)	26
Birth date	17/05/81
Height	5ft 8ins
Other clubs	Carlisle United, Derby County
Honours (Youth)	1998 FA Youth Cup
Everton debut	12/01/03 v Tottenham Hotspur
Everton appearances	98 + 23 as substitute
Everton goals	15

Steven Pienaar (on loan from Bor. Dortmund)

Position	Midfield
Born	Johannesburg, South Africa
Age (at start of 07/08)	25
Birth date	17/03/82
Height	5ft 9ins
Other clubs	Ajax, Borussia Dortmund
Honours	2002 Dutch Cup, 2004 Dutch League
Everton debut	-
Everton appearances	-
Everton goals	-
International caps	20 (0 goals)

Anderson Silva de Franca

Position	Central Midfield
Born	Sao Paulo, Brazil
Age (at start of 07/08)	24
Birth date	29/08/82
Height	6ft 1ins
Other clubs	Nacional, Santiago Wanderers, Racing Santander, Malaga
Honours	-
Everton debut	15/04/07 v Charlton Athletic
Everton appearances	0 + 1 as substitute
Everton goals	0

Andy Van der Meyde

Position	Left/Right Midfield
Born	Arnhem, Holland
Age (at start of 07/08)	27
Birth date	30/09/79
Height	5ft 10ins
Other clubs	Ajax, FC Twente, Inter Milan
Honours	1998, 2002 Dutch League, 1998, 1999, 2002 Dutch Cup
Everton debut	26/10/05 v Middlesbrough
Everton appearances	14 + 7 as substitute
Everton goals	0
International caps	18 (1 goal)

Bjarni Vidarsson

Position	Central Midfield
Born	Reykjavik, Iceland
Age (at start of 07/08)	19
Birth date	05/03/88
Height	6ft 1ins
Other clubs	Bournemouth
Honours	-
Everton debut	-
Everton appearances	-
Everton goals	-

Ayegbeni Yakubu

Position	Centre Forward
Born	Benin City, Nigeria
Age (at start of 07/08)	24
Birth date	22/11/82
Height	6ft 1ins
Other clubs	Julius Berger, Hapoel Kfar Saba, Maccabi Haifa, Portsmouth, Middlesbrough
Honours	2001, 2002 Israeli League, 2002 Toto Cup (Israel), 2003 C'ship winner
Everton debut	-
Everton appearances	-
Everton goals	-
International caps	19 (5 goals)

Victor Anichebe

Position	Centre Forward
Born	Lagos, Nigeria
Age (at start of 07/08)	19
Birth date	23/04/88
Height	6ft 1ins
Other clubs	-
Honours	-
Everton debut	28/01/06 v Chelsea
Everton appearances	7 + 19 as substitute
Everton goals	5

Andrew Johnson

Position	Centre Forward
Born	Bedford
Age (at start of 07/08)	26
Birth date	10/02/81
Height	5ft 7ins
Other clubs	Birmingham City, Crystal Palace
Honours	2004 Championship Play-Off Winner
Everton debut	19/08/06 v Watford
Everton appearances	35
Everton goals	12
International caps	7 (0 goals)

Lukas Jutkiewicz

Position	Forward
Born	Southampton
Age (at start of 07/08)	18
Birth date	28/03/89
Height	6ft 1ins
Other club	Swindon Town
Honours	-
Everton debut	-
Everton appearances	0
Everton goals	0

James McFadden

Position	Left/Centre Midfield or Forward
Born	Glasgow, Scotland
Age (at start of 07/08)	24
Birth date	14/04/83
Height	5ft 10ins
Other club	Motherwell
Honours	-
Everton debut	21/09/03 v Middlesbrough
Everton appearances	65 + 53 as substitute
Everton goals	13
International caps	31 (10 goals)

James Vaughan

Position	Centre Forward
Born	Birmingham
Age (at start of 07/08)	19
Birth date	14/07/88
Height	5ft 11ins
Other clubs	-
Honours	-
Everton debut	10/04/05 v Crystal Palace
Everton appearances	7 + 11 as substitute
Everton goals	5

SQUAD NUMBERS
2007/08

2 Tony Hibbert
3 Leighton Baines
4 Joseph Yobo
5 Joleon Lescott
6 Mikel Arteta
7 Andy Van der Meyde
8 Andy Johnson
10 Thomas Gravesen
11 James McFadden
12 Iain Turner
14 James Vaughan
15 Alan Stubbs
16 Phil Jagielka
17 Tim Cahill

18 Phil Neville
19 Nuno Valente
20 Steven Pienaar
21 Leon Osman
22 Ayegbeni Yakubu
24 Tim Howard
25 Anderson de Silva Franca
26 Lee Carsley
27 Lukas Jutkiewicz
28 Victor Anichebe
29 Patrick Boyle
30 John Ruddy
31 Bjarni Vidarsson
33 Stefan Wessels

RESERVES

RESERVES APPEARANCES & GOALS 2006/07

	Appearances	Goals
Kieran Agard	9	1
Victor Anichebe	8	1
Patrick Boyle	1	0
Stephen Connor	11	0
Darren Dennehy	11	0
Shaun Densmore	7	1
Aidan Downes	5	0
Matthew Elder	4	0
Ryan Harpur	4	0
Tony Hibbert	4	0
Mark Hughes	7	4
John Irving	17	0
Jamie Jones	2	0
Alan Kearney	12	0
John Paul Kissock	13	0
James McFadden	3	4
Lee Molyneux	13	1
Steven Morrison	8	0
Gary Naysmith	3	0
Scott Phelan	15	0
Alessandro Pistone	2	0
Jack Rodwell	4	0
John Ruddy	7	0
Anderson Silva de Franca	6	0
Scott Spencer	5	0
Iain Turner	4	0
Nuno Valente	2	1
Andy Van der Meyde	5	0
James Vaughan	9	3
Bjarni Vidarsson	14	1
David Weir	3	0
Richard Wright	5	0

RESERVES LEAGUE NORTH TABLE 2006/07

		Pld	W	D	L	F	A	Pts
1	Bolton Wan.	18	10	3	5	21	16	33
2	Man Utd	18	9	4	5	24	17	31
3	Middlesboro	18	9	3	6	31	25	30
4	Man City	18	9	2	7	27	24	29
5	Liverpool	18	8	2	8	24	19	26
6	Blackburn R.	18	7	5	6	16	15	26
7	Sheff. Utd	18	8	2	8	23	23	26
8	Newcastle U.	18	6	5	7	29	29	23
9	**Everton**	**18**	**3**	**7**	**8**	**18**	**25**	**16**
10	Wigan Ath.	18	2	5	11	8	28	11

Jack Rodwell, the first Everton player to score at the new Wembley Stadium

RESERVE LEAGUE RESULTS 2006/07

			Result
29.08.06	Newcastle United	A	2-2
03.10.06	Sheffield United	H	1-1
10.10.06	Liverpool	H	2-1
16.10.06	Blackburn Rovers	A	0-1
31.10.06	Manchester City	H	1-1
15.11.06	Wigan Athletic	A	2-0
21.11.06	Middlesbrough	A	0-3
05.12.06	Bolton Wanderers	H	2-2
13.02.07	Sheffield United	A	1-2
06.03.07	Blackburn Rovers	H	0-0
13.03.07	Manchester City	A	1-2
22.03.07	Manchester United	A	0-1
27.03.07	Manchester United	H	1-2
03.04.07	Newcastle United	H	2-1
10.04.07	Middlesbrough	H	0-0
18.04.07	Bolton Wanderers	A	1-2
24.04.07	Wigan Athletic	H	1-1
30.04.07	Liverpool	A	1-3

RESERVE LEAGUE FIXTURES 2007/08

7pm Kick-Off times apply unless stated

30.08.07	Manchester United	A	
04.09.07	Sunderland	H	
18.09.07	Blackburn Rovers	H	
02.10.07	Middlesbrough	A	
09.10.07	Manchester City	H	
24.10.07	Bolton Wanderers	A	
06.11.07	Newcastle United	H	
28.11.07	Wigan Athletic	A	
04.12.07	Liverpool	A	
08.01.08	Manchester United	H	
21.01.08	Blackburn Rovers	A	
12.02.08	Middlesbrough	H	
19.02.08	Bolton Wanderers	H	
26.02.08	Manchester City	A	KO TBC
03.03.08	Newcastle United	A	KO TBC
11.03.08	Wigan Athletic	H	KO TBC
19.03.08	Sunderland	A	
01.04.08	Liverpool	H	

RESERVES : POST-WAR RECORDS

RECORD VICTORY

9-1	Blackburn Rovers Res. (h)	28th November 1981
8-0	Manchester City Res. (h)	16th November 1963

MOST GOALS IN A GAME

6	Robbie Wakenshaw	Bradford City Res. (a)	11th December 1984
5	Steve Melledew	Huddersfield Town Res. (a)	22nd November 1969
5	Imre Varadi	Preston North End Res. (h)	23rd April 1979
5	Kevin Richardson	Blackburn Rovers Res. (h)	28th November 1981

6 GOALS IN A GAME FOR EVERTON REPRESENTATIVE TEAMS (SINCE 1970)

George Telfer	Chorley Res. v Everton 'A'	20th November 1971
Barry Wellings	Altrincham Res. v Everton 'A'	18th October 1975
Robbie Wakenshaw	Bradford City Res. v Everton Res.	11th December 1984
Stuart Barlow	Everton 'B' v Carlisle 'B'	30th March 1991

LEADING RESERVE SCORERS (SINCE 1960)

Season	Player	Goals	Season	Player	Goals
1960/61	Keith Webber	12	1985/86	Paul Wilkinson	13
1961/62	Keith Webber	15	1986/87	Warren Aspinall	13
1962/63	Frank Wignall	23	1987/88	Gary Powell	15
1963/64	Jimmy Hill	14	1988/89	Wayne Clarke	13
1964/65	Jimmy Hill	19	1989/90	Gary Powell	12
1965/66	Jimmy Husband	21	1990/91	Stuart Barlow	10
1966/67	Mike Trebilcock	17	1991/92	Stuart Barlow	15
1967/68	Mike Trebilcock	24	1992/93	Stuart Barlow	21
1968/69	Terry Owen	11	1993/94	Stuart Barlow	16
1969/70	Mick Lyons	22	1994/95	Stuart Barlow	15
1970/71	Billy Kenny	14	1995/96	Stuart Barlow	7
1971/72	Alan Wilson	21	1996/97	Paul Rideout	7
1972/73	Billy Kenny	8	1997/98	Phil Jevons/	4
1973/74	David Irving	10		Michael Branch/	
1974/75	Billy Kenny	9		Nick Barmby	
1975/76	Dave Esser	13	1998/99	Phil Jevons	11
1976/77	Jim Pearson	7	1999/00	Phil Jevons	10
1977/78	Ross Jack	14	2000/01	Phil Jevons	9
1978/79	Ross Jack	15	2001/02	Nick Chadwick	8
1979/80	Imre Varadi	14	2002/03	Nick Chadwick	16
1980/81	George Telfer	11	2003/04	Leon Osman	8
1982/83	Stuart Rimmer/	6	2004/05	James Vaughan	7
	Mick Ferguson		2005/06	Victor Anichebe	9
1983/84	Stuart Rimmer	15	2006/07	Mark Hughes/	4
1984/85	Robbie Wakenhaw	26		James McFadden	

THE ACADEMY

The aim of the club's academy has always been to provide quality players for the first-team squad. The recent success in a blue shirt of Leon Osman, Tony Hibbert, James Vaughan and Victor Anichebe suggests a rich seam of players looking to follow in their footsteps, and 2006/07 has brought some notable success. Defender Jack Rowell became the first Everton player to both appear and score at the new Wembley after netting for England U19s, while the club's youngsters picked up silverware in the form of the Liverpool Senior Cup.

FA PREMIER ACADEMY 2006/07 GROUP C

	P	W	D	L	F	A	Pts
1 Man City	28	21	3	4	63	28	66
2 Bolton	28	14	6	8	38	26	48
3 Blackburn	28	13	7	8	47	34	46
4 Man Utd	28	12	4	12	51	42	40
5 West Brom	28	12	2	14	44	45	38
6 Everton	**28**	**6**	**13**	**9**	**38**	**38**	**31**
7 Crewe	28	9	3	16	44	57	30
8 Liverpool	28	7	8	13	29	37	29
9 Wolves	28	6	7	15	30	52	25
10 Stoke	28	3	5	20	14	53	14

John Irving (left) and Shaun Densmore show off the Liverpool Senior Cup

U18s' LEAGUE & CUP RESULTS 2006/07

Date	Opponent		Result*
19.08.06	Watford	A	2-3
26.08.06	Charlton Athletic	H	1-2
02.09.06	Middlesbrough	A	2-2
09.09.06	Nottingham Forest	H	0-2
16.09.06	Derby County	A	1-1
23.09.06	Manchester United	H	1-1
30.09.06	Manchester City	A	1-1
07.10.06	Liverpool	H	0-0
14.10.06	West Bromwich Albion	H	1-2
21.10.06	Bolton Wanderers	A	1-2
04.11.06	Blackburn Rovers	A	2-2
11.11.06	Crewe Alexandra	H	1-0
18.11.06	Stoke City	A	2-2
01.12.06	Wolverhampton W.	H	3-0
05.01.07	Macclesfield T (FAYC)	A	3-0
17.01.07	Millwall (FAYC)	H	0-1
20.01.07	Crewe Alexandra	A	1-1
29.01.07	Bolton Wanderers	H	1-1
03.02.07	Stoke City	H	3-0
17.02.07	Manchester United	A	0-2
24.02.07	Manchester City	H	1-3
03.03.07	Liverpool	A	1-1
08.03.07	Prescot Cables (LSC)	H	3-1
17.03.07	Sunderland	A	2-1
24.03.07	Sheffield United	H	0-1
30.03.07	Blackburn Rovers	H	1-1
21.04.07	Barnsley	A	2-0
27.04.07	Sheffield Wednesday	H	2-0
01.05.07	Wolverhampton W.	A	2-2
05.05.07	Newcastle United	H	3-3
08.05.07	Tranmere Rovers (LSC)	A	2-1

* Everton score shown first

U18s' LEAGUE FIXTURES 2007/08

11am Kick-Off times apply unless stated

18.08.07	Bristol City	H	
25.08.07	Tottenham Hotspur	A	
01.09.07	Leeds United	H	
08.09.07	Newcastle United	A	
15.09.07	Sheffield United	A	KO TBC
22.09.07	Sunderland	H	KO TBC
29.09.07	Wolves	A	KO TBC
06.10.07	Manchester City	H	KO TBC
13.10.07	Crewe Alexandra	A	KO TBC
20.10.07	Blackburn Rovers	H	KO TBC
27.10.07	Stoke City	A	KO TBC
03.11.07	Crewe Alexandra	A	KO TBC
10.11.07	West Bromwich Albion	H	KO TBC
17.11.07	Manchester United	H	KO TBC
01.12.07	Bolton Wanderers	A	
08.12.07	Blackburn Rovers	A	
15.12.07	Stoke City	H	
05.01.08	West Bromwich Albion	A	
12.01.08	Liverpool	H	
19.01.08	Bolton Wanderers	H	
26.01.08	Manchester United	A	
09.02.08	Wolves	H	
16.02.08	Manchester City	A	
01.03.08	Crewe Alexandra	H	
15.03.08	Derby County	H	
29.03.08	Nottingham Forest	A	
05.04.08	Middlesbrough	A	
12.04.08	Barnsley	H	

THE ACADEMY

EVERTON IN THE LIVERPOOL SENIOR CUP 2006/07

Quarter-Final	8th March 2007	
	Everton 3-1 Prescot Cables	(Halton Stadium, Widnes)
Scorers:	Spencer (16, 69), Irving (18)	
Semi-Final		
Liverpool scratched from the competition and Everton were given a walkover		
Final	8th May 2007	
	Tranmere Rovers 1-2 Everton	(Prenton Park)
Scorers:	Rodwell (19), Morrison (20)	

Two goals in a minute were enough for Everton to lift the Liverpool Senior Cup for the second time in three seasons. Skipper John Irving was presented with the trophy before travelling back across the Mersey to pick up his Reserve Player of the Year gong at the End of Season Awards. Irving and Academy Player of the Year Shaun Densmore paraded the trophy at the St. George's Hall event.

EVERTON IN THE FA YOUTH CUP 2006/07

Round 3	5th January 2007
	Macclesfield Town 0-3 Everton
Scorers:	Connor (20) Morrison (73, 75 pen)
Everton:	Jones; Densmore, Rodwell, Irving, Dennehy, Harpur, Molyneux (71, Stewart), Morrison, Agard, Kissock (71, Spencer), Connor.
Round 4	17th January 2007
	Everton 0-1 Millwall
Everton:	Jones; Densmore, Rodwell, Irving, Dennehy, Harpur, Connor, Morrison, Agard, Kissock, Molyneux (70, Elder).

EVERTON FA YOUTH CUP RECORDS

Winners (final played over two legs, aggregate scores shown)

1964/65	Everton 3-2 Arsenal
1983/84	Everton 4-2 Stoke City
1997/98	Everton 5-3 Blackburn Rovers

Finalists

1960/61	Everton 3-5 Chelsea
1976/77	Everton 0-1 Crystal Palace
1982/83	Everton 5-5 Norwich (Norwich won third game 1-0 at Goodison Park)
2001/02	Everton 2-4 Aston Villa

Record victory:	Everton 12-1 Wigan Athletic, 14th January 1964
Record attendance:	29,908 Everton v Arsenal (home), final second leg, 3rd May 1965

Most appearances:	19, Robbie Wakenshaw (1982-84)
Most goals:	14, Keith Webber (1960-61)

Most goals in a game:

5	J. Gregory	South Liverpool (a), 17th September 1952
5	Keith Webber	Tranmere Rovers (a), 19th September 1960
4	Bert Llewellyn	Middlesbrough (a), 8th December 1956
4	Keith Webber	Burnley (h), 3rd October 1960
4	John Hurst	Wigan Athletic (h), 14th January 1964
4	Mark Farrington	Sheffield Wednesday (h), 7th April 1983

EVERTON LADIES

Mo Marley's Everton Ladies side enjoyed a highly successful season, and their second place in the FA Nationwide Premier League, behind the all-conquering Arsenal, was enough to secure a fully deserved UEFA Cup place. Captained by England midfielder and Blues Player of the Year Fara Williams, the Blues have already booked a place in the second qualifying round group stage, where they will meet 1. FFC Frankfurt, Valur Reykjavik and KFC Rapide Wezemaal in October.

Everton have six players in the England squad for the 2007 World Cup in China, which means domestic fixtures are sure to be heavily hit so keep tabs on www.evertonfc.com for the latest news. Note that home games are played at Marine's Rossett Park in Crosby.

WOMEN'S LEAGUE & CUP RESULTS 2006/07

Date	Opponent		Result*
02.08.06	Arsenal (FACShield)	N	0-3
20.08.06	Charlton	A	2-1
27.08.06	Birmingham	H	2-1
03.09.06	Leeds United	H	1-1
10.09.06	Crystal Palace (PLC)	H	4-0
17.09.06	Doncaster R. Belles	A	1-2
08.10.06	Bristol Academy (PLC)	H	2-0
22.10.06	Arsenal	H	1-4
05.11.06	Chelsea (PLC)	H	1-2
08.11.06	Blackburn	A	3-2
12.11.06	Birmingham	A	4-0
19.11.06	Sunderland	A	4-0
26.11.06	Bristol Academy	A	2-0
17.12.06	Charlton	H	0-1
14.01.07	Millwall L. (FAC)	A	6-0
04.02.07	Langford (FAC)	A	4-0
11.02.07	Charlton (FAC)	A	0-1
18.02.07	Sunderland	H	5-0
25.02.07	Bristol Academy	H	3-0
28.02.07	Blackburn	H	1-0
04.03.07	Cardiff City	A	3-0
18.03.07	Liverpool (LSC)	A	2-1
25.03.07	Cardiff City	H	2-0
01.04.07	Fulham	H	9-0
08.04.07	Fulham	A	2-0
29.04.07	Doncaster R. Belles	H	3-0
03.05.07	Leeds United	A	1-0
05.05.07	Chelsea	A	1-0
09.05.07	Arsenal	A	2-3
20.05.07	Chelsea	H	4-0

FA WOMEN'S PREMIER LEAGUE 2006/07

	P	W	D	L	F	A	Pts
1 Arsenal	22	22	0	0	119	10	66
2 Everton	22	17	1	4	56	15	52
3 Charlton	22	16	2	4	63	32	50
4 Bristol Ac.	22	13	1	8	53	41	40
5 Leeds Utd	22	12	1	9	50	44	37
6 Blackburn	22	10	2	10	37	36	32
7 Birmingham	22	8	4	10	34	29	28
8 Chelsea	22	8	4	10	33	34	28
9 Doncaster	22	7	2	13	29	54	23
10 Cardiff	22	3	3	16	26	64	12
11 Sunderland	22	3	2	17	15	72	11
12 Fulham	22	1	2	19	12	96	5

WOMEN'S LEAGUE FIXTURES 2007/08

2pm Kick-Off times apply unless stated

09.08.07	Gintra (UEFA)	N	4-0
11.08.07	Glentoran (UEFA)	N	11-0
14.08.07	Zuchwil (UEFA)	N	5-0
23.09.07	Charlton	A	
26.09.07	Liverpool	H	7pm
30.09.07	Barnet (FAPLC)	H	
07.10.07	Birmingham	A	
21.10.07	Chelsea	H	
28.10.07	Cardiff City	A	
31.10.07	Liverpool	A	7pm
11.11.07	Watford	H	
14.11.07	Leeds Utd/UEFA QF1	A	7pm
18.11.07	Doncaster R. Belles	A	
22.11.07	UEFA QFL2		
25.11.07	Charlton	H	
02.12.07	Arsenal	H	
09.12.07	Bristol Academy	A	
13.12.07	Watford	A	7.45pm
16.12.07	Cardiff City	H	
20.12.07	Birmingham	H	7.45pm
06.01.08	FA CUP ROUND 4		
13.01.08	Watford	A	
20.01.08	Birmingham	H	
27.01.08	Blackburn/FAC5	H	
10.02.08	FA CUP ROUND 6		
09.03.08	FA CUP SEMI-FINAL		
29.03.08	UEFA SF1		
06.04.08	UEFA SF2		
05.05.08	FA CUP FINAL		
17.05.08	UEFA CUP FINAL L1		
24.05.08	UEFA CUP FINAL L2		
TBC	Chelsea	A	
TBC	Doncaster R. Belles	H	
TBC	Blackburn	A	
TBC	Arsenal	A	
TBC	Bristol Academy	H	
TBC	Leeds United	H	

EVERTON LADIES - SQUAD 2007/08

GOALKEEPERS

Rachel Brown, Danielle Hill

DEFENDERS

Lindsay Johnson,Becky Easton,Fern Whelan, Rachel Unitt

MIDFIELDERS

Fara Williams, Leanne Duffy, Amy Kane, Kelly McDougall, Emily Westwood, Michelle Evans, Jill Scott, Josanne Potter

FORWARDS

Jody Handley, Faye McCoy, Natasha Dowie, Toni Duggan

Celebrations for Everton Ladies following the 4-0 final-day victory over Chelsea which secured UEFA Cup qualification at the end of the 2006/07 campaign.

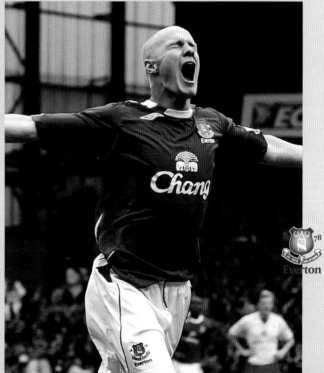

10 ▶

4-goal show

It was a Good Friday for all Evertonians as the Blues kept their UEFA Cup qualification charge on track with a 4-1 victory over Fulham, with youngsters James Vaughan (right) and Victor Anichebe both on target.

9

AJ worth the wait

After failing to hit the target in pre-season, record signing Andy Johnson finally broke his duck when it mattered in the Premiership, against Watford.

Mikel lights up Goodison

A freezing Saturday with little on-field cheer is suddenly transformed on the hour-mark as Player of the Season Mikel Arteta rockets home the only goal against Bolton.

Ball tribute

The first game after the untimely death of Goodison legend Alan Ball saw the Blues entertain Manchester United. A moving occasion included Alan's children laying a wreath in front of the Gwladys Street and the minute's applause proved fitting.

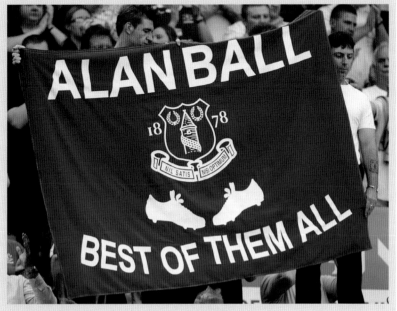

Our Vic

Everton youth product Victor Anichebe struck the first brace of his Blues career in the 3-0 victory over Newcastle United, the club's last game of 2006.

Goal of the season

Charlton had just levelled late on, close to securing a vital point in their fight to beat the drop. Enter James McFadden, who moments later collected a headed clearance, flicked the ball over Madjid Bougherra and volleyed home from 20 yards beyond Scott Carson.

4

Rocky show

Hollywood royalty visited Goodison back in January, when Sylvestor Stallone (friend of director Robert Earl) was paraded ahead of the game against Reading.

3

10 men end Spurs woe

Without a win at Spurs in 21 years and seeing Kevin Kilbane sent off in the first half, there seemed little reason for this statistic to change. But thanks to an inspired 10-man display and goals from Calum Davenport (own goal) and Andy Johnson, the Blues had secured the win!

Gunners late show

A hard-fought 0-0 draw seemed on the cards late on at Goodison. But almost as soon as the hailstones rained down, the home side seemed to draw a second wind. From Mikel Arteta's corner, the ball fell for Andy Johnson – and the points were snatched!

And so the long wait is ended

Everton's biggest derby win at Goodison since April 1909 saw Andy Johnson enter Evertonian folklore with two goals in the 3-0 triumph, and for a few hours the Blues were top of the table.

BACK IN '85 - THE EARLY ROUNDS

The Toffees' qualification for Europe in 2007/08 gives an opportunity to look back at the 1984/85 Cup Winners' Cup campaign, which ended in the club lifting a European trophy for the first time.

First Round

UCD	**0-0**	**Everton**	**19/9/1984**
Everton Sharp 11	**1-0**	**UCD**	**2/10/1984**

The Road to Rotterdam began in the not-so-glamorous surroundings of Tolka Park against University College Dublin. Despite dominating the play to an almost embarrassing degree, the English side were unable to find the net from a plethora of opportunities.

The second leg saw more of the same after Graeme Sharp put Everton – playing in their change strip of yellow shirts and blue shorts – ahead early on. After the Irishmen had restricted the home team to the one goal, they broke out in the last 10 minutes and centre-forward Joe Hanrahan missed a golden opportunity at the end to put the Toffees out. Hard to believe now but Everton were booed off the pitch at the end!

Second Round

Slovan Bratislava	**0-1**	**Everton** Bracewell 6	**24/10/1984**
Everton Sharp 12 Sheedy 44 Heath 63	**3-0**	**Slovan Bratislava**	**7/11/1984**

A comfortable 4-0 aggregate victory over the Czech side put the Toffees safely through to the quarter-finals. The first-leg win – courtesy of a Paul Bracewell header in the opening minutes – was sandwiched between two famous league victories over Liverpool and Manchester United. The return at Goodison saw Sharp score early on to end the tie as a contest.

Quarter-final

Everton Gray 48,74,76	**3-0**	**Fortuna Sittard**	**6/3/1985**
Fortuna Sittard	**0-2**	**Everton** Sharp 16 Reid 75	**20/3/1985**

Fortuna Sittard journeyed to Goodison 27 years after appearing there in a friendly game in April 1958. After a goalless first half it was Andy Gray who put Everton ahead – his first goal on the ground that season – and then adding a second with a typical diving header. The forward completed a famous hat-trick with a left-footed volley.

BACK IN '85 - THE SEMI-FINAL

Semi-final

Bayern Munich	**0-0**	**Everton**	**10/4/1985**

Everton	**3-1**	**Bayern Munich**	**24/4/1985**
Sharp 48		Hoeness 38	
Gray 73			
Steven 86			

The Toffees travelled to West Germany and, with Graeme Sharp playing as a lone striker, a disciplined performance was enough for a goalless draw – and a then British record of seven European matches without conceding a goal – in front of a capacity crowd of 67,000.

The second leg has quite rightly gone down as Goodison's greatest night, driven on by a cauldron of noise Everton fought back brilliantly in the second half to triumph in what many thought was the final of the competition, if one round early.

Everton players in the 1984/85 Cup Winners' Cup

	Games (subs apps)	Goals
Atkins	0 (1)	
Bailey	4	
Bracewell	8	1
Curran	3 (1)	
Gray	3	5
Harper	3 (1)	
Heath	4	1
Morrissey	0 (1)	
Mountfield	9	
Ratcliffe	9	
Reid	9	1
Richardson	2 (1)	
Sharp	8	4
Sheedy	5	2
Southall	9	
Steven	9	2
Stevens	9	
Van den Hauwe	5	
Wakenshaw	0 (2)	

BACK IN '85 - THE FINAL

Everton overwhelmed their outclassed opponents on a never-to-be-forgotten night in Holland to secure both their first European trophy and legendary status for the players in the victorious side.

After Everton dominated the opening half it took Andy Gray 12 minutes of the second period before putting the Blues ahead with his fifth European goal in three matches, after Graeme Sharp had intercepted an attempted back-pass.

Trevor Steven scored a second at the far post after a Kevin Sheedy corner-kick and although Rapid captain Hans Krankl sneaked though to pull a goal back, the Austrians were hit by an immediate riposte, with Sheedy adding a third.

Everton skipper Kevin Ratcliffe holds aloft the European Cup Winners' Cup

Team line-ups

Everton (4-4-2):

Gray   Sharp

Sheedy   Bracewell   Reid   Steven

Van den Hauwe   Ratcliffe   Mountfield   Stevens

Southall

Subs (not used): Arnold, Richardson, Atkins, Bailey, Harper

Rapid Vienna (4-4-2):

Krankl   Pacult

Weinhofer   Hrstic   Kienast   Kranjcar

Weber   Garger   Brauneder   Lainer

Konsel

Subs: Panenka (Weinhofer), Gross (Pacult)

EVERTON 3
RAPID VIENNA 1

European Cup Winners' Cup final, Rotterdam,
Wednesday, May 15, 1985.
Attendance: 38,500

Goals: Gray (57), Steven (72), Krankl (83), Sheedy (85)
Referee: Paolo Casarin (Italy)

EVERTON'S FULL LIST OF RESULTS IN EUROPE

Season	Round	Venue	Opponents	Opponent Country	Score	Scorers	Att
1962-63	**INTER-CITIES FAIRS CUP**						
24th Oct	1 Leg 1	(h)	Dunfermline Ath.	Sco	W 1-0	Stevens	40,244
31st Oct	1 Leg 2	(a)	Dunfermline Ath	"	L 0-2		21,813
1963-64	**EUROPEAN CUP**						
18th Sept	1 Leg 1	(h)	Inter Milan	Ita	D 0-0		62,408
25th Sept	1 Leg 2	(a)	Inter Milan	"	L 0-1		70,000
1964-65	**INTER-CITIES FAIRS CUP**						
23rd Sept	1 Leg 1	(a)	Valerengens IF	Nor	W 5-2	Pickering 2,Harvey,Temple, Scott	17,952
14th Oct	1 Leg 2	(h)	Valerengens IF	"	W 4-2	Young 2,Hansen (og),Vernon	20,717
11th Nov	2 Leg 1	(a)	Kilmarnock	Sco	W 2-0	Temple,Morrissey	20,000
23rd Nov	2 Leg 2	(h)	Kilmarnock	"	W 4-1	Harvey,Pickering 2,Young	30,727
20th Jan	3 Leg 1	(a)	Manchester Utd	Eng	D 1-1	Pickering	49,075
4th Feb	3 Leg 2	(h)	Manchester Utd	"	L 1-2	Pickering	54,397
1965-66	**INTER-CITIES FAIRS CUP**						
28th Sept	1 Leg 1	(a)	FC Nuremburg	W.Ger	D 1-1	Harris	10,000
12th Oct	1 Leg 2	(h)	FC Nuremburg	"	W 1-0	Gabriel	39,033
3rd Nov	2 Leg 1	(a)	Ujpest Dozsa	Hun	L 0-3		4,000
16th Nov	2 Leg 2	(h)	Ujpest Dozsa	"	W 2-1	Harris,Nosko (og)	24,201
1966-67	**EUROPEAN CUP WINNERS' CUP**						
28th Sept	1 Leg 1	(a)	AaB Aalborg	Den	D 0-0		13,000
11th Oct	1 Leg 2	(h)	AaB Aalborg	"	W 2-1	Morrissey,Ball	36,628
9th Nov	2 Leg 1	(a)	Real Zaragoza	Spa	L 0-2		20,000
23rd Nov	2 Leg 2	(h)	Real Zaragoza	"	W 1-0	Brown	56,077
1970-71	**EUROPEAN CUP**						
16th Sept	1 Leg 1	(h)	IBK Keflavik	Ice	W 6-2	Ball 3,Royle 2,Kendall	28,444
30th Sept	1 Leg 2	(a)	IBK Keflavik	"	W 3-0	Whittle,Royle 2	9,500
21st Oct	2 Leg 1	(a)	B. Moench'bach	W. Ger	D 1-1	Kendall	32,000
4th Nov	2 Leg 2	(h)	B. Moench'bach (Everton won 5-4 on penalties)	"	D 1-1	Morrissey	42,744
9th Mar	3 Leg 1	(h)	Panathinaikos	Gre	D 1-1	Johnson	46,047
24th Mar	3 Leg 2	(a)	Panathinaikos	"	D 0-0		25,000
1975-76	**UEFA CUP**						
17th Sept	1 Leg 1	(h)	AC Milan	Ita	D 0-0		31,917
1st Oct	1 Leg 2	(a)	AC Milan	"	L 0-1		60,000
1978-79	**UEFA CUP**						
12th Sept	1 Leg 1	(a)	Finn Harps	Ire	W 5-0	Thomas,King 2,Latchford, Walsh	5,000
26th Sept	1 Leg 2	(h)	Finn Harps	"	W 5-0	King,Latchford,Walsh,Ross, Dobson	21,611
18th Oct	2 Leg 1	(h)	Dukla Prague	Cze	W 2-1	Latchford,King	32,857
1st Nov	2 Leg 2	(a)	Dukla Prague	"	L 0-1		35,000

EVERTON'S FULL LIST OF RESULTS IN EUROPE

Season	Round	Venue	Opponents	Opponent Country	Score	Scorers	Att
1978-79	UEFA CUP						
19th Sept	1 Leg 1	(a)	Feyenoord	Hol	L 0-1		36,000
3rd Oct	1 Leg 2	(h)	Feyenoord	"	L 0-1		28,203
1984-85	EUROPEAN CUP WINNERS' CUP						
19th Sept	1 Leg 1	(a)	UC Dublin	Ire	D 0-0		10,000
2nd Oct	1 Leg 2	(h)	UC Dublin	"	W 1-0	Sharp	16,277
24th Oct	2 Leg 1	(a)	Slovan Bratislava	Cze	W 1-0	Bracewell	15,000
7th Nov	2 Leg 2	(h)	Slovan Bratislava	"	W 3-0	Sharp,Sheedy,Heath	25,007
6th Mar	3 Leg 1	(h)	Fortuna Sittard	Hol	W 3-0	Gray 3	25,782
20th Mar	3 Leg 2	(a)	Fortuna Sittard	"	W 2-0	Sharp,Reid	20,000
10th Apr	SF Leg 1	(a)	Bayern Munich	W. Ger	D 0-0		67,000
24th Apr	SF Leg 2	(h)	Bayern Munich	"	W 3-1	Sharp,Gray,Steven	49,476
15th May	Final	N	Rapid Vienna	Aus	W 3-1	Gray,Steven,Sheedy	38,500
1995-96	EUROPEAN CUP WINNERS' CUP						
14th Sept	1 Leg 1	(a)	KR Reykjavik	Ice	W 3-2	Ebbrell,Unsworth (pen), Amokachi	6,000
28th Sept	1 Leg 2	(h)	KR Reykjavik	"	W 3-1	Stuart,Grant,Rideout	18,422
19th Oct	2 Leg 1	(h)	Feyenoord	Hol	D 0-0		27,526
2nd Nov	2 Leg 2	(a)	Feyenoord	"	L 0-1		40,000
2005-06	EUROPEAN CUP						
9th Aug	Q.3 Leg 1	(h)	Villarreal	Spa	L 1-2	Beattie	37,685
24th Aug	Q.3 Leg 2	(a)	Villarreal	"	L 1-2	Arteta	16,000
2005-06	UEFA CUP						
15th Sept	1 Leg 1	(a)	D. Bucharest	Rom	L 1-5	Yobo	11,500
29th Sept	1 Leg 2	(h)	D. Bucharest	"	W 1-0	Cahill	21,843

Tim Cahill's goal against Bucharest was not enough to prevent an early UEFA Cup exit in 2005

EUROPEAN RECORDS

Biggest victories

Date	Opponents	Venue	Score	Scorers	Attendance
12th Sept 1978	Finn Harps	A	5-0	Thomas, King 2, Latchford, Walsh	5,000
26th Sept 1978	Finn Harps	H	5-0	King, Latchford, Walsh, Ross, Dobson	21,611
16th Sept 1970	Keflavik	H	6-2	Ball 3, Royle 2, Kendall	28,444

Biggest defeats

Date	Opponents	Venue	Score	Scorer	Attendance
29th Sept 2005	D. Bucharest	A	1-5	Yobo	11,500
3rd Nov 1965	Ujpest Dozsa	A	0-3		4,000
31st Oct 1962	Dunfermline	A	0-2		21,813
9th Nov 1966	R. Zaragoza	A	0-2		20,000

Highest Home Attendance

Attendance	Opponents	Competition	Date
62,408	Inter Milan	European Cup	18th Sep 1963

Everton Sendings-off

Date	Name	Competition	Against	Venue	Mins
9th Nov 1966	Johnny Morrissey	ECW Cup	Real Zaragoza	A	45
17th Sept 1975	Mike Bernard	UEFA Cup	AC Milan	H	89
2nd Nov 1995	Craig Short	ECW Cup	Feyenoord	A	90

Opponents' Sendings-off

Date	Name	Competition	Against	Venue	Mins
11th Oct 1966	Morten Larsen	ECW Cup	AaB Aalborg	H	87

The victorious Everton squad celebrate in Rotterdam folllowing the 3-1 victory over Rapid Vienna in the 1985 European Cup Winners' Cup

Bob Latchford is thwarted by a linesman's flag during the 5-0 UEFA Cup romp over Finn Harps at Goodison in 1978, Everton's biggest home win in European competition

LOOKING BACK ON 06/07

Where did it all go? We kept tabs on the goings on during 2006/07, and are sure we'll bring back some fond memories from a season which secured European qualification.

August
The opening-day triumph against newly-promoted Watford not only saw Everton earn victory in the first game of the season for the first time in five years, it also sees a debut goal for record signing Andy Johnson, bought for £8.6m from Crystal Palace in the summer.

A stunning 2-0 victory at Tottenham Hotspur (Everton were down to 10 men for just under an hour) yields a first three-pointer at White Hart Lane in 21 years. The performance of Leon Osman encourages manager David Moyes to demand England recognition for the midfielder.

Chief executive Keith Wyness warms to the idea of a possible play-off system being introduced to determine the Premier League champions every season.

Everton legend Andy King believes Andy Johnson to be the signing of the summer while Kevin Kilbane leaves Goodison for Wigan Athletic, the only transfer business involving the Blues before the August transfer window closes.

Scorers on Premiership debut:

Player	Opposition (venue)	Date
Barry Horne	Sheffield Wednesday (h)	15th August 1992
Gary Speed	Newcastle United (h)	17th August 1996
Mickael Madar	Crystal Palace (a)	10th January 1998
Brian McBride	Tottenham Hotspur (a)	12th January 2003
James Vaughan	Crystal Palace (h)	10th April 2005
Andrew Johnson	Watford (h)	19th August 2006

Outgoing: Kevin Kilbane (Wigan Athletic).

Quotes of the month:
"I want to score in the big games and I want to score week in, week out. I just love scoring goals."
Andy Johnson gunning for goals

"I was concerned about coming here but we put a marker down, probably even more so with 10 men. I think this has to be the best performance I've been involved with at Everton because of the way the game went and because of the opposition."
David Moyes, delighted by the victory at Spurs

"Since I came to the club that is the best we have played in terms of footballing quality. It was amazing really because when it was XI versus XI I think maybe Tottenham shaded it a little bit."
Phil Neville, on a similar theme

AUGUST

THE GAMES

19	Watford	H	2-1	Johnson, Arteta pen
23	Blackburn R.	A	1-1	Cahill
26	Tottenham H.	A	2-0	Davenport o.g., Johnson

WHERE THEY STOOD

1. Manchester United
2. Portsmouth
3. Aston Villa
4. **Everton**
5. Chelsea
6. West Ham
7. Liverpool

MOYES ON NEW SEASON

'I am a dreamer. And the dream is that we get Everton into a similar position to a year ago.'

LOOKING BACK ON 06/07

September

The memorable derby victory over Liverpool dominates the thoughts of Evertonians throughout the month, while the Blues maintain an unbeaten start to the season. The 3-0 success over the Reds inspires a whole host of new records:

Biggest derby victories at Goodison Park:

9th April 1909	5-0
11th January 1902	4-0
1st April 1904	5-2
13th October 1894	3-0
16th October 1897	3-0
9th September 2006	3-0

Two goals in a post-War league derby:

20th January 1951	Jimmy McIntosh	Anfield	W 2-0
8th February 1964	Roy Vernon	Goodison Park	W 3-1
27th August 1966	Alan Ball	Goodison Park	W 3-1
18th November 1995	Andrei Kanchelskis	Anfield	W 2-1
9th September 2006	Andrew Johnson	Goodison Park	W 3-0

Scorers in both league derbies in calendar year (post-War):

Alan Whittle	1970
Joe Royle	1970
Andy King	1979
Wayne Clarke	1988
Tim Cahill	2006

Tim Cahill becomes the first Everton player since Alex Young from 1901-1904 to score in league derbies in three successive seasons.

Andy Johnson's goal in the 2-2 draw with Wigan Athletic takes the striker to five goals in five games (he would eventually land September's Player of the Month award).

Best scoring start to a season in post-War era (first five games):

Eddie Wainwright	5 goals	1949/50
Fred Pickering	5 goals	1965/66
Francis Jeffers	5 goals	2000/01
Andy Johnson	5 goals	2006/07

Quotes of the month:

"We know how important this game is...it is not just about the game at the weekend, it is about the bragging rights after. I know a lot of people who feel every single kick. You can't play for this club unless it is in the blood. You hear so many stories of what it means to be an Evertonian and I can tell you every single player relishes this game and is honoured to play for this football club."

Tim Cahill on the derby

"It is amazing, it is probably the best day of my life."

Andy Johnson on a high

"It feels as good as any other victory an Everton manager has had in a Merseyside derby. We have not won many in the past and Liverpool have a terrific team with some fabulous players. I have to give credit to our players for how they played."

David Moyes, likewise...

SEPTEMBER

THE GAMES

9	Liverpool	H	3-0	Cahill, Johnson 2
16	Wigan Athletic	H	2-2	Johnson, Beattie pen
19	Peterborough U.	A	2-1	Stirling o.g., Cahill
24	Newcastle Utd	A	1-1	Cahill
30	Manchester City	H	1-1	Johnson

WHERE THEY STOOD

2	Bolton Wanderers
3	Manchester United
4	Portsmouth
5	**Everton**
6	Aston Villa
7	Arsenal
8	Reading

MOYES ON CURRENT SIDE

'That was a terrific team for grinding out results (in 2004/05) but this is a better footballing side.'

LOOKING BACK ON 06/07

October

Defeat at Middlesbrough (for whom a certain Yakubu also saw a penalty saved by Tim Howard) brings to an end a 10-match unbeaten run for the Blues, the club's best since December 1988. The seven-match unbeaten start to 2006/07 is also the best since last winning the title in 1986/87.

Premiership penalty saves by Everton goalkeepers:

Date	Goalkeeper and Penalty Taker	Opposition (venue)
4th May 1993	Neville Southall from Glyn Hodges	Sheffield United (h)
19th April 1997	Neville Southall from Paul Kitson	West Ham United (a)
17th April 1999	Thomas Myhre from Alan Shearer	Newcastle United (a)
28th April 2001	Paul Gerrard from Robbie Blake	Bradford City (h)
24th August 2002	Richard Wright from Kevin Phillips	Sunderland (a)
14th October 2006	Tim Howard from Ayegbeni Yakubu	Middlesbrough (a)

Ayegbeni Yakubu is only the second player, after Alan Shearer in April 1999 (see above) to both score and miss a penalty in a match against Everton.

Illness and injury plague the Blues in the run-up to the Sheffield United fixture, but the Blues still manage to come up with the three points. Off the field Robert Earl, the multi-millionaire owner of the *Planet Hollywood* chain, purchases a significant shareholding in the club.

October also sees some other notable occurances. The gate of 60,047 at Arsenal's Emirates Stadium was the first 60,000+ attendance for an Everton away league match other than at Old Trafford since 60,626 at Tottenham Hotspur in December 1962.
The comfortable League Cup victory over Luton Town also equals the biggest win under David Moyes.

Biggest wins under David Moyes:

Date	Opposition	Competition	Venue	Score
28th September 2003	Leeds United	Premier League	H	4-0
19th April 2005	Crystal Palace	Premier League	H	4-0
24th October 2006	Luton Town	League Cup	H	4-0

Quotes of the month:

"I didn't expect him to turn up. When he did he looked even worse, he was sweating...he made a great save in the first half when they could have got back into it from a set-piece but he's been like that all season."

Phil Neville hails Tim Howard after revealing the keeper was ill before and during the Sheffield United clash

"I have met David Moyes and he comes across as a really good guy. He is doing extremely well there."

Thierry Henry, impressed with the manager

OCTOBER

THE GAMES

14	Middlesboro	A	1-2	Cahill
21	Sheff Utd	H	2-0	Arteta, Beattie pen
24	Luton Town	H	4-0	Cahill, Keane o.g., McFadden, Anichebe
28	Arsenal	A	1-1	Cahill

WHERE THEY STOOD

3	Bolton Wanderers
4	Portsmouth
5	Arsenal
6	**Everton**
7	Aston Villa
8	Liverpool
9	Fulham

MOYES ON BLADES WIN

'It was probably our best win of the season as far as I'm concerned.'

LOOKING BACK ON 06/07

November

Only one win is yielded during the month, as Everton experience their most difficult period of the campaign. The Aston Villa defeat also sees Tim Cahill, who had already hit seven goals this season, suffer a serious knee injury after colliding with Lee Carsley.

Goalkeeper Iain Turner enjoys a brief loan spell at Crystal Palace, while it is confirmed that Everton will take on Barcelona at Goodison in March – the Legends team that is, in aid of the David France Collection.

The defeat at Manchester United sees more landmarks involving the Blues. For the first time in Premiership history brothers were opposing captains.

Brothers in opposition in Everton games:

Everton player	Brother	Period
Nick Ross	Jimmy Ross (Preston North End)	1888-89
Jack Cock	Donald Cock (Notts County)	1923-24
Bob Latchford	Dave Latchford (Birmingham City)	1974-77
Ian Snodin	Glynn Snodin (Sheffield Wednesday)	1986-87
Phil Neville	Gary Neville (Manchester United)	2005-07

Away attendances over 70,000:

Date	Opposition	Competition	Attendance
3rd March 1956	Manchester City	FA Cup	76,129
29th November 2006	Manchester United	Premier League	75,723
25th Sep 1963	Inter Milan	European Cup	70,000

Quotes of the month:

"It was a nice goal, I wouldn't like to say it was my best but it was an important one."

Mikel Arteta, mildly pleased with his Bolton winner

"Hopefully he will get some recognition from Spain because for a player of his calibre not to be playing in the Spanish team is baffling."

Tim Cahill calls for a Spain call-up for Mikel Arteta

"It is good to see that he has settled in so well at Goodison. He is a top professional and you can be sure that wherever he is, he will give nothing but his whole-hearted best."

Sir Alex Ferguson salutes his former player Phil Neville

NOVEMBER

THE GAMES

4	Fulham	A	0-1	
8	Arsenal	H	0-1	
11	Aston Villa	H	0-1	
18	Bolton W.	H	1-0	Arteta
25	Charlton Ath.	A	1-1	Hriedarsson o.g.
29	Man Utd	A	0-3	

WHERE THEY STOOD

6	Arsenal
7	Liverpool
8	Reading
9	**Everton**
10	Fulham
11	Tottenham Hotspur
12	Manchester City

MOYES ON ARTETA WINNER

'It was a really tight game that needed something special and we got it.'

LOOKING BACK ON 06/07

December

Three of the four home games in the month bring about rare events. The meeting with West Ham sees the youngest and oldest Premiership goalscorers on opposite sides – namely James Vaughan and Teddy Sheringham, who are both on the bench. It would be Vaughan who has the final say, scoring his second goal for the Blues, the second in the 2-0 win.

The goalless draw with Middlesbrough proves to be the only 0-0 scoreline at Goodison Park in the campaign, while Victor Anichebe becomes the fifth youngest post-War scorer of two goals for the club following his brace in the 3-0 defeat of Newcastle United. The other goalscorer in the game, Phil Neville (it was his first for the Blues) was the first by a right-back for Everton since Steve Watson netted at Arsenal in May 2002.

Incidentally the 61 points achieved by Everton in the calendar year of 2006 was the club's best since 1988.

Youngest players to score two goals in a match post-War:

Age	Player	Opposition & Venue	Date
16 years 342 days	Wayne Rooney	Wrexham (League Cup, a)	1st October 2002
18 years 11 days	Joe Royle	Chelsea (h)	19th April 1967
18 years 81 days	Derek Mayers	Bury (h)	15th April 1953
18 years 177 days	Alan Whittle	Tranmere (League Cup, h)	3rd September 1968
18 years 251 days	Victor Anichebe	Newcastle United (h)	30th December 2006

Other matters during the month include confirmation that Brazilian midfielder Anderson Silva de Franca would be allowed to join the club after acquiring an EU passport following his loan spell in Spain with Malaga.

Quotes of the month:

"...it was a terrific goal and a great finish. He is capable of that because he has good feet and good ability and we want to see more of that from him."

David Moyes hails Leon Osman's West Ham strike

"James Vaughan is someone we have a lot of hope for and to get a goal when we are struggling to get some is great. When he scored it was one of those new dance routines that he probably practised last night. Not the type of dancing I'm used to."

David Moyes, on the other goalscorer in the Hammers game

"The fans have been brilliant, they haven't murmured or moaned so I'd like to say thanks to the fans. They keep believing in me and if they keep believing, I'll keep scoring goals."

Andy Johnson thanks the fans for their support

"I know Yakubu well and I don't think he really fancies playing against me."

Joseph Yobo, confident of snuffing out Middlesbrough's striking threat

DECEMBER

THE GAMES

3	West Ham	H	2-0	Osman, Vaughan
9	Portsmouth	A	0-2	
17	Chelsea	H	2-3	Arteta pen, Yobo
23	Reading	A	2-0	Johnson, McFadden
26	Middlesboro	H	0-0	
30	Newcastle U.	H	3-0	Anichebe 2, Neville

WHERE THEY STOOD

4	Liverpool
5	Arsenal
6	Portsmouth
7	**Everton**
8	Tottenham Hotspur
9	Reading
10	Manchester City

MOYES ON TWO-GOAL VIC

'They were terrific poachers goals from Victor but he got a rollicking at half-time. He soon shut me up and that is what I want players to do.'

LOOKING BACK ON 06/07

January

It proves a mixed month for the Blues, with the disappointment of an early exit in the FA Cup tempered by Premiership improvement and the visit of a Hollywood legend to Goodison.

Indeed, Sylvester Stallone's appearance at Goodison Park for the Reading fixture (as a guest of major shareholder Robert Earl) makes front page headlines as he promotes his new film *Rocky Balboa*, while he is even pictured sporting his new Everton scarf while promoting the film in Paris. The 2-0 win at Wigan Athletic is also Everton's first over the Latics in the league, which means that Carlisle United – courtesy of two defeats in 1974/75 – are the only side Everton have failed to beat in league matches.

Portugal midfielder Manuel Fernandes is the only new addition to the Everton squad (Anderson Silva de Franca having already agreed his deal back in 2005) before the transfer deadline closes, joining on loan until the end of the season from Benfica having already played for Portsmouth this season. Leaving the Blues are Simon Davies, young defender Mark Hughes and veteran David Weir after almost eight years at Goodison.

Incoming: Manuel Fernandes (Benfica).

Outgoing: Simon Davies (Fulham), David Weir (Rangers), Mark Hughes (Northampton Town).

Quotes of the month:

"There is no doubt that Distin doesn't get his foot to the ball and so in my mind that's a penalty-kick. At worst it should have been a corner. I don't like criticising but when it's like that we have to accept it. But we are getting pretty fed up with it now."

David Moyes, upset by the failure to earn a penalty at Manchester City

"I've never seen anything like this level. This is a legendary club."

Sylvester Stallone, impressed by the Blues

"Would I have preferred the three points or would I have preferred Sly being here? I have to admit I would have taken the three points. But it was a great privilege him coming here."

Bill Kenwright, post Reading

"We thank him for everything he has done. He was great around the club and was someone I enjoyed working with and I wish him all the best."

David Moyes on David Weir's departure

JANUARY

THE GAMES

1	Man City	A	1-2	Osman
7	Blackburn R.	H	1-4	Johnson pen
14	Reading	H	1-1	Johnson
21	Wigan Ath.	A	2-0	Arteta 2 – 1 pen

WHERE THEY STOOD

6	Portsmouth
7	Reading
8	**Everton**
9	Newcastle United
10	Tottenham Hotspur
11	Middlesbrough
12	Blackburn Rovers

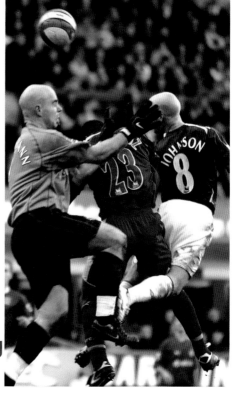

MOYES ON WIGAN WIN

'We've played much better and only drawn games but today we dug it out.'

LOOKING BACK ON 06/07

February

Unbeaten in derbies for the season, revenge against Blackburn Rovers and late disappointment against Spurs – it proves an up-and-down month for Evertonians. However, February ends on a high with the victory at Watford (where Manuel Fernandes nets his first goal for the Blues) being amongst the club's biggest away from home in the Premiership.

Goalkeeper Iain Turner agrees a loan move to Sheffield Wednesday, while first choice Tim Howard makes his loan deal with the Blues permanent, agreeing a five-year contract with the club.

Biggest Premiership away wins:

Date	Opposition	Scoreline
26th February 2000	West Ham United	4-0
8th May 1993	Manchester City	5-2
27th April 1996	Sheffield Wednesday	5-2
19th August 1992	Manchester United	3-0
30th March 1996	Blackburn Rovers	3-0
6th February 2000	Wimbledon	3-0
24th February 2007	Watford	3-0

Quotes of the month:

"It was a real team performance. We've played them twice now and not conceded, so credit to the defenders."

David Moyes hails Blues' derby rearguard

"Osman's goal was a great goal. I was on the bench and I didn't even stand up because I was stunned. It was an unbelievable goal and Ossie is a really nice player."

Manuel Fernandes impressed with Leon's Watford strike

"Any player that gets booed should pat themselves on the back because it shows what a good player they are. He is a very good player and £8.6m has proved to be a snip for them. I don't think he is a cheat, not at all. That's not fair."

Adrian Boothroyd praises Andy Johnson

"I went through and cut inside and got tangled up and went down. It was a penalty and I was pleased to put it away. It was a great performance by the team."

Andy Johnson, happy with his penalty at Vicarage Road

FEBRUARY

THE GAMES

3	Liverpool	A	0-0	
10	Blackburn R.	H	1-0	Johnson
21	Tottenham H.	H	1-2	Arteta
24	Watford	A	3-0	Fernandes, Johnson pen, Osman

WHERE THEY STOOD

5	Bolton Wanderers
6	Reading
7	**Everton**
8	Portsmouth
9	Tottenham Hotspur
10	Blackburn Rovers
11	Newcastle United

MOYES HIGHLIGHTS AMBITIONS

'I've always said I want to compete. I want to manage in Europe regularly. I want to take Everton there.'

LOOKING BACK ON 06/07

March

A quiet, but unbeaten month for the Blues, who come from behind to earn a point at Bramall Lane (where Tim Cahill suffers a foot injury) before Andy Johnson strikes in the last minute against Arsenal. It is only the second time in the Premiership that Everton have scored the only goal of the game in the last minute – while another late winner would follow in April.

Last-minute winners in the Premiership:

Date	Opposition	Venue	Scoreline	Last-minute scorer
18th March 1995	QPR	A	W 3-2	Hinchcliffe
19th October 2002	Arsenal	H	W 2-1	Rooney
22nd February 2003	Southampton	H	W 2-1	Radzinski
26th April 2003	Aston Villa	H	W 2-1	Rooney
31st December 2005	Sunderland	A	W 1-0	Cahill
18th March 2007	Arsenal	H	W 1-0	Johnson
15th April 2007	Charlton Athletic	H	W 2-1	McFadden

Quotes of the month:

"People said Everton paid a lot of money, but there are not many exceptional players at that price, yet Andy is one of them. He's very unfortunate his face does not seem to fit England-wise, but personally I would love to see him have two or three games in the team. Everton may have spent £8.6m on him, but he has been the best buy of the season – value for money."

Neil Warnock, singles out Andy Johnson for praise

"Can I get 10 goals? I will try my best. I want to score as many as I can to help the team. The gaffer keeps asking me to improve the number of goals I score and I want to become a better player. If I can score a lot of goals, that will help the team."

Mikel Arteta, gunning for goals

"I've put a plan for the next five years together and presented it to the board. It's how I think the club should be run, even if I'm not here. It's necessary to plan that far ahead."

David Moyes' view on the club's future

"If I could sign here for the rest of my career I would do it tomorrow. I am more than happy here, I love the club, the fans and the lads in the dressing room. I am sure the fans can see how much I love it here in my football but I want to make it clear there is no truth in this report – I am loving being an Everton player and I regard it as a great honour to put that blue shirt on every week. I would love to think I will still be here in seven years."

Andy Johnson, enjoying Everton life, despite Press reports to the contrary

MARCH

THE GAMES

| 3 | Sheff Utd | A | 1-1 | Arteta pen |
| 18 | Arsenal | H | 1-0 | Johnson |

WHERE THEY STOOD

4	Arsenal
5	Bolton Wanderers
6	**Everton**
7	Tottenham Hotspur
8	Reading
9	Portsmouth
10	Blackburn Rovers

MOYES ON PAST COMMENTS

'I stick by the People's Club statement I made when I joined. If that ruffled a few feathers at Liverpool, it wasn't meant to.'

LOOKING BACK ON 06/07

April

From the highs of another last-minute winner and an impressive defeat of Fulham to the huge setback of Manchester United on a day when the life of Alan Ball was remembered following his death from a heart attack on April 25.

Mikel Arteta pledges his future to the club while goalkeeper John Ruddy agrees an emergency loan deal with Bristol City, having already enjoyed spells at Stockport County and Wrexham this term. The defeat to United is only the fifth suffered by the Blues at Goodison after being two goals ahead since 1970.

Matches lost at Goodison after leading by two goals (since 1970):

Date	Opposition	Scoreline
21st December 1974	Carlisle United	L 2-3
19th April 1975	Sheffield United	L 2-3
19th January 1994	Bolton Wanderers (FA Cup)	L 2-3
4th October 1995	Millwall (League Cup)	L 2-4
28th April 2007	Manchester United	L 2-4

Quotes of the month:

"It would mean almost everything to me to play for Everton in Europe. We had an experience of playing there a couple of years ago but it wasn't the best and it didn't last very long. We went out too early and because of that, everyone is hungry."

Joseph Yobo relishing potential European adventures

"It was a good goal but the most important thing is that it was a winning goal and keeps us on the march. I saw the lad closing me down so I flicked it over him and it nestled in the bottom corner."

James McFadden after his Goal of the Month against Charlton

"The main thing is that it is in our hands. To finish fourth you need one of the big teams to have an off season but, no disrespect, Arsenal haven't had the greatest of years and they are still fourth, so it shows there is still a long way to go for us. But we are improving and we just want to keep getting closer every year."

Joleon Lescott eyes Blues progress

"When you've got a team like ours, you need one individual special player, and he's our icing on the cake. He is well and truly one of the lads and I'm just glad he's committed his future to the club."

Phil Neville salutes Mikel Arteta

APRIL

THE GAMES

2	Aston Villa	A	1-1	Lescott
6	Fulham	H	4-1	Carsley, Stubbs, Vaughan, Anichebe
9	Bolton Wan.	A	1-1	Vaughan
15	Charlton Ath.	H	2-1	Lescott, McFadden
21	West Ham	A	0-1	
28	Man Utd	H	2-4	Stubbs, Fernandes

WHERE THEY STOOD

4	Arsenal
5	Bolton Wanderers
6	**Everton**
7	Reading
8	Portsmouth
9	Tottenham Hotspur
10	Blackburn Rovers

MOYES AFTER CHARLTON

'We are pleased with the position and I always knew this could be a defining weekend if we won.'

LOOKING BACK ON 06/07

May

European qualification is sealed before the final day of the season at Chelsea. The 3-0 victory over fellow UEFA Cup challengers Portsmouth also meant it is only the ninth season in the club's history when the Blues had been awarded 10 penalties or more is a single campaign – and the first time since 1988/89. The Pompey game also sees Gary Naysmith complete the scoring, in what would be his final game for the club before his summer switch to Sheffield United. Incidentally, the goal was his final touch of the ball for the club.

End-of-season internationals see Joleon Lescott turn out for England B, while James Vaughan earns a call-up to England's squad for the U21 European Championships in Holland. Swindon Town midfielder/forward Lukas Jutkiewicz completes his move to Goodison having agreed the switch in March, the youngster having helped the Robins to promotion from League Two at the end of the campaign.

Penalties by Everton players 2006/07:

Player	Opposition	Venue	Outcome
Arteta	Watford	H	Scored
Beattie	Wigan Athletic	H	Scored
Beattie	Sheffield United	H	Scored
Arteta	Luton Town (League Cup)	H	Missed
Arteta	Chelsea	H	Scored
Johnson	Blackburn Rovers (FA Cup)	H	Scored
Arteta	Wigan Athletic	A	Scored
Johnson	Watford	A	Scored
Arteta	Sheffield United	A	Scored
Arteta	Portsmouth	H	Scored

Scoring in final game for Everton (since 1965):

Date	Player	Opposition	Venue
13th March 1965	Roy Vernon	Aston Villa	H
6th March 1979	Ross Jack	Middlesbrough	A
10th May 1986	Gary Lineker	Liverpool (FA Cup)	N
8th May 1993	Peter Beardsley	Manchester City	A
18th January 1998	Gary Speed	Chelsea	H
4th January 2003	Niclas Alexandersson	Shrewsbury Town (FA Cup)	A
5th May 2007	Gary Naysmith	Portsmouth	H

It was Ross Jack's only match for the club.

Incoming: Lukas Jutkiewicz (Swindon Town).

Quotes of the month:

"The noise, particularly in the second half, was incredible and I firmly believe it made a difference. I knew full well that our supporters were great but to actually be amongst them in such a cracking atmosphere was a pleasure and a privilege for me."

Andy Johnson, impressed with Pompey atmosphere

"Cars has had a great season, He is one of those players that does his job and no one notices until they look at the game afterwards and say 'didn't Lee Carsley play well.'"

Alan Stubbs hails Everton's unsung hero of the season

MAY

THE GAMES

5	Portsmouth	H	3-0	Arteta pen, Yobo, Naysmith
13	Chelsea	A	1-1	Vaughan

WHERE THEY FINISHED

4	Arsenal
5	Tottenham Hotspur
6	**Everton**
7	Bolton Wanderers
8	Reading
9	Portsmouth
10	Blackburn Rovers

MOYES ON THE FANS

'Probably the biggest thing was the support. They acted like a proper football club and the supporters were the difference.'

Date	Opposition		Res	Att	Pts	Pos	Line-up					
August												
Sat 19	**Watford**	H	2-1	39,691	3	7	Howard	Neville	Valente	Yobo	Stubbs	Davies
Wed 23	Blackburn	A	1-1	22,015	4	6	Howard	Neville	Naysmith	Yobo	Stubbs	Osman
Sat 26	Tottenham	A	2-0†	35,540	7	4	Howard	Neville	Naysmith	Yobo	Lescott	Osman
September												
Sat 9	**Liverpool**	H	3-0	40,004	10	3	Howard	Hibbert	Naysmith	Yobo	Lescott	Osman
Sat 16	**Wigan**	H	2-2	37,117	11	4	Howard	Hibbert	Naysmith	Yobo	Lescott	Osman
Tues 19	Peterborough U (CC2)	A	2-1†	10,756	-	-	Wright	Neville	Valente	Hughes	Lescott	Van der M
Sun 24	Newcastle	A	1-1	50,107	12	4	Howard	Hibbert	Naysmith	Yobo	Lescott	Osman
Sat 30	**Man City**	H	1-1	38,250	13	5	Howard	Neville	Valente	Yobo	Lescott	Osman
October												
Sat 14	Middlesbrough	A	1-2	27,156	13	7	Howard	Hibbert	Valente	Yobo	Lescott	Davies
Sat 21	**Sheff Utd**	H	2-0	37,900	16	6	Howard	Neville	Lescott	Yobo	Weir	Davies
Tues 24	Luton Town (CC3)	H	4-0†	27,149	-	-	Turner	Davies	Lescott	Stubbs	Weir	Arteta
Sat 28	Arsenal	A	1-1	60,047	17	6	Howard	Neville	Lescott	Yobo	Stubbs	Arteta
November												
Sat 4	Fulham	A	0-1	23,327	17	7	Howard	Neville	Lescott	Yobo	Stubbs	Arteta
Wed 8	Arsenal (CC4)	H	0-1	31,045	-	-	Howard	Neville	Valente	Yobo	Lescott	Arteta
Sat 11	**Aston Villa**	A	0-1	36,376	17	7	Howard	Neville	Lescott	Yobo	Stubbs	Osman
Sat 18	**Bolton**	H	1-0	34,417	20	7	Howard	Yobo	Lescott	Stubbs	Valente	Osman
Sat 25	Charlton	A	1-1†	26,435	21	8	Howard	Neville	Lescott	Yobo	Valente	Davies
Wed 29	Man Utd	A	0-3	75,723	21	9	Wright	Yobo	Lescott	Stubbs	Valente	Osman
December												
Sun 3	**West Ham**	H	2-0	32,968	24	7	Howard	Yobo	Lescott	Stubbs	Valente	Van der M
Sat 9	Portsmouth	A	0-2	19,528	24	10	Howard	Yobo	Weir	Stubbs	Lescott	Van der M
Sun 17	**Chelsea**	H	2-3	33,970	24	10	Howard	Neville	**Yobo**	Stubbs	Lescott	Davies
Sat 23	Reading	A	2-0	24,053	27	10	Howard	Neville	Lescott	Yobo	Naysmith	Davies
Tues 26	**Middlesbrough**	H	0-0	38,126	28	8	Howard	Davies	Lescott	Yobo	Naysmith	Arteta
Sat 30	**Newcastle**	H	3-0	38,682	31	7	Howard	**Neville**	Lescott	Yobo	Valente	Van der M
January												
Mon 1	Man City	A	1-2	39,836	31	8	Howard	Neville	Lescott	Yobo	Valente	Davies
Sun 7	Blackburn (FAC3)	H	1-4	24,426	-	-	Howard	Neville	Lescott	Yobo	Valente	Van der M
Sun 14	**Reading**	H	1-1	34,722	32	7	Howard	Neville	Lescott	Yobo	Naysmith	Van der M
Sun 21	Wigan	A	2-0	18,149	35	7	Howard	Neville	Stubbs	Yobo	Lescott	Davies
February												
Sat 3	Liverpool	A	0-0	44,234	36	8	Howard	Hibbert	Stubbs	Yobo	Lescott	Arteta
Sat 10	**Blackburn**	H	1-0	35,593	39	8	Howard	Neville	Stubbs	Yobo	Lescott	Van der M
Wed 21	**Tottenham**	H	1-2	34,121	39	8	Howard	Neville	Stubbs	Yobo	Lescott	Osman
Sat 24	Watford	A	3-0	18,761	42	7	Howard	Neville	Lescott	Yobo	Naysmith	Cahill
March												
Sat 3	Sheff Utd	A	1-1	32,019	43	6	Howard	Neville	Lescott	Yobo	Naysmith	Cahill
Sun 18	**Arsenal**	H	1-0	37,162	46	6	Howard	Neville	Stubbs	Yobo	Lescott	Osman
April												
Mon 2	Aston Villa	A	1-1	36,407	47	7	Howard	Hibbert	Stubbs	Yobo	**Lescott**	Osman
Fri 6	**Fulham**	H	4-1	35,612	50	5	Howard	Hibbert	**Stubbs**	Yobo	Lescott	Osman
Mon 9	Bolton	A	1-1	25,179	51	6	Howard	Hibbert	Stubbs	Yobo	Lescott	Osman
Sun 15	**Charlton**	H	2-1	34,028	54	5	Howard	Hibbert	Stubbs	Yobo	**Lescott**	Osman
Sat 21	West Ham	A	0-1	34,945	54	5	Howard	Hibbert	Stubbs	Yobo	Lescott	Osman
Sat 28	**Man Utd**	H	2-4	39,682	54	6	Turner	Hibbert	**Stubbs**	Yobo	Lescott	Osman
May												
Sat 5	**Portsmouth**	H	3-0	39,619	57	5	Howard	Neville	Stubbs	**Yobo**	Lescott	Osman
Sun 13	Chelsea	A	1-1	41,746	58	6	Howard	Hibbert	Stubbs	Yobo	Lescott	Osman

---

Pre-season Friendly 14.07.07

BURY   0
EVERTON   1

Attendance: 3,612
Referee: J. Moss

Everton: Ruddy, Hibbert, Stubbs, Dennehy, Boyle, Morrison, Neville, Vidarsson, Kissock, Jutkiewicz, (Barnett 56), Anichebe
Subs not used: Jones, Densmore, Spencer, Hall, Downes

Goal: Jutkiewicz (56)

Pre-season Friendly 14.07.07

N.IRELAND XI 0
EVERTON   2

Attendance: 4,000
Referee: M. Courtney

Everton: Turner, Irving, Rodwell, Lescott, Valente, van der Meyde, de Franca, Carsley, Molyneux (Harpur 85), Vaughan (Connor 72), Johnson (Agard 66)
Subs not used: Stubhaug, Akpan, Stewart

Goals: Vaughan (27), Agard (79)

Pre-season Friendly 18.07

PRESTON
EVERTON

Attendance: 8,047
Referee: N. Swarbrick

Everton: Howard, Hibbert, Lesc... Stubbs (Jagielka 46), Valente, ... de Franca, Carsley (Neville 46), van der Meyde, Vaughan (Beattie 15), Anichebe
Subs not used: Yobo, Turner

Goals: Anichebe (80)

					Substitutes				
Carsley	Cahill	**Arteta**	**Johnson**	Beattie ■	Lescott	McFadden ■	Anichebe	Kilbane	Wright
Carsley	Arteta	Kilbane ■	Johnson	Beattie ■	Lescott ■	McFadden	**Cahill** ■	Davies	Wright
Carsley	Arteta	Cahill	Kilbane ■	**Johnson**	Weir	McFadden	Beattie	Hibbert	Wright
Carsley	Arteta ■	**Cahill**	Neville	**Johnson 2**	Weir	Beattie	Van der Meyde	Valente ■	Wright
Carsley	Arteta	Cahill	Neville	**Johnson**	Weir	**Beattie** ■	Van der Meyde	Valente ■	Wright
Carsley	Davies	Naysmith ■	Anichebe	Beattie	**Cahill** ■	Arteta ■	Hibbert	Johnson	Turner
Carsley	Arteta ■	**Cahill**	Neville	Johnson	Weir	Beattie ■	Davies	Valente ■	Wright
Carsley	Arteta ■	Cahill	Beattie	**Johnson**	Weir ■	Anichebe	Van der Meyde	Davies ■	Wright
Carsley	Arteta	**Cahill**	Neville	Johnson	Weir	Beattie ■	Van der Meyde	McFadden ■	Wright
Carsley	Cahill	**Arteta**	**Beattie** ■	Johnson	Osman	McFadden ■	Anichebe	Boyle	Turner
Carsley	**Cahill**	Osman	**McFadden**	Johnson ■	Beattie ■	**Anichebe** ■	Hughes	Vidarsson	Howard
Carsley	**Cahill**	Davies	Osman	Johnson	Beattie	Anichebe	Hughes	McFadden	Turner
Carsley ■	Cahill	Davies ■	Osman	Johnson	Beattie ■	Anichebe ■	McFadden	Valente	Turner
Carsley ■	Cahill	Osman	McFadden ■	Johnson	Anichebe ■	Weir	Stubbs	Davies	Turner
Carsley	Arteta	Davies	Cahill ■	Johnson	Beattie ■	Anichebe ■	Weir	Hughes	Turner
Carsley	**Arteta**	Neville	Beattie ■	Johnson	Weir	Anichebe ■	Van der Meyde	Vaughan	Wright
Carsley	Arteta	Osman	Beattie ■	McFadden	Weir	Stubbs	Anichebe	Vaughan ■	Wright
Carsley	Arteta	Neville	Beattie	McFadden	Weir	Anichebe	Van der Meyde	Vaughan ■	Ruddy
Carsley	**Osman** ■	McFadden	Beattie ■	Johnson	Weir ■	**Vaughan**	Hughes ■	Vidarsson	Wright
Carsley	Davies	Valente	Beattie ■	Johnson	McFadden	Vaughan ■	Anichebe ■	Hughes	Wright
Carsley ■	Osman	**Arteta**	Anichebe ■	Johnson	McFadden	Beattie ■	Weir	Naysmith	Wright
Carsley	Osman	Arteta	**McFadden** ■	**Johnson**	Beattie ■	Van der Meyde	Weir	Vaughan	Wright
Carsley	Osman	McFadden ■	Anichebe	Johnson ■	Beattie ■	Van der Meyde	Valente	Weir	Wright
Carsley	Osman	Arteta	**Anichebe 2** ■	Johnson	Beattie ■	McFadden ■	Davies ■	Weir	Wright
Carsley	**Osman** ■	Arteta	Beattie	Johnson	Anichebe	McFadden ■	Naysmith	Weir	Wright
Carsley	Osman	Arteta	Anichebe	**Johnson**	Naysmith ■	Vaughan ■	McFadden	Weir	Wright
Carsley	Osman	McFadden ■	Cahill	**Johnson**	Beattie ■	Anichebe	Davies	Stubbs	Wright
Carsley	Osman	**Arteta 2**	Cahill	Johnson	Beattie ■	Anichebe	Van der Meyde	Pistone	Wright
Carsley	Osman	Neville	Cahill	Johnson	Beattie	Anichebe	Fernandes	Naysmith	Wright
Carsley	Fernandes	Arteta	Cahill	**Johnson**	Beattie ■	Vaughan	de Franca	Naysmith	Wright
Carsley	Fernandes ■	**Arteta**	Anichebe	Beattie	Naysmith ■	Hibbert ■	Vaughan ■	de Franca	Wright
Carsley	**Fernandes** ■	Arteta	Beattie	**Johnson**	Vaughan ■	**Osman** ■	Hibbert	Anichebe	Wright
Carsley	Fernandes	**Arteta**	Beattie ■	Johnson	Osman ■	Vaughan ■	Hibbert	Stubbs	Wright
Carsley	Fernandes	Arteta	Vaughan ■	**Johnson**	Anichebe ■	Beattie	Hibbert	Naysmith	Wright
Carsley	Neville	Arteta	Vaughan	Johnson	Anichebe	Beattie	Naysmith	Valente	Wright
Carsley	Neville	Arteta ■	**Vaughan**	Johnson	**Anichebe** ■	Beattie ■	Naysmith	McFadden	Ruddy
Carsley	Neville	Arteta	**Vaughan**	Johnson	Beattie ■	McFadden	Naysmith	de Franca	Wright
Carsley	Neville	Arteta	Beattie ■	Johnson	**McFadden** ■	Naysmith ■	Van der Meyde	de Franca	Wright
Carsley	Neville ■	Arteta	Beattie	Johnson	McFadden ■	Fernandes ■	Naysmith	de Franca	Wright
Carsley ■	Neville	Arteta	**Fernandes**	Vaughan	Beattie ■	McFadden ■	Van der Meyde ■	Naysmith	Wright
Carsley	Fernandes ■	**Arteta**	Anichebe ■	Vaughan ■	McFadden ■	Beattie ■	**Naysmith** ■	Hibbert	Turner
Carsley	Neville	Arteta	Fernandes ■	**Vaughan**	Beattie ■	McFadden ■	Naysmith	Valente	Turner

TOTAL APPEARANCES 2006/2007

	LEAGUE			FA CUP			LEAGUE CUP			TOTAL		
	Apps	Subs	Total	Apps	Subs	Total	Apps	Subs	Total	Apps	Subs	Total
ANDERSON DA SILVA FRANCA	0	1	0	0	0	0	0	0	0	0	1	1
ANICHEBE VICTOR	5	14	19	1	0	1	1	2	3	7	16	23
ARTETA MIKEL	35	0	35	1	0	1	2	1	3	38	1	39
BEATTIE JAMES	15	18	33	0	0	0	1	1	2	16	19	35
CAHILL TIM	17	1	18	0	0	0	2	1	3	19	2	21
CARSLEY LEE	38	0	38	1	0	1	3	0	3	42	0	42
DAVIES SIMON	13	2	15	0	0	0	2	0	2	15	2	17
FERNANDES MANUEL	8	1	9	0	0	0	0	0	0	8	1	9
HIBBERT TONY	12	1	13	0	0	0	0	0	0	12	1	13
HOWARD TIM	36	0	36	1	0	1	1	0	1	38	0	38
HUGHES MARK	0	1	1	0	0	0	1	1	2	1	2	3
JOHNSON ANDREW	32	0	32	1	0	1	2	0	2	35	0	35
KILBANE KEVIN	2	0	2	0	0	0	0	0	0	2	0	2
LESCOTT JOLEON	36	2	38	1	0	1	3	0	3	40	2	42
McFADDEN JAMES	6	13	19	0	0	0	2	0	2	8	13	21
NAYSMITH GARY	10	5	15	0	1	1	1	0	1	11	6	17
NEVILLE PHIL	35	0	35	1	0	1	2	0	2	38	0	38
OSMAN LEON	31	3	34	1	0	1	2	0	2	34	3	37
STUBBS ALAN	23	0	23	0	0	0	1	0	1	24	0	24
TURNER IAIN	1	0	1	0	0	0	1	0	1	2	0	2
VALENTE NUNO	10	4	14	1	0	1	2	0	2	13	4	17
VAN DER MEYDE ANDY	5	3	8	1	0	1	1	0	1	7	3	10
VAUGHAN JAMES	7	7	14	0	1	1	0	0	0	7	8	15
WEIR DAVID	2	3	5	0	0	0	1	0	1	3	3	6
WRIGHT RICHARD	1	0	1	0	0	0	1	0	1	2	0	2
YOBO JOSEPH	38	0	38	1	0	1	1	0	1	40	0	40

Lee Carsley – The only player to start every Everton match in 2006/07

PLAYER GOALS 2006/2007 SEASON

ALL COMPETITIONS				
	LEAGUE	FA CUP	LEAGUE CUP	TOTAL
JOHNSON	11	1	0	12
ARTETA	9	0	0	9
CAHILL	5	0	2	7
ANICHEBE	3	0	1	4
VAUGHAN	4	0	0	4
OWN GOALS	2	0	2	4
McFADDEN	2	0	1	3
OSMAN	3	0	0	3
LESCOTT	2	0	0	2
YOBO	2	0	0	2
BEATTIE	2	0	0	2
FERNANDES	2	0	0	2
STUBBS	2	0	0	2
NEVILLE	1	0	0	1
CARSLEY	1	0	0	1
NAYSMITH	1	0	0	1
TOTAL	52	1	6	59

FINAL TABLE 2006/2007 SEASON

BARCLAYS PREMIERSHIP STANDINGS													
		HOME					AWAY						
Team	Pld	W	D	L	F	A	W	D	L	F	A	Pts	GD
1 Man Utd	38	15	2	2	46	12	13	3	3	37	15	89	+56
2 Chelsea	38	12	7	0	37	11	12	4	3	27	13	83	+40
3 Liverpool	38	14	4	1	39	7	6	4	9	18	20	68	+30
4 Arsenal	38	12	6	1	43	16	7	5	7	20	19	68	+28
5 Tottenham	38	12	3	4	34	22	5	6	8	23	32	60	+3
6 Everton	38	11	4	4	33	17	4	9	6	19	19	58	+16
7 Bolton	38	9	5	5	26	20	7	3	9	21	32	56	-5
8 Reading	38	11	2	6	29	20	5	5	9	23	27	55	+5
9 Portsmouth	38	11	5	3	28	15	3	7	9	17	27	54	+3
10 Blackburn	38	9	3	7	31	25	6	4	9	21	29	52	-2
11 Aston Villa	38	7	8	4	20	14	4	9	6	23	27	50	+2
12 Middlesbrough	38	10	3	6	31	24	2	7	10	13	25	46	-5
13 Newcastle	38	7	7	5	23	20	4	3	12	15	27	43	-9
14 Man City	38	5	6	8	10	16	6	3	10	19	28	42	-15
15 West Ham	38	8	2	9	24	26	4	3	12	11	33	41	-24
16 Fulham	38	7	7	5	18	18	1	8	10	20	42	39	-22
17 Wigan	38	5	4	10	18	30	5	4	10	19	29	38	-22
18 Sheff Utd	38	7	6	6	24	21	3	2	14	8	34	38	-23
19 Charlton	38	7	5	7	19	20	1	5	13	15	40	34	-26
20 Watford	38	3	9	7	19	25	2	4	13	10	34	28	-30

APPEARANCES & GOALS FOR EVERTON

	LEAGUE		FA CUP		LGE CUP		EUROPE		EFC CAREER	
	GMS	GLS	GMS	GLS	GMS	GLS	GMS	GLS	GMS	GLS
ANICHEBE	21	4	2	0	3	1	0	0	26	5
ARTETA	76	11	6	1	4	0	3	1	89	13
BEATTIE	76	13	5	1	3	0	2	1	86	15
CAHILL	83	22	5	2	6	2	4	1	98	27
CARSLEY	132	11	8	0	9	1	0	0	149	12
DA SILVA FRANCA	1	0	0	0	0	0	0	0	1	0
DAVIES	45	1	2	0	3	0	3	0	53	1
FERNANDES	9	2	0	0	0	0	0	0	9	2
HIBBERT	140	0	9	0	9	0	4	0	162	0
HOWARD	36	0	1	0	1	0	0	0	38	0
HUGHES	1	0	0	0	2	0	0	0	3	0
JOHNSON	32	11	1	1	2	0	0	0	35	12
KILBANE	104	4	10	1	3	0	4	0	121	5
LESCOTT	38	2	1	0	3	0	0	0	42	2
MCFADDEN	97	9	8	3	9	1	4	0	118	13
NAYSMITH	134	6	14	0	7	1	0	0	155	7
NEVILLE	69	1	5	0	3	0	4	0	81	1
OSMAN	104	13	8	2	7	0	1	0	121	15
PISTONE	103	1	6	0	7	0	1	0	117	1
RUDDY	1	0	0	0	0	0	0	0	1	0
STUBBS	161	5	11	1	8	0	0	0	180	6
TURNER	4	0	1	0	1	0	0	0	6	0
VALENTE	34	0	5	0	2	0	2	0	43	0
VAN DER MEYDE	18	0	1	0	2	0	0	0	21	0
VAUGHAN	17	5	1	0	0	0	0	0	18	5
WEIR	235	9	19	0	11	0	4	0	269	9
WRIGHT	60	0	4	0	7	0	0	0	71	0
YOBO	146	5	5	0	9	0	4	1	164	6

David Weir – Over 250 appearances for the Blues

MAN OF THE SEASON

Mikel Arteta landed the Player of the Year honour for a second successive season at the club's end-of-season awards ceremony at St. George's Hall in Liverpool. The Players' Player of the Year award was secured by Joleon Lescott, while James Vaughan scooped the Young Player of the Year accolade.

EVERTON'S EVER-PRESENTS

In 2006/07 Nigerian international Joseph Yobo became the first outfielder since Kevin Ratcliffe in 1986/87 to remain on the pitch for every single minute of Everton's league campaign. The centre-half was one of only two outfielders to achieve this feat in the Premiership last season – the other was Reading's Ivar Ingimarsson.

Yobo's feat overshadowed the fact that Lee Carsley also started every game – although he was substituted on a number of occasions – and Joleon Lescott also featured in all 38 league games, albeit two were from the bench. Lee Carsley was the only player to start all 42 matches in all competitions.

Prior to Yobo, the last ever-present in a league season was goalkeeper Thomas Myhre in 1998/99 with the last outfielder to achieve the feat being Peter Beardsley in 1991/92 – the England international remaining on the pitch for all but 32 minutes of the league campaign.

Since the expansion of the top flight to 38 matches in 1905/06 the following players have started every league match in a single season. Not surprisingly the great Neville Southall leads the way, doing so on seven occasions.

EVER-PRESENTS IN THE LEAGUE

7 SEASONS:

Neville Southall	1984/85
	1988/89
	1989/90
	1990/91
	1991/92
	1993/94
	1995/96

3 SEASONS:

Brian Labone	1960/61	Gordon West	1968/69
	1964/65		1969/70
	1968/69		1971/72

2 SEASONS:

Peter Farrell	1950/51	Ted Sagar	1932/33
	1955/56		1947/48
John Hurst	1968/69	Dennis Stevens	1962/63
	1969/70		1963/64
Cyril Lello	1953/54	George Wood	1977/78
	1954/55		1978/79
Mike Lyons	1975/76	Tommy Wright	1966/67
	1977/78		1969/70
Joe Royle	1968/69		
	1969/70		

EVERTON'S EVER-PRESENTS

1 SEASON:

John Maconnachie	1908/09	Jimmy Tansey	1956/57
Hunter Hart	1923/24	Jimmy Harris	1958/59
Wilf Chadwick	1923/24	Bobby Collins	1959/60
Alec Troup	1927/28	Albert Dunlop	1960/61
John O'Donnell	1927/28	Jimmy Gabriel	1961/62
Arthur Davies	1928/29	Alex Young	1962/63
Billy Coggins	1930/31	Colin Harvey	1966/67
Warney Cresswell	1930/31	David Lawson	1973/74
Cliff Britton	1933/34	Martin Dobson	1975/76
Jimmy Stein	1933/34	Ken McNaught	1976/77
Jock Thomson	1934/35	Andy King	1977/78
Torry Gillick	1936/37	John Bailey	1979/80
Norman Greenhalgh	1938/39	Kevin Ratcliffe	1986/87
Jackie Grant	1950/51	Peter Beardsley	1991/92
Tommy E.Jones	1952/53	Thomas Myhre	1998/99
Don Donovan	1953/54	Joseph Yobo	2006/07
Eric Moore	1955/56		

MINUTES ON THE PITCH: PREMIER LEAGUE 2006/07

Player	Mins
Joseph Yobo	3,420
Lee Carsley	3,377
Joleon Lescott	3,314
Tim Howard	3,240
Mikel Arteta	3,129
Phil Neville	3,105
Leon Osman	2,792
Andy Johnson	2,790
Simon Davies	2,315
Alan Stubbs	1,960
James Beattie	1,487
Tim Cahill	1,448
Gary Naysmith	972
Tony Hibbert	948
Nuno Valente	919
James McFadden	782
Manuel Fernandes	718
Victor Anichebe	630
James Vaughan	597
Andy Van der Meyde	386
David Weir	151
Kevin Kilbane	93
Iain Turner	90
Richard Wright	90
Anderson da Silva	2
Mark Hughes	2

EVERTON OBITUARIES

Alan Ball (12th May 1945 – 25th April 2007)

On the morning of April 25, 2007 football fans woke to the shocking news of the death of one of Everton and England's finest players. During his time at the club from 1966-1971, Alan Ball firmly established himself as one of the greatest to wear the blue jersey. The midfielder would be one of the first names on any all-time Everton teamsheet. Although he had success at other clubs, there is no doubting that his best days were at Goodison in the great side of Harry Catterick. For Everton supporters his name will be forever associated with the names of Colin Harvey and Howard Kendall.

The youngest member of England's 1966 World Cup team, he joined Everton shortly after and typically his first goals at Goodison were in a match-winning performance against Liverpool – a side he always saved his best games for wherever he was playing – in August 1966. Ball played more than 250 games for Everton before his much-lamented move to Arsenal in 1971 and his final top-flight game was appropriately against the Toffees for Southampton in 1982. During his career he became the first player to make more than 100 league appearances for four different clubs.

The maestro played 72 times for his country from 1965-75 – winning 39 at Everton, which is still a club record for England. His life and playing career was commemorated before an emotional meeting with Manchester United three days after his untimely death at the age of 61.

What They Said:

"He was always bubbly, on and off the field, and he was undoubtedly the best player I ever played with. When things were going wrong on the pitch he was the one who put them right."

Howard Kendall

"In my time as a supporter and a player Alan was the greatest I have seen at Everton. The fact that he was Man of the Match in a World Cup final at 21 says it all."

Colin Harvey

"I would think he was probably the best footballer I played alongside."

Alex Young

"He was the youngest member of the team and Man of the Match in the 1966 World Cup final."

Sir Geoff Hurst

"If it had not been for his impact in 1966 the result could have been totally different. He did not appear to have a nerve in his body and he was an inspiration to us all."

Sir Bobby Charlton

"Once Everton has touched you, nothing will be the same"

Alan Ball

ALAN BALL AT EVERTON

Record club-by-club

Opponents	Games	Goals
AaB Aalborg	2	1
Arsenal	9	1
Aston Villa	2	1
Blackburn Rovers	1	0
Blackpool	4	0
B. M'Gladbach	2	0
Bristol City	1	0
Bristol Rovers	1	0
Burnley	11	5
Carlisle United	1	0
Chelsea	11	2
Colchester United	1	1
Coventry City	8	2
Crystal Palace	4	0
Darlington	1	1
Derby County	8	1
Fulham	4	3
Huddersfield Town	2	1
IBK Keflavik	2	3
Ipswich Town	8	1
Leeds United	11	1
Leicester City	8	4

Opponents	Games	Goals
Liverpool	13	5
Luton Town	1	1
Manchester City	11	2
Manchester Utd	12	5
Middlesbrough	1	0
Newcastle United	10	2
Nottingham Forest	10	0
Panathinaikos	2	0
QPR	2	0
Real Zaragoza	2	0
Sheffield United	6	4
Sheffield Wed.	6	2
Southampton	9	6
Southport	1	0
Stoke City	12	4
Sunderland	8	2
Tottenham H.	10	1
Tranmere Rovers	1	1
WBA	12	10
West Ham United	10	2
Wolves	10	4
Grand Total	**251**	**79**

Season by Season Record

(Apps/Goals)	League		FA Cup		Lge Cup		Europe		C. Shield		Total	
	A	G	A	G	A	G	A	G	A	G	A	G
1966/67	41	15	6	2	0	0	4	1	-	-	51	18
1967/68	34	20	4	0	2	0	-	-	-	-	40	20
1968/69	40	16	5	0	4	2	-	-	-	-	49	18
1969/70	37	10	1	1	3	1	-	-	-	-	41	12
1970/71	39	2	6	3	1	0	6	3	1	0	53	8
1971/72	17	3	0	0	0	0	-	-	-	-	17	3
	208	**66**	**22**	**6**	**10**	**3**	**10**	**4**	**1**	**0**	**251**	**79**

(Figures include 3rd/4th place play-off match in 1970/71 FA Cup)

EVERTON OBITUARIES

Jack Bentley (17th February 1942 – 27th May 2007)

After progressing through the youth and reserve ranks, the local-born Jack Bentley's only appearance for the club was against Bolton Wanderers in February 1961. He then left Everton and played for two seasons at Stockport County. After joining Wellington Town in the Southern League in 1963 he scored a remarkable 431 goals in 835 games, before retiring in 1977.

Jock Dodds (7th September 1915 – 23rd February 2007)

Ephraim "Jock" Dodds was one of the most prolific goalscorers of the years immediately before and after World War Two. After appearing for Sheffield United in the 1936 FA Cup final, he left for Blackpool in 1939 where he was a prolific scorer in wartime matches. The centre-forward joined Everton in November 1946 and his strike rate of 37 goals in 58 matches is one of the best for the club.

George Heslop (1st July 1940 – 16th September 2006)

The centre-half arrived at Goodison in March 1962 from Newcastle United – where he had made his debut in an 8-2 win over Everton in 1959 – in a deal that saw Jimmy Fell go the other way. The presence of Brian Labone meant that he made just 11 appearances when with the Toffees before moving to Manchester City in 1965. He was an integral part of the side that won the Second (1966) and First Division (1968) titles and the FA Cup (1969) and Cup Winners' Cups (1970).

Oscar Hold (19th October 1918 – 16th October 2006)

This much-travelled forward scored five goals in 22 games for Everton from 1950-52 but is better known in the game for his managerial career that encompassed Fenerbahce in Turkey, Saudi Arabia, Cyprus, Kuwait and Nigeria.

Harry Leyland (12th May 1930 – 7th December 2006)

Goalkeeper Harry Leyland made 40 appearances in six years as a professional at Goodison from 1950-56 before joining Blackburn Rovers, where he played in the 1960 FA Cup final. He then enjoyed a successful spell at Tranmere Rovers, making 180 league appearances from 1961-67.
Following his playing days, he became heavily involved with New Brighton Rugby Club where he was a life member. But his heart always remained at Everton as far as football was concerned and in his later years, he was a Goodison Park regular.

MOST POINTS WON BY TEAMS IN PREMIER LEAGUE HISTORY

		POINTS	HIGHEST POS	SEASONS IN PREMIERSHIP
1	MANCHESTER UNITED	1232	1st (9 times)	15
2	ARSENAL	1081	1st (3 times)	15
3	CHELSEA	1013	1st (2 times)	15
4	LIVERPOOL	999	2nd (2001/2002)	15
5	NEWCASTLE UNITED	829	2nd (2 times)	14
6	ASTON VILLA	817	2nd (1992/1993)	15
7	TOTTENHAM HOTSPUR	788	5th (2 times)	15
8	BLACKBURN ROVERS	747	1st (1994/1995)	13
9	EVERTON	735	4th (2004/2005)	15
10	LEEDS UNITED	692	3rd (1999/2000)	12
11	WEST HAM UNITED	596	5th (1998/1999)	12
12	SOUTHAMPTON	587	8th (2002/2003)	13
13	MIDDLESBROUGH	559	7th (2004/2005)	12
14	MANCHESTER CITY	452	8th (2004/2005)	10
15	COVENTRY CITY	409	11th (2 times)	9
16	SHEFFIELD WEDNESDAY	392	7th (3 times)	8
17	WIMBLEDON (MK DONS)	391	6th (1993/1994)	8
18	BOLTON WANDERERS	376	6th (2004/2005)	8
19	CHARLTON ATHLETIC	361	7th (2003/2004)	8
20	LEICESTER CITY	342	8th (1999/2000)	8
21	FULHAM	275	9th (2003/2004)	6
22	DERBY COUNTY	263	8th (1998/1999)	6
23	NOTTINGHAM FOREST	239	3rd (1994/1995)	5
24	SUNDERLAND	229	7th (2 times)	6
25	IPSWICH TOWN	224	5th (2000/2001)	5
26	QUEENS PARK RANGERS	216	5th (1992/1993)	4
27	NORWICH CITY	201	3rd (1992/1993)	4
28	BIRMINGHAM CITY	177	10th (2003/2004)	4
29	PORTSMOUTH	176	9th (2006/2007)	4
30	CRYSTAL PALACE	160	18th (2004/2005)	4
31	SHEFFIELD UNITED	132	14th (1992/1993)	3
32	WEST BROMWICH ALB.	90	17th (2004/2005)	3
33	OLDHAM ATHLETIC	89	19th (1992/1993)	2
=	WIGAN ATHLETIC	89	10th (2005/2006)	2
35	BRADFORD CITY	62	17th (1999/2000)	2
36	READING	55	8th (2006/2007)	1
37	WATFORD	52	20th (2 times)	2
38	BARNSLEY	35	19th (1997/1998)	1
39	WOLVERHAMPTON W.	33	20th (2003/2004)	1
40	SWINDON TOWN	30	22nd (1994/1995)	1

Duncan Ferguson – Everton's top goalscorer in Premiership history

PREMIERSHIP RECORD: CLUB-BY-CLUB

EVERTON'S LEAGUE RECORD – CLUB-BY-CLUB (2006/07 PREMIERSHIP TEAMS ONLY)						
	PLAYED	WON	DREW	LOST	FOR	AGAINST
ARSENAL	172	54	36	82	213	278
ASTON VILLA	184	70	45	69	284	282
BLACKBURN ROVERS	138	55	29	54	228	221
BOLTON WANDERERS	128	64	30	34	213	172
CHARLTON ATHLETIC	48	20	10	18	78	68
CHELSEA	136	45	42	49	210	214
FULHAM	38	18	8	12	62	43
LIVERPOOL	176	56	55	65	212	238
MANCHESTER CITY	148	52	39	57	203	214
MANCHESTER UNITED	156	52	37	67	228	242
MIDDLESBROUGH	108	51	27	30	183	141
NEWCASTLE UNITED	146	56	31	59	212	220
PORTSMOUTH	52	22	8	22	81	94
READING	4	3	1	0	8	3
SHEFFIELD UNITED	120	48	30	42	184	154
TOTTENHAM HOTSPUR	140	44	43	53	189	220
WATFORD	16	13	1	2	41	20
WEST HAM UNITED	104	51	21	32	177	121
WIGAN ATHLETIC	4	1	2	1	5	4

EVERTON'S GOALS v PREMIERSHIP OPPONENTS					
	GAMES PLAYED	GOALS IN FIXTURE	AVE. PER GAME	EVERTON GOALS	AVE. PER GAME
ARSENAL	30	82	2.73	22	0.73
ASTON VILLA	30	67	2.23	26	0.87
BARNSLEY	2	10	5	6	3
BIRMINGHAM CITY	8	12	1.5	5	0.63
BLACKBURN ROVERS	26	55	2.12	26	1
BOLTON WANDERERS	16	44	2.75	23	1.44
BRADFORD CITY	4	8	2	8	2
CHARLTON ATHLETIC	16	39	2.44	22	1.38
CHELSEA	30	79	2.63	30	1
COVENTRY CITY	18	34	1.89	15	0.83
CRYSTAL PALACE	8	24	3	16	2
DERBY COUNTY	12	29	2.42	14	1.17
FULHAM	12	30	2.5	15	1.25
IPSWICH TOWN	10	20	2	11	1.1
LEEDS UNITED	24	53	2.21	29	1.21
LEICESTER CITY	16	38	2.38	20	1.25
LIVERPOOL	30	66	2.2	31	1.03
MANCHESTER CITY	20	58	2.9	25	1.25
MANCHESTER UNITED	30	88	2.93	23	0.77
MIDDLESBROUGH	24	62	2.58	36	1.5
NEWCASTLE UNITED	28	72	2.57	31	1.11
NORWICH CITY	8	21	2.63	8	1
NOTTINGHAM FOREST	10	24	2.4	16	1.6
OLDHAM ATHLETIC	4	9	2.25	5	1.25
PORTSMOUTH	8	15	1.88	10	1.25
QUEENS PARK RANGERS	8	35	4.38	14	1.75
READING	2	4	2	3	1.5
SHEFFIELD UNITED	6	13	2.17	7	1.17
SHEFFIELD WEDNESDAY	16	50	3.13	22	1.38
SOUTHAMPTON	26	62	2.38	36	1.38
SUNDERLAND	12	32	2.67	16	1.33
SWINDON TOWN	2	10	5	7	3.5
TOTTENHAM HOTSPUR	30	80	2.67	29	0.97
WATFORD	4	16	4	12	3
WEST BROMWICH ALBION	6	16	2.67	7	1.17
WEST HAM UNITED	24	62	2.58	42	1.75
WIGAN ATHLETIC	4	9	2.25	5	1.25
WIMBLEDON (MK DONS)	16	45	2.81	24	1.5
WOLVERHAMPTON WANDERERS	2	5	2.5	3	1.5

(Up to and including end of 2006/07 season)

PREMIERSHIP RECORD: CLUB-BY-CLUB

EVERTON'S HEAD-TO-HEAD v PREMIERSHIP OPPONENTS						
	PLAYED	WON	DREW	LOST	FOR	AGAINST
ARSENAL	30	5	7	18	24	58
ASTON VILLA	30	7	9	14	27	40
BARNSLEY	2	1	1	0	6	4
BIRMINGHAM CITY	8	3	4	1	6	6
BLACKBURN ROVERS	26	11	4	11	26	29
BOLTON WANDERERS	16	7	5	4	23	21
BRADFORD CITY	4	3	1	0	7	1
CHARLTON ATHLETIC	16	7	3	6	21	18
CHELSEA	30	4	11	15	30	49
COVENTRY CITY	18	3	9	6	15	19
CRYSTAL PALACE	8	5	0	3	16	8
DERBY COUNTY	12	5	2	5	14	15
FULHAM	12	6	0	6	16	14
IPSWICH TOWN	10	4	2	4	11	9
LEEDS UNITED	24	7	10	7	29	24
LEICESTER CITY	16	4	11	1	20	18
LIVERPOOL	30	8	11	11	31	35
MANCHESTER CITY	20	8	4	8	25	33
MANCHESTER UNITED	30	3	4	23	24	64
MIDDLESBROUGH	24	10	7	7	36	26
NEWCASTLE UNITED	28	9	6	13	31	41
NORWICH CITY	8	3	2	3	8	13
NOTTINGHAM FOREST	10	6	0	4	16	8
OLDHAM ATHLETIC	4	2	1	1	5	4
PORTSMOUTH	8	6	0	2	10	5
QUEENS PARK RANGERS	8	2	1	5	14	21
READING	2	1	1	0	3	1
SHEFFIELD UNITED	6	2	2	2	7	6
SHEFFIELD WEDNESDAY	16	3	5	8	20	30
SOUTHAMPTON	26	11	8	7	36	26
SUNDERLAND	12	5	2	5	16	16
SWINDON TOWN	2	1	1	0	7	3
TOTTENHAM HOTSPUR	30	3	10	17	30	50
WATFORD	4	4	0	0	12	4
WEST BROMWICH ALBION	6	3	1	2	7	9
WEST HAM UNITED	24	12	6	6	42	20
WIGAN ATHLETIC	4	1	2	1	5	4
WIMBLEDON (MK DONS)	16	6	6	4	24	21
WOLVERHAMPTON WANDERERS	2	1	0	1	3	2
TOTAL	**582**	**192**	**159**	**231**	**703**	**775**

(Up to and including end of 2006/07 season)

PREMIERSHIP NUMBERS GAME

SQUAD NUMBERS

Number Players (with Premiership appearances in brackets)

1	Southall (207),	Myhre (42),	Gerrard (45),	Wright (60)	
2	Jackson (67),	Barrett (57),	Cleland (27),	S. Watson (126),	Kroldrup (1),	Hibbert (13)
3	Hinchcliffe (143),	Ball (62),	Pistone (101),	Naysmith (22)	
4	Snodin (32),	Barrett (17),	Unsworth (65),	Williamson (15),	Dacourt (30),	Gough (38),
	Stubbs (124),	Yobo (67)			
5	D. Watson (183),	Weir (186)			
6	Ablett (71),	Phelan (24),	Unsworth (187),	Arteta (76)	
7	Ma. Ward (27),	Samways (19),	Stuart (78),	Madar (17),	Collins (55),	Alexandersson (58),
	Bent (54),	Van der Meyde (8)			
8	Stuart (58),	Rideout (34),	Barmby (91),	Nyarko (22),	Radzinski (91),	Beattie (43),
	Johnson (32)				
9	Cottee (42),	Ferguson (116),	Campbell (145),	Ferguson (27),	Beattie (33)	
10	Horne (89),	Speed (58),	Hutchison (75),	S. Hughes (18),	Ferguson (84),	Davies (45)
11	Beagrie (29),	Amokachi (18),	Limpar (30),	Spencer (9),	Gemmill (14),	Pembridge (60),
	Jeffers (18),	McFadden (75)			
12	Holmes (16),	Amokachi (25),	Barmby (25),	Short (53),	Pembridge (31),	Ball (29),
	Blomqvist (15),	Tie (34)			
13	Kearton (1),	Gerrard (43),	Simonsen (29),	Turner (4)	
14	Ebbrell (97),	Grant (23),	Weir (35),	Jeffers (12),	Tal (7),	Kilbane (102)
15	Rideout (53),	Jackson (14),	Thomsen (24),	Beagrie (6),	Materazzi (27),	Dunne (34),
	Naysmith (112),	Stubbs (37)			
16	Radosavljevic (23),	Burrows (19),	Samways (4),	Branch (32),	Cadamarteri (17),	Gravesen (141),
	Carsley (5),	Lescott (38)			
17	Limpar (36),	Kanchelskis (52),	Farrelly (27),	Jeffers (21),	Gemmill (76),	Cahill (83)
18	Parkinson (90),	Madar (17),	Weir (14),	Phelan (1),	S. Hughes (11),	Gascoigne (31),
	Rooney (67),	Neville (69)			
19	Barlow (36),	Hottiger (17),	Oster (40),	Xavier (20),	J. Moore (37),	McBride (8),
	Chadwick (1),	Valente (34)			
20	Warzycha (7),	Durrant (5),	Grant (35),	Thomas (8),	Gemmill (7),	Jevons (3),
	Cleland (8),	Yobo (79),	Ferrari (8)		
21	Rowett (4),	Short (46),	Mi. Ward (24),	Cadamarteri (19),	Weifeng (1),	Nyarko (11),
	Osman (98)				
22	Angell (20),	McCann (11),	Degn (4),	Linderoth (40),	Hibbert (65),	Vaughan (14)
23	Branch (28),	Tiler (21),	J. Moore (15),	M. Hughes (9)*,	Rodrigo (4),	Pistone (2)
24	O'Connor (5),	Grant (2),	Ferguson (12),	Ginola (5),	Xavier (12),	McFadden (23),
	Howard (36)				
25	N. Moore (4),	Ball (30),	Baardsen (1),	Martyn (86)	
26	Unsworth (46),	Allen (6),	Bakayoko (23),	Johnson (3),	M. Hughes (9)*,	Jevons (4),
	Carsley (89),	Westerveld (2),	Carsley (38)		
27	Dunne (26),	Clarke (8),	Van der Meyde (10)		
28	Cadamarteri (1),	Bilic (28),	Xavier (11),	Hibbert (59),	Anichebe (19)	
29	Cadamarteri (56),	McLeod (5),	Vaughan (1)		
30	Jevons (1),	Clarke (1),	Chadwick (13),	Ruddy (1)	
31	Myhre (22),	Osman (6),	Vaughan (2),	M. Hughes (1)	
32	O'Kane (14),	Hibbert (3)			
33	Tal (22)				
34	Holmes (1),	Jeffers (16)			
35	Hills (3),	Simonsen (1),	Myhre (6),	Gerrard (2)	
36	Milligan (4)				
37	Farley (1),	Fernandes (9)			
38	Anichebe (2),	Silva de Franca (1)			

*Please note 'M. Hughes' (No. 23 & 26) was striker Mark Hughes (D.O.B. 1/11/1963);
'M. Hughes' (No. 31) was defender Mark Hughes (D.O.B. 9/12/1986)

PREMIERSHIP NUMBERS GAME

Top 10 total appearances in Premier League

David Unsworth	302
Duncan Ferguson	239
David Weir (right)	235
Dave Watson	223
Neville Southall	207
Alan Stubbs	**161**
Joseph Yobo	**146**
Kevin Campbell	145
Andy Hinchcliffe	143
Thomas Gravesen	141

Top 10 goalscorers in Premier League

Duncan Ferguson	60
Kevin Campbell	45
David Unsworth	33
Paul Rideout (right)	29
Tony Cottee	28
Tomasz Radzinski	25
Tim Cahill	**22**
Graham Stuart	22
Andrei Kanchelskis	20
Nick Barmby	18
Francis Jeffers	18

Kevin Campbell in scoring action against Charlton Athletic in 1999. The striker lies second behind Duncan Ferguson in Everton's all-time Premiership goalscoring charts

Record win v Southampton – Andrei Kanchelskis is congratulated by Joe Parkinson and Graham Stuart after scoring the second goal (top); Gary Speed completes the rout (above)

PREMIER LEAGUE FACTS & FIGURES

PREMIER LEAGUE RECORD

Season	P	W	D	L	F	A	Pts	Pos
1992/1993	42	15	8	19	53	55	53	13
1993/1994	42	12	8	22	42	63	44	18
1994/1995	42	11	17	14	44	51	50	15
1995/1996	38	17	10	11	64	44	61	6
1996/1997	38	10	12	16	44	57	42	15
1997/1998	38	9	13	16	41	56	40	17
1998/1999	38	11	10	17	42	47	43	14
1999/2000	38	12	14	12	59	49	50	13
2000/2001	38	11	9	18	45	59	42	16
2001/2002	38	11	10	17	45	57	43	15
2002/2003	38	17	8	13	48	49	59	7
2003/2004	38	9	12	17	45	57	39	17
2004/2005	38	18	7	13	45	46	61	4
2005/2006	38	14	8	16	34	49	50	11
2006/2007	38	15	13	10	52	36	58	6

BIGGEST PREMIERSHIP WINS

Date	Opponents	Venue	Score	Scorers	Attendance
16th November 1996	Southampton	Home	7-1	Stuart, Kanchelskis 2, Speed 3, Barmby	35,669
8th May 1999	West Ham United	Home	6-0	Campbell 3, Ball (pen), Hutchison, Jeffers	40,049
29th September 2001	West Ham United	Home	5-0	Campbell, Hutchison (og), Gravesen, Watson, Radzinski	32,049
26th December 1999	Sunderland	Home	5-0	Hutchison 2, Jeffers, Pembridge, Campbell	40,017
17th February 1999	Middlesbrough	Home	5-0	Barmby 2, Dacourt, Materazzi, Unsworth	31,606

BIGGEST PREMIERSHIP DEFEATS

Date	Opponents	Venue	Score	Scorers	Attendance
11th May 2005	Arsenal	Away	0-7		38,073
9th December 2000	Manchester City	Away	0-5		34,516
29th March 2002	Newcastle United	Away	2-6	Ferguson, Alexandersson	51,921
15th May 2004	Manchester City	Away	1-5	Campbell	47,284
4th December 1999	Manchester United	Away	1-5	Jeffers	55,193
2nd April 1994	Sheffield Wednesday	Away	1-5	Cottee	24,096
25th September 1993	Norwich City	Home	1-5	Rideout	20,531

AVERAGE HOME ATTENDANCES

Season	High	Low	Average	
1992/1993	35,826	14,051	20,457	**LOWEST AVERAGE FOR SEASON**
1993/1994	38,157	13,667	23,129	**LOWEST ATTENDANCE v S'TON, 4/12/93**
1994/1995	40,011	23,293	31,035	
1995/1996	40,127	30,009	35,424	
1996/1997	40,177	30,368	36,188	
1997/1998	40,112	28,533	35,355	
1998/1999	40,185	30,357	35,760	
1999/2000	40,056	30,490	33,342	
2000/2001	40,260	27,670	34,131	
2001/2002	39,948	28,138	33,582	
2002/2003	40,168	32,240	38,481	
2003/2004	40,228	35,775	38,837	**HIGHEST AVERAGE FOR SEASON**
2004/2005	40,552	32,406	36,834	**HIGHEST ATTENDANCE, v L'POOL, 11/12/04**
2005/2006	40,158	34,333	36,860	
2006/2007	40,004	32,968	36,739	

PREMIER LEAGUE RED CARDS - EVERTON

Date	Player	Opponents	Venue	Minute of Dismissal	Result (Everton first)
28th December 1992	Neville Southall	Queens Park Rangers	(a)	19	2-4
28th December 1992	Paul Rideout	Queens Park Rangers	(a)	44	2-4
6th February 1993	Neville Southall	Sheffield Wednesday	(a)	43	1-3
14th January 1995	Duncan Ferguson	Arsenal	(a)	53	1-1
1st February 1995	Earl Barrett	Newcastle United	(a)	61	0-2
1st February 1995	Barry Horne	Newcastle United	(a)	66	0-2
4th March 1995	Vinny Samways	Leicester City	(a)	49	2-2
4th March 1995	Duncan Ferguson	Leicester City	(a)	61	2-2
9th May 1995	Stuart Barlow	Ipswich Town	(a)	87	1-0
9th September 1995	David Unsworth	Manchester United	(h)	80	2-3
14th October 1995	Barry Horne	Bolton Wanderers	(a)	61	1-1
30th December 1995	Dave Watson	Leeds United	(h)	17	2-0
21st September 1996	Duncan Ferguson	Blackburn Rovers	(a)	88	1-1
16th April 1997	David Unsworth	Liverpool	(h)	81	1-1
13th September 1997	Andy Hinchcliffe	Derby County	(a)	67	1-3
24th September 1997	Slaven Bilic	Newcastle United	(a)	62	0-1
26th November 1997	Slaven Bilic	Chelsea	(a)	90	0-2
14th February 1998	Duncan Ferguson	Derby County	(h)	15	1-2
7th March 1998	Slaven Bilic	Southampton	(a)	68	1-2
12th September 1998	Olivier Dacourt	Leeds United	(h)	55	0-0
5th December 1998	Richard Dunne	Chelsea	(h)	75	0-0
18th January 1999	Alec Cleland	Aston Villa	(a)	15	0-3
13th March 1999	Don Hutchison	Arsenal	(h)	18	0-2
11th April 1999	Marco Materazzi	Coventry City	(h)	85	2-0
11th August 1999	John Collins	Aston Villa	(a)	64	0-3
28th August 1999	Richard Dunne	Derby County	(a)	25	0-1
27th September 1999	Francis Jeffers	Liverpool	(a)	75	1-0
30th October 1999	David Weir	Middlesbrough	(a)	76	1-2
8th May 2000	Richard Dunne	Leeds United	(a)	50	1-1
8th May 2000	Don Hutchison	Leeds United	(a)	87	1-1
29th October 2000	Tommy Gravesen	Liverpool	(a)	75	1-3
24th February 2001	Alex Nyarko	Ipswich Town	(a)	71	0-2
8th April 2001	Alessandro Pistone	Manchester City	(h)	88	3-1
21st April 2001	Abel Xavier	Arsenal	(a)	80	1-4
8th December 2001	David Weir	Fulham	(a)	77	0-2
16th March 2002	Tommy Gravesen	Fulham	(h)	29	2-1
1st April 2002	Duncan Ferguson	Bolton Wanderers	(h)	20	3-1
28th August 2002	Alan Stubbs	Birmingham City	(h)	48	1-1
10th October 2002	David Weir	Manchester United	(a)	89	0-3
1st December 2002	Joseph Yobo	Newcastle United	(a)	21	1-2
7th December 2002	David Unsworth	Chelsea	(h)	87	1-3
26th December 2002	Wayne Rooney	Birmingham City	(a)	81	1-1
19th April 2003	David Weir	Liverpool	(h)	81	1-2
19th April 2003	Gary Naysmith	Liverpool	(h)	90	1-2
16th August 2003	Li Tie	Arsenal	(a)	87	1-2
13th September 2003	Gary Naysmith	Newcastle United	(h)	58	2-2
20th March 2004	Duncan Ferguson	Leicester City	(a)	41	1-1
21st August 2004	Gary Naysmith	Crystal Palace	(a)	70	3-1
11th September 2004	Tim Cahill	Manchester City	(a)	60	1-0
28th December 2004	Duncan Ferguson	Charlton Athletic	(a)	83	0-2
12th February 2005	James Beattie	Chelsea	(h)	8	0-1
27th August 2005	Phil Neville	Fulham	(a)	90	0-1
28th December 2005	Phil Neville	Liverpool	(h)	68	1-3
28th December 2005	Mikel Arteta	Liverpool	(h)	90	1-3
31st January 2006	Duncan Ferguson	Wigan Athletic	(a)	80	1-1
11th February 2006	Iain Turner	Blackburn Rovers	(h)	9	1-0
25th March 2006	Andy Van der Meyde	Liverpool	(a)	73	1-3
26th August 2006	Kevin Kilbane	Tottenham Hotspur	(a)	32	2-0
24th September 2006	Tony Hibbert	Newcastle United	(a)	79	1-1

PREMIER LEAGUE RED CARDS - OPPONENTS

Date	Player	Opponents	Venue	Minute of	Result (Everton first) Dismissal
3rd March 1993	Tim Sherwood	Blackburn Rovers	(h)	61	2-1
10th April 1993	Andy Kernaghan	Middlesbrough	(a)	55	2-1
15th January 1994	Andy Mutch	Swindon Town	(h)	48	6-2
5th March 1994	Graeme Sharp	Oldham Athletic	(h)	69	2-1
30th August 1994	Steve Chettle	Nottingham Forest	(h)	85	1-2
15th March 1995	Terry Phelan	Manchester City	(h)	61	1-1
14th April 1995	Robert Lee	Newcastle United	(h)	88	2-0
14th October 1995	Richard Sneekes	Bolton Wanderers	(a)	51	1-1
11th December 1995	Ludek Miklosko	West Ham United	(h)	43	3-0
16th December 1995	John Beresford	Newcastle United	(a)	33	0-1
13th January 1996	Mark Hughes	Chelsea	(h)	62	1-1
10th February 1996	Michael Frontzeck	Manchester City	(h)	86	2-0
30th March 1996	Garry Flitcroft	Blackburn Rovers	(a)	3	3-0
16th April 1997	Robbie Fowler	Liverpool	(h)	81	1-1
11th May 1997	Frode Grodas	Chelsea	(h)	20	1-2
7th March 1998	Ken Monkou	Southampton	(a)	36	1-2
11th April 1998	Lucas Radebe	Leeds United	(h)	17	2-0
25th April 1998	Andy Booth	Sheffield Wednesday	(h)	80	1-3
26th September 1998	Martin Dahlin	Blackburn Rovers	(h)	78	0-0
5th December 1998	Dennis Wise	Chelsea	(h)	36	0-0
13th March 1999	Emmanuel Petit	Arsenal	(h)	60	0-2
27th September 1999	Sander Westerveld	Liverpool	(a)	75	1-0
27th September 1999	Steven Gerrard	Liverpool	(a)	90	1-0
20th November 1999	Frank Lebouef	Chelsea	(h)	56	1-1
18th December 1999	Neil Cox	Watford	(a)	90	3-1
8th May 2000	Michael Duberry	Leeds United	(a)	54	1-1
23rd August 2000	Carl Tiler	Charlton Athletic	(h)	36	3-0
25th November 2000	J.F. Hasselbaink	Chelsea	(h)	71	2-1
31st March 2001	Stuart Pearce	West Ham United	(a)	45	2-0
8th April 2001	Paul Dickov	Manchester City	(h)	88	3-1
16th April 2001	Igor Biscan	Liverpool	(h)	77	2-3
19th May 2001	Don Hutchison	Sunderland	(h)	64	2-2
20th August 2001	Gary Doherty	Tottenham Hotspur	(h)	62	1-1
20th August 2001	Gus Poyet	Tottenham Hotspur	(h)	65	1-1
3rd November 2001	Souleymane Diawara	Bolton Wanderers	(a)	87	2-2
8th December 2001	Luis Boa Morte	Fulham	(a)	77	0-2
3rd March 2002	Dominic Matteo	Leeds United	(h)	38	0-0
1st April 2002	Kostas Konstandinis	Bolton Wanderers	(h)	30	3-1
31st August 2002	Shaun Wright-Phillips	Manchester City	(a)	27	1-3
14th December 2002	Lucas Neill	Blackburn Rovers	(h)	76	2-1
16th August 2003	Sol Campbell	Arsenal	(a)	30	1-2
13th September 2003	Laurent Robert	Newcastle United	(h)	40	2-2
9th April 2004	Stephen Carr	Tottenham Hotspur	(h)	75	3-1
13th November 2004	Muzzy Izzet	Birmingham City	(h)	69	1-0
26th December 2004	Christian Negouai	Manchester City	(h)	83	2-1
20th March 2005	Milan Baros	Liverpool	(a)	77	1-2
20th April 2005	Gary Neville	Manchester United	(h)	71	1-0
20th April 2005	Paul Scholes	Manchester United	(h)	90	1-0
30th April 2005	Papa Bouba Diop	Fulham	(a)	75	0-2
7th May 2005	Shola Ameobi	Newcastle United	(h)	56	2-0
15th May 2005	Bruno N'Gotty	Bolton Wanderers	(a)	45	2-3
3rd December 2005	Andy Todd	Blackburn Rovers	(a)	31	2-0
4th February 2006	Stephen Jordan	Manchester City	(h)	90	1-0
21st January 2006	Cesc Fabregas	Arsenal	(h)	90	1-0
31st January 2006	Jason Roberts	Wigan Athletic	(a)	83	1-1
25th March 2006	Steven Gerrard	Liverpool	(a)	18	1-3
24th September 2006	Titus Bramble	Newcastle United	(a)	78	1-1
21st October 2006	Claude Davis	Sheffield United	(h)	32	2-0

THE FOOTBALL LEAGUE RECORD

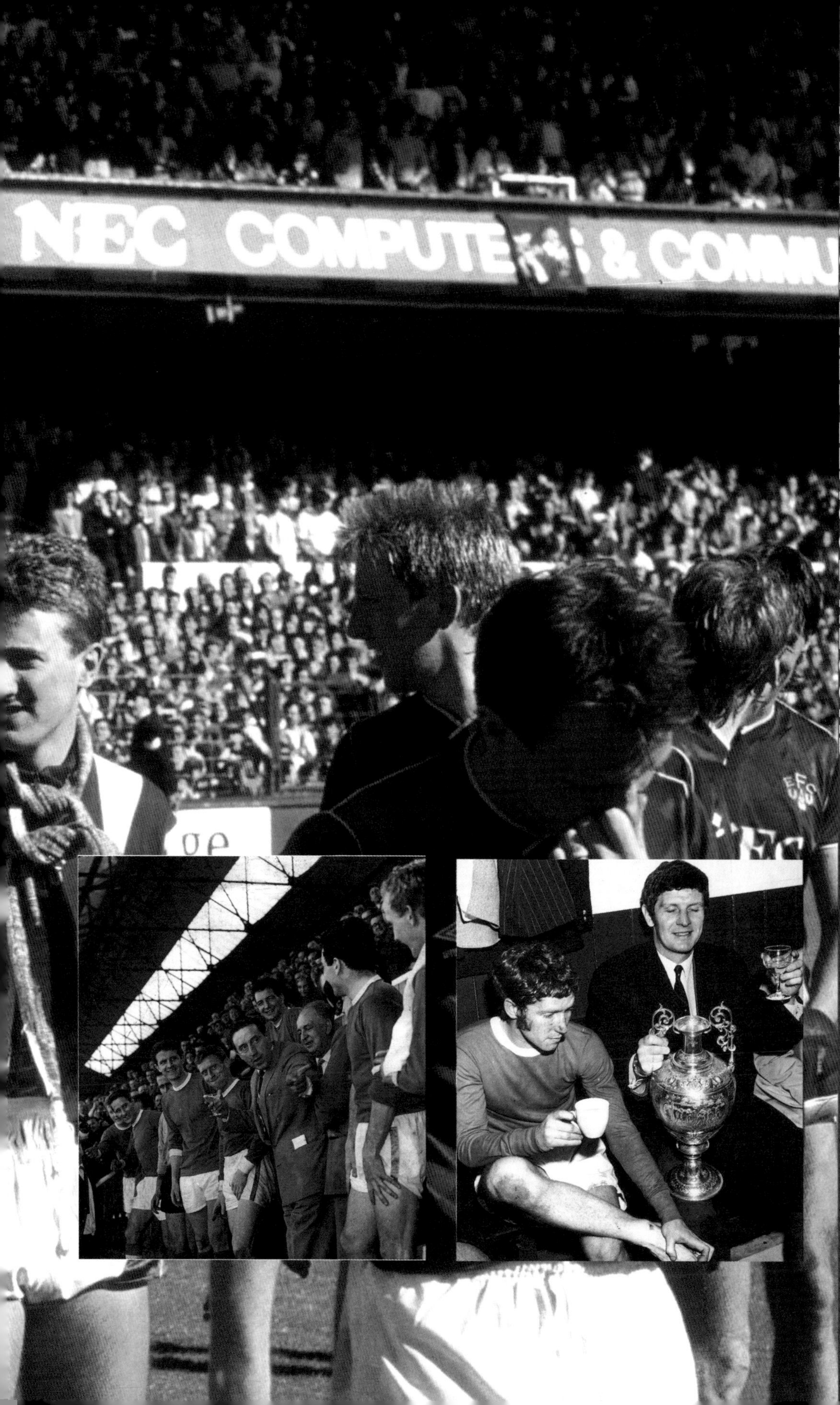

EVERTON'S CHAMPIONSHIP-WINNING SEASONS

1890/91

	PLD	WON	DRAWN	LOST	GOALS FOR	GOALS AGAINST	POINTS
1 EVERTON	22	14	1	7	63	29	29
2 PRESTON NORTH END	22	12	3	7	44	23	27

Everton clinched their first title in only the third season of English League football. They made a blistering start and dropped only a single point from their first six matches, with goal machine Fred Geary scoring 11 goals out of a season's total for the forward of 20 in all.

Everton and Wolves were initially the pacesetters at the top and Everton clinched the title on 3rd January 1891 with a 4-2 home victory over Notts County.

The campaign was characterised by some outrageous scoring: Derby conceded 13 goals in their two matches and Burnley were hammered 7-3 at Anfield. However, old rivals Preston continued to be a jinx and they completed a double over the new champions.

Apart from Geary, the star men were his magnificent forward partners Edgar Chadwick and Alf Milward while Johnny Holt and Dan Doyle were rocks in defence.

Appearances:

Jack Angus	11	Patrick Gordon	3	Alf Milward	22
Alexander Brady	21	Andrew Hannah	20	Duncan McLean	5
Billy Campbell	13	Johnny Holt	21	Charlie Parry	13
Edgar Chadwick	22	David Jardine	10	Hope Robertson	3
Dan Doyle	20	David Kirkwood	19	Robert Smalley	1
Jack Elliott	1	Alex Latta	10	Tom Wylie	4
Fred Geary	22	Alex Lochhead	1		

Goals:

Geary	20	Milward	12	Chadwick	10
Brady	9	Latta	4	Wylie	4
Campbell	1	Holt	1	Kirkwood	1
Robertson	1				

1914/15

	PLD	WON	DRAWN	LOST	GOALS FOR	AGAINST	POINTS
1 EVERTON	**38**	**19**	**8**	**11**	**76**	**47**	**46**
2 OLDHAM ATHLETIC	38	17	11	10	70	56	45

Goodison witnessed its first league title victory before organised football was halted after the outbreak of World War One. With many clubs drained of players it was a far more open title race than normal and Everton topped the table with just 46 points from 38 games.

Star man was another prolific Scottish forward, Bobby Parker, who netted 36 goals in just 35 matches. One purple patch before Christmas saw Parker score 17 goals in 11 matches, including four hat-tricks. One treble came in a record 5-0 victory at Anfield.

Oldham were our strongest rivals and they led the race for the title at the end of March by a point with a game in hand, but a strong finish by the Goodison side – nine points from the last five matches – secured the championship after Oldham lost their final game, crucially to Liverpool!

Appearances:

William Brown	4	John Houston	1	Billy Palmer	17
Sam Chedgzoy	30	Horace Howarth	1	Bobby Parker	35
Joe Clennell	36	Frank Jefferis	18	Jimmy Roberts	1
Tom Fern	36	Billy Kirsopp	16	Bob Simpson	9
Tom Fleetwood	35	John Maconnachie	28	Bob Thompson	33
Jimmy Galt	32	Harry Makepeace	23	William Wareing	8
Alan Grenyer	14	Frank Mitchell	2	Louis Weller	6
George Harrison	26	Tom Nuttall	5	Billy Wright	2

Goals:

Parker	36	Clennell	14	Kirsopp	9
Harrison	4	Jefferis	4	Chedgzoy	2
Fleetwood	2	Galt	2	Grenyer	1
Makepeace	1	Palmer	1		

1927/28

	PLD	WON	DRAWN	LOST	GOALS FOR	GOALS AGAINST	POINTS
1 EVERTON	42	20	13	9	102	66	53
2 HUDDERSFIELD TOWN	42	22	7	13	91	68	51

Everton's third title was arguably overshadowed by the greatest individual feat in English football history: Dixie Dean's 60 league goals.

The season was split into three distinct parts with the first seeing Everton lose just one of their first 14 matches and were top after a 3-0 victory at Derby in November. Dean at that stage had netted an astonishing 24 goals in 13 appearances, with the game he missed – a 7-0 victory over West Ham – proving that Everton were not a one-man side.

However, a poor run results followed and Everton lost top spot in early March. Between early January and the end of March there was not a single victory in nine league matches as Huddersfield went top of the table. But Dean had regained his scoring touch and his two goals in a home draw against Derby acted as a springboard for an assault on the title. The great man scored 17 goals in the final nine matches – six wins and three draws – as Goodison celebrated a third championship and a new scoring record for the legendary centre-forward.

Appearances:

David Bain	2	Dick Forshaw	23	John O'Donnell	42
William Brown	2	Henry Hardy	6	David Raitt	6
Warney Cresswell	36	Hunter Hart	41	Walter Rooney	4
Ted Critchley	40	Harold Houghton	1	Ted Taylor	26
Arthur Davies	10	Bobby Irvine	9	Alec Troup	42
Dixie Dean	39	Jeremiah Kelly	40	Albert Virr	39
Arthur Dominy	1	George Martin	10	Tony Weldon	38
William Easton	3	Samuel Meston	1	Tommy White	1

Goals:

Dean	60	Troup	10	Weldon	7
Critchley	6	Forshaw	5	Irvine	3
Martin	3	White	2	Easton	1
Hart	1	Kelly	1	O'Donnell	1
Virr	1	Own Goals	1		

1931/32

	PLD	WON	DRAWN	LOST	GOALS FOR	AGAINST	POINTS
1 EVERTON	**42**	**26**	**4**	**12**	**116**	**64**	**56**
2 ARSENAL	42	22	10	10	90	48	54

Everton became only the second side to lift the First Division title after winning the Second Division the previous season. Once again they had Dean to thank for an enormous contribution, but this time the side were considerably much stronger throughout. Tom Johnson was a perfect foil and the former Manchester City player netted 22 goals with fine support from Tommy White (18 goals). Ted Sagar was beginning his extraordinary Goodison career and he missed just one game.

An incredible scoring run of 50 goals in 10 league matches – with Dean twice scoring five goals in a match – from October onwards took Everton top of the table and they stayed there, finishing four points ahead of Arsenal. A league double was completed over Liverpool, with Dean memorably scoring inside a minute as part of a 20-minute hat-trick at Anfield in a 3-1 win in September.

Appearances:

William Bocking	10	Charlie Gee	38	Arthur Rigby	3
Archie Clark	39	Philip Griffiths	7	Ted Sagar	41
Billy Coggins	1	Tommy Johnson	41	Jimmy Stein	37
Warney Cresswell	40	Henry Lowe	1	Jock Thomson	39
Ted Critchley	37	George Martin	2	Tommy White	23
Dixie Dean	38	Joseph McClure	7	Ben Williams	33
Jimmy Dunn	22	Lachie McPherson	3		

Goals:

Dean	45	Thomson	22	White	18
Dunn	10	Stein	9	Critchley	8
Griffiths	3	Clark	1		

1938/39

	PLD	WON	DRAWN	LOST	GOALS FOR	GOALS AGAINST	POINTS
1 EVERTON	42	27	5	10	88	52	59
2 WOLVERHAMPTON W.	42	22	11	9	88	39	55

Like 1915 an Everton championship preceded the cessation of League football due to the outbreak of hostilities. The 1939 side was almost certainly the best to play for the club before the 1960s, containing fine full-backs in Billy Cook and Norman Greenhalgh, a superb centre-half in T.G. Jones and a well-balanced middle in the form of Cliff Britton, Joe Mercer and Alex Stevenson. Up front the majestic Tommy Lawton was the division's top-scorer with 34 goals while still a teenager.

The season began in explosive fashion with six straight wins – including an important 2-1 victory at Highbury in front of 65,000 – and Everton vied for supremacy with Derby County and Wolves for the rest of the campaign. Everton won 3-0 at Anfield in February to complete a derby double and they stayed top as the title was secured with 59 points.

Appearances:

Arthur Barber	2	Charlie Gee	2	Harry Morton	1
Robert Bell	4	Torry Gillick	40	Ted Sagar	41
Stan Bentham	41	Norman Greenhalgh	42	Alex Stevenson	36
Wally Boyes	36	George Jackson	2	Jock Thomson	26
Cliff Britton	1	TG Jones	39	Douglas Trentham	1
James Caskie	5	Tommy Lawton	38	Gordon Watson	16
Billy Cook	40	Joe Mercer	41		
Jimmy Cunliffe	7	George Milligan	1		

Goals:

Lawton	34	Gillick	14	Stevenson	11
Bentham	9	Cook	5	Boyes	4
Bell	3	Cunliffe	3	Own Goals	2
Caskie	1	Greenhalgh	1	Trentham	1

1962/63

	PLD	WON	DRAWN	LOST	GOALS FOR	AGAINST	POINTS
1 EVERTON	42	25	11	6	84	42	61
2 TOTTENHAM HOTSPUR	42	23	9	10	111	62	55

Harry Catterick's team brought the championship crown to Goodison for the first time in the post-War era with a club record 61 points, as they uniquely went through a whole season unbeaten at home in the league. Alex Young and Roy Vernon formed a productive partnership up-front and both players passed the 20-goal mark. Gordon West and Brian Labone were now established as Goodison favourites but unsung heroes like Jimmy Gabriel and Dennis Stevens also made major contributions.

After top-five finishes in the previous two campaigns, Everton started strongly with four straight wins and were in the top-three all season. The harsh winter resulted in only six matches being played from December-February and when the season resumed only two of the last 17 matches were lost.

The side finished with a flourish with four straight wins and the title was clinched in spectacular fashion with a 4-1 win over Fulham in the final match at Goodison. The 60,000 crowd witnessed both a Roy Vernon hat-trick and the trophy returning to the club for the first time since 1939.

Appearances:

Billy Bingham	23	Mick Meagan	32	George Thomson	19
Albert Dunlop	4	Johnny Morrissey	28	Ray Veall	11
Jimmy Gabriel	40	Alex Parker	33	Roy Vernon	41
Brian Harris	24	Alex Scott	17	Gordon West	38
George Heslop	1	George Sharples	2	Frank Wignall	1
Tony Kay	19	Dennis Stevens	42	Alex Young	42
Brian Labone	40	Derek Temple	5		

Goals:

Vernon	24	Young	22	Morrissey	7
Stevens	7	Bingham	5	Gabriel	5
Scott	4	Own Goals	3	Parker	2
Harris	1	Kay	1	Temple	1
Veall	1	Wignall	1		

1969/70

	PLD	WON	DRAWN	LOST	GOALS FOR	AGAINST	POINTS
1 EVERTON	42	29	8	5	72	34	66
2 LEEDS UNITED	42	21	15	6	84	49	57

"We won by playing pure football – there were no destroyers in the team," was manager Harry Catterick's view as Everton romped to their seventh title with a club record 66 points and 29 wins in a season. The triumph was of course built around the talents of Ball, Harvey and Kendall and the midfield trio ensured that the team played with a fluency and style in keeping with the best Goodison traditions. Elsewhere Joe Royle scored 23 goals and in the spring Alan Whittle fired six crucial goals.

The team started with an incredible run of 15 wins and a draw from their first 18 matches. Perennial challengers Leeds had their record run of 34 league matches ended in August 1969 while there were fine victories over Stoke (6-2) and a double over Manchester United in the space of a week.

After a shaky spell in mid-season, the side were unbeaten in the final 14 games, with eight consecutive victories in March-April 1970 securing another title. Highlights were plenty – especially a 2-0 derby win at Anfield – and the Easter weekend was especially memorable with a 5-2 home win over Chelsea and a 1-0 victory at Stoke. The trophy was presented after a 2-0 home victory over West Brom on 1st April 1970.

Appearances:

Alan Ball	37	Jimmy Husband	30	Keith Newton	12
Sandy Brown	36	Tommy Jackson	15	Joe Royle	42
Frank D'Arcy	5	Howard Kendall	36	Gordon West	42
Colin Harvey	35	Roger Kenyon	9	Alan Whittle	15
Gerry Humphreys	1	Brian Labone	34	Tommy Wright	42
John Hurst	42	Johnny Morrissey	41		

Goals:

Royle	23	Whittle	11	Ball	10
Morrissey	9	Husband	6	Hurst	5
Kendall	4	Harvey	3	Wright	1

1984/85

	PLD	WON	DRAWN	LOST	GOALS		POINTS
					FOR	AGAINST	
1 EVERTON	**42**	**28**	**6**	**8**	**88**	**43**	**90**
2 LIVERPOOL	42	22	11	9	68	35	77

Fifteen years after he had played in a championship-winning side, Howard Kendall joined an elite group who have also managed one as his Everton team romped to the title with a record 90 points, as well as lifting the Cup Winners' Cup and appearing in the FA Cup final.

But that outcome seemed a long way off after the season opened with two defeats. From then on there was such an upswing in fortunes that the Toffees were top by the first weekend in November, for the first time since 1979. Six straight wins in that time produced some of the best football ever seen by an Everton team, especially during a 5-0 defeat of Manchester United while the 14-year Anfield voodoo was laid to rest with Graeme Sharp's volley.

The New Year witnessed 16 victories and two draws in 18 matches as Kendall's side continued their remorseless march to the title. Two matches were crucial – a 2-1 victory at Spurs which effectively ended their threat and then a famous 4-1 win over Sunderland at Goodison thanks to a fabulous pair of headers by Andy Gray.

The championship was effectively theirs after a 2-0 win over QPR on May Day and the trophy was presented two days later against West Ham.

Appearances:

Ian Atkins	6	Johnny Morrissey jnr	1	Neville Southall	42
John Bailey	15	Derek Mountfield	37	Trevor Steven	40
Paul Bracewell	37	Darren Oldroyd	1	Gary Stevens	37
Terry Curran	9	Kevin Ratcliffe	40	Pat Van den Hauwe	31
Jason Danskin	1	Peter Reid	36	Robbie Wakenshaw	2
Andy Gray	26	Kevin Richardson	15	Derek Walsh	1
Alan Harper	13	Neill Rimmer	1	Paul Wilkinson	5
Adrian Heath	17	Graeme Sharp	36		
Darren Hughes	2	Kevin Sheedy	29		

Goals:

Sharp	21	Steven	12	Heath	11
Sheedy	11	Mountfield	10	Gray	9
Richardson	4	Stevens	3	Bracewell	2
Reid	2	Wilkinson	2	Atkins	1

1986/87

	PLD	WON	DRAWN	LOST	GOALS FOR	GOALS AGAINST	POINTS
1 EVERTON	42	26	8	8	76	31	86
2 LIVERPOOL	42	23	8	11	72	42	77

Everton's ninth and most recent title occurred in a season when they exacted revenge over their neighbours. Such an outcome seemed remote as the season started with six key players injured, but some astute buys during the summer – such as the evergreen Paul Power and future Goodison legend Dave Watson – meant Kendall's side were able to stay in contention.

The run up to Christmas saw some brilliant football in a run of eight wins in nine matches, when 25 goals were scored and just three conceded, and going into the New Year Everton were handily placed in second behind Arsenal.

The side struggled to maintain their form in the first two months of 1987 as Liverpool began what appeared to be another run to the title, one that took then nine points clear, albeit having played two games more than the Toffees.

The tide turned at the end of March when Everton won seven consecutive matches to regain top spot as their rivals slipped. A Pat Van den Hauwe goal at Norwich City on May Day clinched the title in what was the final season of Howard Kendall's first spell in charge.

Appearances:

Neil Adams	12	Derek Mountfield	13	Ian Snodin	16
Warren Aspinall	6	Neil Pointon	12	Neville Southall	31
Wayne Clarke	10	Paul Power	40	Trevor Steven	41
Alan Harper	36	Kevin Ratcliffe	42	Gary Stevens	25
Adrian Heath	41	Peter Reid	16	Pat Van den Hauwe	11
Kevin Langley	16	Kevin Richardson	1	Dave Watson	35
Ian Marshall	2	Graeme Sharp	27	Paul Wilkinson	22
Bobby Mimms	11	Kevin Sheedy	28		

Goals:

Steven	14	Sheedy	13	Heath	11
Clarke	5	Sharp	5	Power	4
Harper	3	Mountfield	3	Own Goals	3
Stevens	3	Watson	3	Wilkinson	3
Langley	2	Marshall	1	Pointon	1
Reid	1	Van den Hauwe	1		

Celebrations from Everton's last two Championship wins – a lap of honour in 1985 (above),
while Kevin Ratcliffe and Peter Reid show off the trophy in 1987 (below)

THE LEAGUE FINISHES

DIVISION ONE/PREMIERSHIP - 104 SEASONS	
Position	Number of times
First	9
Second	7
Third	7
Fourth	9
Fifth	4
Sixth	5
Seventh	8
Eighth	4
Ninth	2
Tenth	2
Eleventh	10
Twelfth	2
Thirteenth	2
Fourteenth	5
Fifteenth	8
Sixteenth	6
Seventeenth	5
Eighteenth	4
Nineteenth	1
Twentieth	2
Twenty-first	0
Twenty-second	2

DIVISION TWO - 4 SEASONS	
Position	Number of times
First	1
Second	1
Seventh	1
Sixteenth	1

David Johnson rounds off the scoring against Southampton in 1971, Everton's biggest post-War league victory

THE LEAGUE RECORDS

HIGHEST

578	Most appearances	–	Neville Southall (1981-1997)
349	Most goals	–	Dixie Dean (1925-1937)
6	Most goals in a game	–	Jack Southworth, WBA (h), 30/12/1893
12	Sequence of consecutive wins	–	24/3/1894-13/10/1894
20	Sequence of unbeaten games	–	29/4/1978-16/12/1978
20	Most penalties in career	–	Trevor Steven (1983-1989)
78,299	Home attendance	–	v Liverpool, 18/9/1948
75,723	Away attendance	–	v Manchester United 29/11/2006
£23m	Transfer fee received	–	Wayne Rooney, Manchester United, 2004
£11.25m	Transfer fee paid	–	Ayegbeni Yakubu, Middlesbrough, 2007

HIGHEST (SEASON)

66	Points total (2 points for a win)	–	1969/70
90	Points total (3 points for a win)	–	1984/85
95	If 3 points for a win	–	1969/70
29	Wins	–	1969/70
18	Draws	–	1925/26, 1971/72, 1974/75
22	Defeats	–	1950/51, 1993/94
121	Goals scored	–	1930/31
35	Players used in a season	–	1888/89, 1919/20
51,603	Average home attendance	–	1962/63

BIGGEST VICTORIES

9-1	v Manchester City (H)	–	3/9/1906
	(Everton goalscorers: Taylor, Settle 2, Young 4, Abbott, Bolton. Attendance: 16,000)		
9-1	v Plymouth Argyle (H)	–	27/12/1930
	(Everton goalscorers: Dean 4, Stein 4, Johnson. Attendance: 37,018)		
8-0	v Stoke City (H)	–	2/11/1889
	(Everton goalscorers: Brady 2, Latta 2, Geary 3, Milward. Attendance: 7,500)		
8-0	v Southampton (H)	–	20/11/1971
	(Everton goalscorers: Royle 4, Johnson 3, Ball. Attendance: 28,718)		

LOWEST

2,079	League attendance	–	v West Bromwich Albion, 1/12/1888
16	Players used in a season	–	1969/70
0	Home defeats in a season	–	1962/63
5	Defeats in a season	–	1969/70

BIGGEST DEFEATS

7-0	4 occasions, most recent	–	v Arsenal (a), 8/5/2005

THE COMPLETE RECORD

EVERTON'S COMPLETE LEAGUE RECORD - CLUB BY CLUB

Name	Played	W	D	L	F	A	% Won	% Lost
Accrington	10	5	3	2	21	16	50%	20%
Arsenal	172	54	36	82	213	278	31%	48%
Aston Villa	184	70	45	69	284	282	38%	38%
Barnsley	8	4	3	1	18	12	50%	13%
Birmingham City	112	57	31	24	206	140	51%	21%
Blackburn Rovers	138	55	29	54	228	221	40%	39%
Blackpool	46	20	11	15	66	55	43%	33%
Bolton Wanderers	128	64	30	34	213	172	50%	27%
Bradford City	26	11	9	6	39	30	42%	23%
Bradford PA	8	5	2	1	19	12	63%	13%
Brentford	16	7	2	7	29	22	44%	44%
Brighton & HA	8	4	3	1	15	11	50%	13%
Bristol City	20	12	3	5	34	22	60%	25%
Bristol Rovers	2	1	1	0	4	0	50%	0%
Burnley	98	41	28	29	161	147	42%	30%
Bury	52	21	16	15	87	72	40%	29%
Cardiff City	30	10	8	12	43	35	33%	40%
Carlisle United	2	0	0	2	2	6	0%	100%
Charlton Athletic	48	20	10	18	78	68	42%	38%
Chelsea	136	45	42	49	210	214	33%	36%
Coventry City	70	29	19	22	106	85	41%	31%
Crystal Palace	26	11	7	8	42	26	42%	31%
Darwen	4	2	1	1	17	10	50%	25%
Derby County	124	61	21	42	237	173	49%	34%
Doncaster Rovers	6	2	2	2	15	11	33%	33%
Fulham	38	18	8	12	62	43	47%	32%
Glossop North End	2	1	1	0	5	2	50%	0%
Grimsby Town	22	12	4	6	46	28	55%	27%
Huddersfield Town	56	22	13	21	80	81	39%	38%
Hull City	6	3	0	3	10	5	50%	50%
Ipswich Town	52	20	18	14	69	61	38%	27%
Leeds United	104	28	29	47	132	150	27%	45%
Leicester City	96	36	30	30	179	151	38%	31%
Leyton Orient	2	1	0	1	3	3	50%	50%
Lincoln City	4	1	2	1	5	6	25%	25%
Liverpool	176	56	55	65	212	238	32%	37%
Luton Town	38	16	8	14	56	46	42%	37%
Manchester City	148	52	39	57	203	214	35%	39%
Manchester United	156	52	37	67	228	242	33%	43%
Middlesbrough	108	51	27	30	183	141	47%	28%
Millwall	6	4	1	1	11	6	67%	17%
Newcastle United	146	56	31	59	212	220	38%	40%
Northampton Town	2	2	0	0	7	2	100%	0%
Norwich City	42	16	13	13	61	54	38%	31%
Nottingham Forest	120	52	26	42	198	147	43%	35%
Notts County	66	37	13	16	126	68	56%	24%
Oldham Athletic	28	9	8	11	42	46	32%	39%
Oxford United	6	2	3	1	7	4	33%	17%
Plymouth Argyle	6	4	0	2	22	12	67%	33%
Port Vale	2	1	0	1	5	4	50%	50%
Portsmouth	52	22	8	22	81	94	42%	42%
Preston North End	88	33	25	30	120	120	38%	34%
Queens Park Rang.	42	18	10	14	69	61	43%	33%
Reading	4	3	1	0	8	3	75%	0%
Rotherham United	6	2	3	1	11	8	33%	17%
Sheffield United	120	48	30	42	184	154	40%	35%
Sheffield Wed.	128	55	37	36	227	193	43%	28%
Southampton	76	37	17	22	133	86	49%	29%
Stoke City	104	50	27	27	183	112	48%	26%
Sunderland	144	61	22	61	235	241	42%	42%
Swansea City	12	8	4	0	31	12	67%	0%
Swindon Town	2	1	1	0	7	3	50%	0%

THE COMPLETE RECORD

EVERTON'S COMPLETE LEAGUE RECORD - CLUB BY CLUB

Name	Played	W	D	L	F	A	% Won	% Lost
Tottenham Hotspur	140	44	43	53	189	220	31%	38%
Watford	16	13	1	2	41	20	81%	13%
West Brom	138	55	32	51	231	230	40%	37%
West Ham United	104	51	21	32	177	121	49%	31%
Wigan Athletic	4	1	2	1	5	4	25%	25%
Wimbledon	28	9	11	8	40	36	32%	29%
Wolverhampton W.	116	55	20	41	198	164	47%	35%
Grand Total	**4,230**	**1,729**	**1,043**	**1,458**	**6,721**	**5,976**	**41%**	**34%**

Joy for the Everton players as Derek Mountfield celebrates a goal against Watford in 1986 – the Blues have enjoyed huge success against the Hornets in league encounters

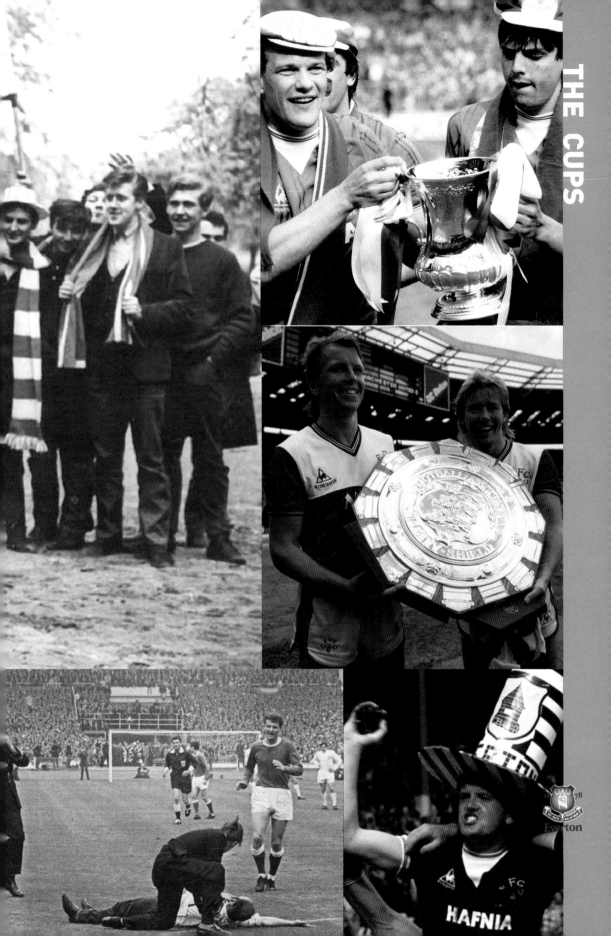

THE FA CUP RESULTS

Date	Round	Venue	Opponents	Score	Scorers	Attendance
1887-88						
15th Oct	1	A	Bolton Wanderers	0-1		5,000
29th Oct	1 Replay	H	Bolton Wanderers	2-2	Farmer, Watson	7,000
12th Nov	1 Replay 2	A	Bolton Wanderers	1-1	Farmer	7,000
19th Nov	1 Replay 3	H	Bolton Wanderers	2-1	Goudie, Watson	8,000
1889-90						
18th Jan	1	H	Derby County	11-2	Brady 3, Geary 3, Milward 3, Doyle, Kirkwood	10,000
3rd Feb	2	A	Stoke City	2-4	Geary, Milward	7,000
1890-91						
17th Jan	1	A	Sunderland	0-1		21,000
1891-92						
16th Jan	1	H	Burnley	2-4	Chadwick, Robertson	3,000
1892-93						
21st Jan	1	H	West Bromwich Alb.	4-1	Maxwell, Latta, Geary 2	23,867
4th Feb	2	H	Nottingham Forest	4-2	E. Chadwick, Milward 2, Geary	25,000
18th Feb	3	H	Sheffield Wednesday	3-0	E. Chadwick, Geary, Kelso (pen)	30,000
4th Mar	SF	N	Preston North End	2-2	E. Chadwick, Gordon	30,000
16th Mar	SF Replay	N	Preston North End	0-0		15,000
20th Mar	SF Replay 2	N	Preston North End	2-1	Maxwell, Gordon	20,000
25th Mar	F	N	Wolverhampton W.	0-1		45,067
1893-94						
27th Jan	1	A	Stoke City	0-1		14,000
1894-95						
2nd Feb	1	A	Southport	3-0	Bell 3	7,000
16th Feb	2	H	Blackburn Rovers	1-1	Chadwick	20,000
20th Feb	2 Replay	A	Blackburn Rovers	3-2	Chadwick 2, Hartley	20,000
2nd March	3	A	Sheffield Wednesday	0-2		9,000
1895-96						
1st Feb	1	A	Nottingham Forest	2-0	Chadwick, Milward	15,000
15th Feb	2	H	Sheffield United	3-0	Milward (pen), Bell, Cameron	20,000
29th Feb	3	A	Sheffield Wednesday	0-4		12,000
1896-97						
30th Jan	1	H	Burton Wanderers	5-2	Holt, Bell, Milward, Chadwick, Archer o.g.	5,000
13th Feb	2	H	Bury	3-0	Milward, Taylor 2	14,171
27th Feb	3	H	Blackburn Rovers	2-0	Hartley 2	16,000
20th Mar	SF	N	Derby County	3-2	Hartley, Milward, Chadwick	25,000
10th Apr	F	N	Aston Villa	2-3	Bell, Boyle	65,891
1897-98						
29th Jan	1	H	Blackburn Rovers	1-0	Williams	12,000
12th Feb	2	A	Stoke City	0-0		25,000
17th Feb	2 Replay	H	Stoke City	5-1	L Bell 2, Taylor, Chadwick, Cameron	10,000

Date	Round	Venue	Opponents	Score	Scorers	Attendance
1897-98 (cont)						
26th Feb	3	A	Burnley	3-1	Taylor 2, L Bell	20,000
19th Mar	SF	N	Derby County	1-3	Chadwick	30,000
1898-99						
28th Jan	1	H	Jarrow	3-1	Taylor, Chadwick, Proudfoot	3,000
11th Feb	2	H	Nottingham Forest	0-1		23,000
1899-00						
27th Jan	1	A	Southampton	0-3		10,000
1900-01						
9th Feb	1	A	Southampton	3-1	Chadwick, Settle, Taylor	12,000
23rd Feb	2	A	Sheffield United	0-2		24,659
1901-02						
25th Jan	1	A	Liverpool	2-2	Young, Sharp	25,000
30th Jan	1 Replay	H	Liverpool	0-2		20,000
1902-03						
7th Feb	1	H	Portsmouth	5-0	Sharp, Brearley, Abbott, Bell 2	32,000
21st Feb	2	H	Manchester United	3-1	Abbott, Taylor, Booth (pen)	15,000
7th Mar	3	A	Millwall	0-1		14,000
1903-04						
6th Feb	1	H	Tottenham Hotspur	1-2	Taylor	25,000
1904-05						
2nd Feb	1	A	Liverpool	1-1	Makepeace (pen)	28,000
8th Feb	1 Replay	H	Liverpool	2-1	McDermott, Hardman	40,000
18th Feb	2	A	Stoke City	4-0	McDermott 2, Makepeace (pen), Settle	25,700
4th Mar	3	H	Southampton	4-0	McDermott, Settle 3	30,000
25th Mar	SF	N	Aston Villa	1-1	Sharp	35,000
29th Mar	SF Replay	N	Aston Villa	1-2	Sharp	25,000
1905-06						
13th Jan	1	H	West Bromwich Alb.	3-1	Hardman, Sharp, Makepeace	18,023
3rd Feb	2	H	Chesterfield	3-0	Settle, Young, Taylor	12,000
24th Feb	3	H	Bradford City	1-0	Makepeace	18,000
10th Mar	4	H	Sheffield Wednesday	4-3	Sharp, Taylor, Bolton, Booth	30,000
31st Mar	SF	N	Liverpool	2-0	Abbott, Hardman	37,000
21st Apr	F	N	Newcastle United	1-0	Young	75,609
1906-07						
12th Jan	1	H	Sheffield United	1-0	Johnson o.g.	35,000
2nd Feb	2	A	West Ham United	2-1	Settle, Sharp	14,000
23rd Feb	3	H	Bolton Wanderers	0-0		52,455
27th Feb	3 Replay	A	Bolton Wanderers	3-0	Taylor, Abbott, Settle	54,470
9th Mar	4	A	Crystal Palace	1-1	Taylor	35,000
13th Mar	4 Replay	H	Crystal Palace	4-0	Hardman, Settle 2, Young	34,340
25th Mar	SF	N	West Bromwich Alb.	2-1	Wilson, Sharp	32,381
20th Apr	F	N	Sheffield Wednesday	1-2	Sharp	84,584

Date	Round	Venue	Opponents	Score	Scorers	Attendance
1907-08						
11th Jan	1	H	Tottenham Hotspur	1-0	Young	21,000
1st Feb	2	A	Oldham Athletic	0-0		25,690
5th Feb	2 Replay	H	Oldham Athletic	6-1	Young, Abbott, Bolton 4	25,800
22nd Feb	3	A	Bolton Wanderers	3-3	Bolton, Settle 2	30,000
26th Feb	3 Replay	H	Bolton Wanderers	3-1	Settle, Young 2	32,000
7th Mar	4	H	Southampton	0-0		40,000
11th Mar	4 Replay	A	Southampton	2-3	Young, Bolton	21,690
1908-09						
16th Jan	1	H	Barnsley	3-1	Sharp, Coleman, White	15,000
6thFeb	2	A	Manchester United	0-1		35,217
1909-10						
15th Jan	1	A	Middlesbrough	1-1	White	25,000
19th Jan	1 Replay	H	Middlesbrough	5-3	Freeman, Taylor, Young, Makepeace, White	20,000
5th Feb	2	H	Arsenal	5-0	Sharp 2 (1 pen), Barlow, Young, Freeman	30,000
9th Feb	3	H	Sunderland	2-0	Makepeace, Young	45,000
5th Mar	4	A	Coventry City	2-0	Freeman 2	19,095
26th Mar	SF	N	Barnsley	0-0		35,000
31st Mar	SF Replay	N	Barnsley	0-3		55,000
1910-11						
14th Jan	1	A	Crystal Palace	4-0	A Young, Magnier, Gourlay, R Young	35,000
4th Feb	2	H	Liverpool	2-1	A Young 2	50,000
25th Feb	3	A	Derby County	0-5		22,892
1911-12						
13th Jan	1	A	Leyton Orient	2-1	Beare, Browell	11,000
3rd Feb	2	H	Bury	1-1	Maconnachie	32,000
8th Feb	2 Replay	A	Bury (Played at Goodison Park)	6-0	Browell 4, Jefferis, Davidson	25,000
24th Feb	3	A	Oldham Athletic	2-0	Browell 2	35,473
9th Mar	4	A	Swindon Town	1-2	Makepeace	13,989
1912-13						
15th Jan	1	H	Stockport County	5-1	Wareing, T Browell 3, Bradshaw	10,000
1st Feb	2	A	Brighton & Hove Alb.	0-0		11,000
5th Feb	2 Replay	H	Brighton & Hove Alb.	1-0	Jefferis	30,000
22nd Feb	3	A	Bristol Rovers	4-0	Jefferis, Fleetwood, Harris, T Browell	15,719
8th Mar	4	H	Oldham Athletic	0-1		43,000
1913-14						
10th Jan	1	A	Glossop North End	1-2	Bradshaw	5,000
1914-15						
9th Jan	1	H	Barnsley	3-0	Galt 2, Parker	18,000
30th Jan	2	H	Bristol City	4-0	Clennell, Kirsopp, Parker, Wareing	24,000
20th Feb	3	A	QPR	2-1	Clennell, Broster o.g.	33,000
6th Mar	4	A	Bradford City	2-0	Chedgzoy, Clennell	26,100
27th Mar	SF	N	Chelsea	0-2		22,000

Date	Round	Venue	Opponents	Score	Scorers	Attendance
1919-20						
10th Jan	1	A	Birmingham City	0-2		44,000
1920-21						
8th Jan	1	H	Stockport County	1-0	Brewster	25,000
29 Jan	2	H	Sheffield Wednesday	1-1	Parker	44,000
3rd Feb	2 Replay	A	Sheffield Wednesday	1-0	Crossley	62,407
19th Feb	3	H	Newcastle United	3-0	Crossley 2, Davies	54,205
5th Mar	4	H	Wolverhampton W.	0-1		53,246
1921-22						
7th Jan	1	H	Crystal Palace	0-6		41,000
1922-23						
13th Jan	1	H	Bradford PA	1-1	Chedgzoy	18,000
17th Jan	1 Replay	A	Bradford PA	0-1		15,000
1923-24						
12th Jan	1	H	Preston North End	3-1	Chadwick, Chedgzoy, Cock	33,000
2nd Feb	2	A	Brighton & Hove Alb.	2-5	Chadwick, Cock	27,450
1924-25						
10th Jan	1	H	Burnley	2-1	Chadwick 2	28,315
31st Jan	2	A	Sunderland	0-0		35,000
4th Feb	2 Replay	H	Sunderland	2-1	Irvine, Chadwick	40,000
21st Feb	3	A	Sheffield United	0-1		51,745
1925-26						
9th Jan	1	H	Fulham	1-1	Dean	46,000
14th Jan	1 Replay	A	Fulham	0-1		20,116
1926-27						
8th Jan	1	H	Poole Town	3-1	Dean, Troup, Irvine	34,250
29th Jan	2	A	Hull City	1-1	Virr	22,000
2nd Feb	2 Replay 1	H	Hull City	2-2	Troup, Dean	45,000
7th Feb	2 Replay 2	N	Hull City	2-3	Dean, Dominy	6,800
1927-28						
14th Jan	1	A	Preston North End	3-0	Ward o.g., Dean, Irvine	39,215
28th Jan	2	A	Arsenal	3-4	Troup, Dean 2	44,328
1928-29						
12th Jan	1	A	Chelsea	0-2		61,316
1929-30						
11th Jan	1	A	Carlisle United	4-2	Critchley 2, Dean 2 (1 pen)	20,000
25th Jan	2	A	Blackburn Rovers	1-4	Martin	53,000
1930-31						
10th Jan	1	A	Plymouth Argyle	2-0	Stein, Dunn	33,000
24th Jan	2	A	Crystal Palace	6-0	Dean 4, Johnson, Wilde o.g.	38,000

Date	Round	Venue	Opponents	Score	Scorers	Attendance
1930-31 (cont)						
14th Feb	3	H	Grimsby Town	5-3	Stein 2, Johnson 2 (1 pen), Dean	65,534
28th Feb	4	H	Southport	9-1	Dean 4, Dunn 2, Critchley 2, Johnson	45,647
14th Mar	SF	N	West Bromwich Alb.	0-1		69,241
1931-32						
19th Jan	1	H	Liverpool	1-2	Dean	57,090
1932-33						
14th Jan	1	A	Leicester City	3-2	Dean, Dunn, Stein	20,000
28th Jan	2	H	Bury	3-1	Johnson 2, Dean	45,478
18th Feb	3	H	Leeds United	2-0	Dean, Stein	58,073
3rd Mar	4	H	Luton Town	6-0	Johnson 2, Stein 2, Dean, Dunn	55,431
18th Mar	SF	N	West Ham United	2-1	Dunn, Critchley	37,936
29th Apr	F	N	Manchester City	3-0	Stein, Dean, Dunn	92,900
1933-34						
13th Jan	1	A	Tottenham Hotspur	0-3		45,637
1934-35						
12th Jan	1	H	Grimsby Town	6-3	Geldard 3, Stevenson 2, Cunliffe	44,850
26th Jan	2	A	Sunderland	1-1	Cunliffe	45,000
30th Jan	2 Replay	H	Sunderland	6-4 aet	Coulter 3, Stevenson, Geldard 2	60,000
16th Feb	3	H	Derby County	3-1	Dean, Coulter 2	62,230
2nd Mar	4	H	Bolton Wanderers	1-2	Coulter	67,696
1935-36						
11th Jan	1	H	Preston North End	1-3	Geldard	35,000
1936-37						
16th Jan	1	H	Bournemouth	5-0	Gillick 2, Cunliffe, Stevenson 2	35,468
30th Jan	2	H	Sheffield Wednesday	3-0	Britton (pen), Dean, Coulter	35,807
20th Feb	3	H	Tottenham Hotspur	1-1	Coulter	57,149
22nd Feb	3 Replay	A	Tottenham Hotspur	3-4	Lawton, Dean 2	46,972
1937-38						
8th Jan	1	A	Chelsea	1-0	Stevenson	41,946
22nd Jan	2	H	Sunderland	0-1		68,158
1938-39						
7th Jan	1	A	Derby County	1-0	Boyes	22,237
21st Jan	2	H	Doncaster Rovers	8-0	Boyes 2, Lawton 4, Stevenson, Gillick	41,115
11th Feb	3	A	Birmingham City	2-2	Boyes, Stevenson	67,341
15th Feb	3 Replay	H	Birmingham City	2-1	Gillick, Cook (pen)	64,796
4th Mar	4	A	Wolverhampton W.	0-2		59,545
1945-46						
5th Jan	3 1st Leg	A	Preston North End	1-2	Catterick	25,000
9th Jan	3 2nd Leg	H	Preston North End	2-2 aet	Mercer (pen), Elliott	25,000

Date	Round	Venue	Opponents	Score	Scorers	Attendance
1946-47						
11th Jan	3	H	Southend United	4-2	Jones, McIlhatton, Wainwright, Fielding	50,124
25th Jan	4	A	Sheffield Wednesday	1-2	Wainwright	62,250
1947-48						
10th Jan	3	A	Grimsby Town	4-1	Wainwright 2, Farrell, Dodds	19,000
24th Jan	4	A	Wolverhampton W.	1-1	Catterick	45,085
31st Jan	4 Replay	H	Wolverhampton W.	3-2	Fielding 2, Grant	72,569
7th Feb	5	A	Fulham	1-1	Eglington	37,500
14th Feb	5 Replay	H	Fulham	0-1		71,587
1948-49						
8th Jan	3	H	Manchester City	1-0	Higgins	63,459
29th Jan	4	A	Chelsea	0-2		56,671
1949-50						
7th Jan	3	A	QPR	2-0	Buckle, Catterick	22,433
28th Jan	4	A	West Ham United	2-1	Catterick 2	26,800
11th Feb	5	H	Tottenham Hotspur	1-0	Wainwright (pen)	72,921
4th Mar	6	A	Derby County	2-1	Wainwright, Buckle	32,128
25th Mar	SF	N	Liverpool	0-2		72,000
1950-51						
6th Jan	3	A	Hull City	0-2		36,465
1951-52						
12th Jan	3	A	Leyton Orient	0-0		21,240
16th Jan	3 Replay	H	Leyton Orient	1-3	Parker	39,750
1952-53						
10th Jan	3	H	Ipswich Town	3-2	Fielding, Hickson 2	42,252
31st Jan	4	H	Nottingham Forest	4-1	Clinton, Parker 2, Eglington	48,904
14th Feb	5	H	Manchester United	2-1	Eglington, Hickson	77,920
28th Feb	6	A	Aston Villa	1-0	Hickson	60,658
21st Mar	SF	N	Bolton Wanderers	3-4	Parker 2, Farrell	75,000
1953-54						
9th Jan	3	H	Notts County	2-1	Eglington, Hickson	49,737
30th Jan	4	H	Swansea City	3-0	Parker 2, Hickson	61,619
20th Feb	5	A	Sheffield Wednesday	1-3	Hickson	65,000
1954-55						
8th Jan	3	H	Southend United	3-1	Potts, Fielding, Hickson	53,043
29th Jan	4	H	Liverpool	0-4		72,000
1955-56						
7th Jan	3	H	Bristol City	3-1	Eglington, Wainwright, J. Harris	46,493
28th Jan	4	A	Port Vale	3-2	Eglington, B. Harris, Wainwright	44,278
18th Feb	5	H	Chelsea	1-0	Farrell	61,572
3rd Mar	6	A	Manchester City	1-2	J. Harris	76,129
1956-57						
5th Jan	3	H	Blackburn Rovers	1-0	J. Harris (pen)	56,293

Date	Round	Venue	Opponents	Score	Scorers	Attendance
1956-57 (cont)						
26th Jan	4	H	West Ham United	2-1	Gauld, Farrell	55,245
16th Feb	5	A	Manchester United	0-1		61,803
1957-58						
4th Jan	3	A	Sunderland	2-2	Hickson 2	34,602
8th Jan	3 Replay	H	Sunderland	3-1	Keeley 2, Hickson	56,952
29th Jan	4	H	Blackburn Rovers	1-2	J. Harris	75,818
1958-59						
10th Jan	3	H	Sunderland	4-0	Hickson 2, J. Harris, Thomas	57,788
24th Jan	4	A	Charlton Athletic	2-2	Thomas, Collins	44,094
28th Jan	4 Replay	H	Charlton Athletic	4-1	Hickson 2, Collins 2	74,782
14th Feb	5	H	Aston Villa	1-4	Hickson	60,225
1959-60						
9th Jan	3	A	Bradford City	0-3		23,550
1960-61						
7th Jan	3	H	Sheffield United	0-1		48,593
1961-62						
6th Jan	3	H	King's Lynn	4-0	Collins, Vernon (pen), Bingham, Fell	44,916
27th Jan	4	H	Manchester City	2-0	Vernon, Lill	56,980
17th Feb	5	A	Burnley	1-3	Collins	50,514
1962-63						
15th Jan	3	A	Barnsley	3-0	B. Harris, Stevens, Vernon	30,011
29th Jan	4	A	Swindon Town	5-1	Vernon 2, Gabriel, Bingham, Morrissey	26,239
16th Mar	5	A	West Ham United	0-1		31,770
1963-64						
4th Jan	3	A	Hull City	1-1	Scott	36,478
7th Jan	3 Replay	H	Hull City	2-1	Scott, B. Harris	56,613
25th Jan	4	A	Leeds United	1-1	Vernon (pen)	48,826
28th Jan	4 Replay	H	Leeds United	2-0	Vernon, Gabriel	66,167
15th Feb	5	A	Sunderland	1-3	B. Harris	62,817
1964-65						
9th Jan	3	H	Sheffield Wednesday	2-2	Burgin o.g., Pickering	44,732
13th Jan	3 Replay	A	Sheffield Wednesday	3-0	Pickering, Harvey, Temple	50,080
30th Jan	4	A	Leeds United	1-1	Pickering (pen)	50,051
2nd Feb	4 Replay	H	Leeds United	1-2	Pickering	65,940
1965-66						
22nd Jan	3	H	Sunderland	3-0	Temple, Pickering, Young	47,893
12th Feb	4	A	Bedford Town	3-0	Temple 2, Pickering	18,407
3rd Mar	5	H	Coventry City	3-0	Young, Temple, Pickering	60,350
26th Mar	6	A	Manchester City	0-0		63,034
29th Mar	6 Replay 1	H	Manchester City	0-0		60,349
5th Apr	6 Replay 2	N	Manchester City	2-0	Temple, Pickering	27,948

Date	Round	Venue	Opponents	Score	Scorers	Attendance
1965-66 (cont)						
23rd Apr	SF	N	Manchester United	1-0	Harvey	60,000
14th May	F	N	Sheffield Wednesday	3-2	Trebilcock 2, Temple	100,000
1966-67						
28th Jan	3	A	Burnley	0-0		42,482
31st Jan	3 Replay	H	Burnley	2-1	Young 2	57,449
18th Feb	4	A	Wolverhampton W.	1-1	Ball (pen)	53,439
21st Feb	4 Replay	H	Wolverhampton W.	3-1	Husband 2, Temple	60,020
11th Mar	5	H	Liverpool	1-0	Ball	64,851
8th Apr	6	A	Nottingham Forest	2-3	Husband 2	47,510
1967-68						
27th Jan	3	A	Southport	1-0	Royle	18,795
17th Feb	4	A	Carlisle United	2-0	Husband, Royle	25,000
9th Mar	5	H	Tranmere Rovers	2-0	Royle, Morrissey	61,982
30th Mar	6	A	Leicester City	3-1	Husband 2, Kendall	43,519
27th Apr	SF	N	Leeds United	1-0	Morrissey (pen)	63,000
18th May	F	N	West Bromwich Alb.	0-1 aet		99,665
1968-69						
4th Jan	3	H	Ipswich Town	2-1	Royle, Hurst	49,047
25th Jan	4	H	Coventry City	2-0	Royle, Hurst	53,289
12th Feb	5	H	Bristol Rovers	1-0	Royle	55,294
1st Mar	6	A	Manchester United	1-0	Royle	63,464
22nd Mar	SF	N	Manchester City	0-1		63,025
1969-70						
3rd Jan	3	A	Sheffield United	1-2	Ball (pen)	29,116
1970-71						
2nd Jan	3	H	Blackburn Rovers	2-0	Husband 2	40,471
23rd Jan	4	H	Middlesbrough	3-0	H. Newton, Harvey, Royle	54,875
13th Feb	5	H	Derby County	1-0	Johnson	53,490
6th Mar	6	H	Colchester United	5-0	Kendall 2, Royle, Husband, Ball	53,028
27th Mar	SF	N	Liverpool	1-2	Ball	62,144
1971-72						
15th Jan	3	A	Crystal Palace	2-2	Whittle, Harvey	32,331
18th Jan	3 Replay	H	Crystal Palace	3-2	Scott, Kenyon, Hurst	45,408
5th Feb	4	H	Walsall	2-1	Johnson, Whittle	45,462
26th Feb	5	H	Tottenham Hotspur	0-2		50,511
1972-73						
13th Jan	3	H	Aston Villa	3-2	Belfitt, Buckley, Harper	42,222
3rd Feb	4	H	Millwall	0-2		37,277
1973-74						
5th Jan	3	H	Blackburn Rovers	3-0	Harper, Hurst, Clements	31,940
27th Jan	4	H	West Bromwich Alb.	0-0		53,509
30th Jan	4 Replay	A	West Bromwich Alb.	0-1		27,556

Date	Round	Venue	Opponents	Score	Scorers	Attendance
1974-75						
4th Jan	3	H	Altrincham	1-1	Clements (pen)	34,519
7th Jan	3 Replay	A	Altrincham	2-0	Latchford, Lyons	35,530
			(Played at Old Trafford)			
25th Jan	4	A	Plymouth Argyle	3-1	Pearson, Lyons 2	38,000
15th Feb	5	H	Fulham	1-2	Kenyon	45,233
1975-76						
3rd Jan	3	A	Derby County	1-2	G. Jones	31,647
1976-77						
8th Jan	3	H	Stoke City	2-0	Lyons, McKenzie (pen)	32,981
29th Jan	4	A	Swindon Town	2-2	McKenzie, Latchford	24,347
1st Feb	4 Replay	H	Swindon Town	2-1	Dobson, Jones	38,063
26th Feb	5	A	Cardiff City	2-1	Latchford, McKenzie	35,582
19th Mar	6	H	Derby County	2-0	Latchford, Pearson	42,409
23rd Apr	SF	N	Liverpool	2-2	McKenzie, Rioch	52,637
27th Apr	SF Replay	N	Liverpool	0-3		52,579
1977-78						
7th Jan	3	H	Aston Villa	4-1	King, Ross (pen), McKenzie, Latchford	46,320
28th Jan	4	A	Middlesbrough	2-3	Telfer, Lyons	33,652
1978-79						
10th Jan	3	A	Sunderland	1-2	Dobson	28,602
1979-80						
5th Jan	3	H	Aldershot	4-1	Latchford, Hartford, King, Kidd	23,700
26th Jan	4	H	Wigan Athletic	3-0	McBride, Latchford, Kidd	51,853
16th Feb	5	H	Wrexham	5-2	Megson, Eastoe 2, Ross (pen), Latchford	44,830
8th Mar	6	H	Ipswich Town	2-1	Latchford, Kidd	45,104
12th Apr	SF	N	West Ham United	1-1	Kidd (pen)	47,685
16th Apr	SF Replay	N	West Ham United	1-2 aet	Latchford	40,720
1980-81						
3rd Jan	3	H	Arsenal	2-0	Sansom o.g., Lyons	34,236
24th Jan	4	H	Liverpool	2-1	Eastoe, Varadi	53,804
14th Feb	5	A	Southampton	0-0		24,152
17th Feb	5 Replay	H	Southampton	1-0 aet	O'Keefe	49,192
7th Mar	6	H	Manchester City	2-2	Eastoe, Ross (pen)	52,791
11th Mar	6 Replay	A	Manchester City	1-3	Eastoe	52,532
1981-82						
2nd Jan	3	A	West Ham United	1-2	Eastoe	24,431
1982-83						
8th Jan	3	A	Newport County	1-1	Sheedy	9,527
11th Jan	3 Replay	H	Newport County	2-1	Sharp, King	18,565
30th Jan	4	H	Shrewsbury Town	2-1	Sheedy, Heath	35,188
19th Feb	5	H	Tottenham Hotspur	2-0	King, Sharp	42,995
12th Mar	6	A	Manchester United	0-1		58,198

Date	Round	Venue	Opponents	Score	Scorers	Attendance
1983-84						
6th Jan	3	A	Stoke City	2-0	Gray, Irvine	16,462
28th Jan	4	H	Gillingham	0-0		22,380
31st Jan	4 Replay 1	A	Gillingham	0-0		15,339
6th Feb	4 Replay 2	A	Gillingham	3-0	Sheedy 2, Heath	17,817
18th Feb	5	H	Shrewsbury Town	3-0	Irvine, Reid, Griffin o.g.	27,106
10th Mar	6	A	Notts County	2-1	Richardson, Gray	19,534
14th Apr	SF	N	Southampton	1-0 aet	Heath	46,587
19th May	F	N	Watford	2-0	Sharp, Gray	100,000
1984-85						
5th Jan	3	A	Leeds United	2-0	Sharp (pen), Sheedy	21,211
26th Jan	4	H	Doncaster Rovers	2-0	Steven, Stevens	37,535
16th Feb	5	H	Telford United	3-0	Reid, Sheedy (pen), Steven	47,402
9th Mar	6	H	Ipswich Town	2-2	Sheedy, Mountfield	36,468
13th Mar	6 Replay	A	Ipswich Town	1-0	Sharp (pen)	27,737
13th Apr	SF	N	Luton Town	2-1 aet	Sheedy, Mountfield	45,289
18th May	F	N	Manchester United	0-1		100,000
1985-86						
5th Jan	3	H	Exeter City	1-0	Stevens	22,726
25th Jan	4	H	Blackburn Rovers	3-1	Van den Hauwe, Lineker 2	41,831
4th Mar	5	A	Tottenham Hotspur	2-1	Heath, Lineker	23,338
8th Mar	6	A	Luton Town	2-2	Donaghy o.g., Heath	15,529
12th Mar	6 Replay	H	Luton Town	1-0	Lineker	44,264
5th Apr	SF	N	Sheffield Wednesday	2-1 aet	Harper, Sharp	47,711
10th May	F	N	Liverpool	1-3	Lineker	98,000
1986-87						
10th Jan	3	H	Southampton	2-1	Sharp 2	32,320
31st Jan	4	A	Bradford City	1-0	Snodin	15,519
22nd Feb	5	A	Wimbledon	1-3	Wilkinson	9,924
1987-88						
9th Jan	3	A	Sheffield Wednesday	1-1	Reid	33,304
13th Jan	3 Replay 1	H	Sheffield Wednesday	1-1 aet	Sharp	32,935
25th Jan	3 Replay 2	H	Sheffield Wednesday	1-1 aet	Steven	37,414
27th Jan	3 Replay 3	A	Sheffield Wednesday	5-0	Sharp 3, Heath, Snodin	38,953
30th Jan	4	H	Middlesbrough	1-1	Sharp	36,564
3rd Feb	4 Replay 1	A	Middlesbrough	2-2 aet	Watson, Steven	25,235
9th Feb	4 Replay 2	H	Middlesbrough	2-1	Sharp, Mowbray o.g.	32,222
21st Feb	5	H	Liverpool	0-1		48,270
1988-89						
7th Jan	3	A	West Bromwich Alb.	1-1	Sheedy (pen)	31,186
11th Jan	3 Replay	H	West Bromwich Alb.	1-0	Sheedy	31,697
28th Jan	4	A	Plymouth Argyle	1-1	Sheedy (pen)	27,566
31st Jan	4 Replay	H	Plymouth Argyle	4-0	Nevin, Sharp 2, Sheedy	28,542
18th Feb	5	A	Barnsley	1-0	Sharp	32,551
19th Mar	6	H	Wimbledon	1-0	McCall	24,562
15th Apr	SF	N	Norwich City	1-0	Nevin	46,553
20th May	F	N	Liverpool	2-3 aet	McCall 2	82,800
1989-90						
6th Jan	3	A	Middlesbrough	0-0		20,075
10th Jan	3 Replay 1	H	Middlesbrough	1-1 aet	Sheedy	24,352
17th Jan	3 Replay 2	H	Middlesbrough	1-0	Whiteside	23,866

Date	Round	Venue	Opponents	Score	Scorers	Attendance
1989-90 (cont)						
28th Jan	4	A	Sheffield Wednesday	2-1	Whiteside 2	31,754
17th Feb	5	A	Oldham Athletic	2-2	Sharp, Cottee	19,320
21st Feb	5 Replay 1	H	Oldham Athletic	1-1 aet	Sheedy (pen)	36,663
10th Mar	5 Replay 2	A	Oldham Athletic	1-2 aet	Cottee	19,346
1990-91						
5th Jan	3	A	Charlton Athletic	2-1	Ebbrell 2	12,234
27th Jan	4	A	Woking	1-0	Sheedy	34,724
			(Played at Goodison Park)			
17th Feb	5	A	Liverpool	0-0		38,323
20th Feb	5 Replay 1	H	Liverpool	4-4 aet	Sharp 2, Cottee 2	37,766
27th Feb	5 Replay 2	H	Liverpool	1-0	Watson	40,201
11th Mar	6	A	West Ham United	1-2	Watson	28,162
1991-92						
4th Jan	3	H	Southend United	1-0	Beardsley	22,606
26th Jan	4	A	Chelsea	0-1		21,152
1992-93						
2nd Jan	3	A	Wimbledon	0-0		7,818
12th Jan	3 Replay	H	Wimbledon	1-2	Watson	15,293
1993-94						
8th Jan	3	A	Bolton Wanderers	1-1	Rideout	21,702
19th Jan	3 Replay	H	Bolton Wanderers	2-3 aet	Barlow 2	34,642
1994-95						
7th Jan	3	H	Derby County	1-0	Hinchcliffe	29,406
29th Jan	4	A	Bristol City	1-0	Jackson	19,816
18th Feb	5	H	Norwich City	5-0	Limpar, Parkinson, Rideout, Ferguson, Stuart	31,616
12th Mar	6	H	Newcastle United	1-0	Watson	35,203
9th Apr	SF	N	Tottenham Hotspur	4-1	Jackson, Stuart, Amokachi 2	38,226
20th May	F	N	Manchester United	1-0	Rideout	79,592
1995-96						
7th Jan	3	H	Stockport County	2-2	Ablett, Stuart	28,921
17th Jan	3 Replay	A	Stockport County	3-2	Ferguson, Stuart, Ebbrell	11,283
27th Jan	4	H	Port Vale	2-2	Amokachi, Ferguson	33,168
14th Feb	4 Replay	A	Port Vale	1-2	Stuart	19,197
1996-97						
5th Jan	3	H	Swindon Town	3-0	Kanchelskis (pen), Barmby, Ferguson	20,411
25th Jan	4	H	Bradford City	2-3	O'Brien o.g., Speed	30,007
1997-98						
4th Jan	3	H	Newcastle United	0-1		20,885
1998-99						
2nd Jan	3	A	Bristol City	2-0	Bakayoko 2	19,608
23rd Jan	4	H	Ipswich Town	1-0	Barmby	28,854

Date	Round	Venue	Opponents	Score	Scorers	Attendance
1998-99 (cont)						
13th Feb	5	H	Coventry City	2-1	Jeffers, Oster	33,907
7th Mar	6	A	Newcastle United	1-4	Unsworth	36,504
1999-2000						
11th Dec	3	A	Exeter City	0-0		6,045
21st Dec	3 Replay	H	Exeter City	1-0	Barmby	16,869
8th Jan	4	H	Birmingham City	2-0	Unsworth 2 (2 pens)	25,405
29th Jan	5	H	Preston North End	2-0	Unsworth, Moore	37,486
20th Feb	6	H	Aston Villa	1-2	Moore	35,331
2000-01						
6th Jan	3	A	Watford	2-1	Hughes, Watson	15,635
27th Jan	4	H	Tranmere Rovers	0-3		39,207
2001-02						
5th Jan	3	A	Stoke City	1-0	Stubbs	28,218
26th Jan	4	H	Leyton Orient	4-1	McGhee o.g., Ferguson, Campbell	35,851
17th Feb	5	H	Crewe Alexandra	0-0		29,939
26th Feb	5 Replay	A	Crewe Alexandra	2-1	Radzinski, Campbell	10,073
10th Mar	6	A	Middlesbrough	0-3		26,950
2002-03						
4th Jan	3	A	Shrewsbury Town	1-2	Alexandersson	7,800
2003-04						
3rd Jan	3	H	Norwich City	3-1	Kilbane, Ferguson 2 (2 pens)	29,955
25th Jan	4	H	Fulham	1-1	Jeffers	27,862
4th Feb	4 Replay	A	Fulham	1-2 aet	Jeffers	11,551
2004-05						
8th Jan	3	A	Plymouth Argyle	3-1	Osman, McFadden, Chadwick	20,112
29th Jan	4	H	Sunderland	3-0	Beattie, McFadden, Cahill	33,186
19th Feb	5	H	Manchester United	0-2		38,664
2005-06						
7th Jan	3	A	Millwall	1-1	Osman	16,440
18th Jan	3 Replay	H	Millwall	1-0	Cahill	25,800
28th Jan	4	H	Chelsea	1-1	McFadden	29,742
8th Feb	4 Replay	A	Chelsea	1-4	Arteta (pen)	39,301
2006-07						
7th Jan	3	H	Blackburn Rovers	1-4	Johnson (pen)	24,426

EVERTON FA CUP RECORDS

Highest Home Attendance:

77,920 v Manchester United, 14th Feb 1953

Biggest Victories:

Date	Opponents	Venue	Score	Scorers	Attendance
18th Jan 1890	Derby County	H	11-2	Brady 3, Geary 3, Milward 3, Doyle Kirkwood	10,000
28th Feb 1931	Southport	H	9-1	Dean 4, Dunn 2, Critchley 2, Johnson	45,647
21st Jan 1939	Doncaster R.	H	8-0	Boyes 2, Lawton 4, Stevenson, Gillick	41,115

Biggest Defeat:

Date	Opponents	Venue	Score	Attendance
7th Jan 1922	Crystal Palace	H	0-6	41,000

Everton sendings-off:

Date	Player	Opponents	Venue	Mins
9th Jan 1915	George Harrison	Barnsley	H	32
9th Jan 1915	Bobby Parker	Barnsley	H	53
20th Feb 1915	Jimmy Gault	Queens Park Rangers	A	44
17th Jan 1923	Hunter Hart	Bradford Park Avenue	A	30
30th Jan 1974	Archie Styles	West Bromwich Albion	A	75
4th Jan 1975	Gary Jones	Altrincham	H	40
26th Jan 1980	Brian Kidd	Wigan Athletic	H	81
12th Apr 1980	Brian Kidd	West Ham United	N	63
7th Mar 1981	Kevin Ratcliffe	Manchester City	H	85
21st Feb 1990	Norman Whiteside	Oldham Athletic	H	50
8th Jan 1994	Barry Horne	Bolton Wanderers	A	56
23rd Jan 1999	Marco Materazzi	Ipswich Town	H	48
6th Jan 2001	Joe-Max Moore	Watford	A	85

Opponents' sendings-off:

Date	Player	For	Venue	Mins
9th Jan 1915	Fred Barson	Barnsley	H	32
8th Jan 1958	Ambrose Fogarty	Sunderland	H	92
24th Jan 1959	Will Duff	Charlton Athletic	A	89
15th Jan 1972	John Hughes	Crystal Palace	A	53
30th Jan 1974	Willie Johnston	West Bromwich Albion	A	75
7th Jan 1978	Leighton Phillips	Aston Villa	H	87
9th Mar 1985	Steve McCall	Ipswich Town	H	72
18th May 1985	Kevin Moran	Manchester United	N	78
18th Feb 1995	Jon Newsome	Norwich City	H	56
5th Jan 1997	Ian Culverhouse	Swindon Town	H	1
5th Jan 1997	Gary Elkins	Swindon Town	H	75
20th Feb 2000	Benito Carbone	Aston Villa	H	90
6th Jan 2001	Robert Page	Watford	A	82

THE LEAGUE CUP RESULTS

Date	Round	Venue	Opponents	Score	Scorers	Attendance
1960-61						
12th Oct	1	H	Accrington Stanley	3-1	Wignall 2, J. Harris	18,246
31st Oct	2	H	Walsall	3-1	Webber, Vernon, Collins	14,137
23rd Nov	3	H	Bury	3-1	Wignall 2, J. Harris	20,724
21st Dec	4	A	Tranmere Rovers	4-0	Wignall 3, Bingham	14,967
15th Feb	5	A	Shrewsbury Town	1-2	Young	15,399
1967-68						
13th Sep	2	A	Bristol City	5-0	Kendall 2, Royle, Hurst, Brown	22,054
11th Oct	3	H	Sunderland	2-3	Young 2	39,914
1968-69						
3rd Sep	2	H	Tranmere Rovers	4-0	Royle, Whittle 2, Ball	35,477
24th Sep	3	H	Luton Town	5-1	Husband, Royle 2 (1 pen), Ball, Morrissey	30,405
16th Oct	4	H	Derby County	0-0		44,705
23rd Oct	4 Replay	A	Derby County	0-1		34,370
1969-70						
3rd Sep	2	A	Darlington	1-0	Ball	18,000
24th Sep	3	A	Arsenal	0-0		36,102
1st Oct	3 Replay	H	Arsenal	1-0	Kendall	41,140
15th Oct	4	A	Manchester City	0-2		45,643
1971-72						
7th Sep	2	A	Southampton	1-2	Johnson	17,833
1972-73						
5th Sep	2	A	Arsenal	0-1		35,230
1973-74						
8th Oct	2	H	Reading	1-0	Buckley	15,772
30th Oct	3	H	Norwich City	0-1		22,046
1974-75						
11th Sep	2	A	Aston Villa	1-1	Latchford	29,640
18th Sep	2 Replay	H	Aston Villa	0-3		24,595
1975-76						
9th Sep	2	H	Arsenal	2-2	Smallman, Lyons	17,174
23rd Sep	2 Replay	A	Arsenal	1-0	Kenyon	21,813
8th Oct	3	H	Carlisle United	2-0	Latchford, Dobson	20,010
11th Nov	4	H	Notts County	2-2	G Jones, Irving	19,169
25th Nov	4 Replay	A	Notts County	0-2		23,404
1976-77						
30th Aug	2	H	Cambridge United	3-0	Latchford, Dobson, King	10,898
20th Sep	3	A	Stockport County	1-0	Latchford	15,031
26th Oct	4	H	Coventry City	3-0	King 2, Lyons	21,572
1st Dec	5	A	Manchester United	3-0	King 2, Dobson	57,738
18th Jan	SF Leg 1	H	Bolton Wanderers	1-1	McKenzie	54,032

Date	Round	Venue	Opponents	Score	Scorers	Attendance
1976-77 (cont)						
15th Feb	SF Leg 2	A	Bolton Wanderers	1-0	Latchford	50,413
12th Mar	F	N	Aston Villa	0-0		96,223
16th Mar	F Replay 1	N	Aston Villa	1-1 aet	Latchford	54,840
13th Apr	F Replay 2	A	Aston Villa	2-3 aet	Latchford, Lyons	54,749
1977-78						
30th Aug	2	A	Sheffield United	3-0	Latchford, McKenzie, King	18,571
25th Oct	3	H	Middlesbrough	2-2	King, Telfer	32,766
31st Oct	3 Replay	A	Middlesbrough	2-1	Lyons, Pearson	28,409
29th Nov	4	A	Sheffield Wednesday	3-1	Lyons, Dobson, Pearson	36,079
18th Jan	5	A	Leeds United	1-4	Thomas	35,020
1978-79						
29th Aug	2	H	Wimbledon	8-0	Latchford 5 (1 pen), Dobson 3	23,137
3rd Oct	3	H	Darlington	1-0	Dobson	23,682
7th Nov	4	H	Nottingham Forest	2-3	Burns o.g., Latchford	48,503
1979-80						
28th Aug	2 Leg 1	H	Cardiff City	2-0	Kidd 2	18,061
5th Sep	2 Leg 2	A	Cardiff City	0-1		9,698
25th Sep	3	A	Aston Villa	0-0		22,635
9th Oct	3 Replay	H	Aston Villa	4-1	Kidd, Latchford 2, Rimmer o.g.	22,088
30th Oct	4	A	Grimsby Town	1-2	Kidd	22,043
1980-81						
26th Aug	2 Leg 1	H	Blackpool	3-0	Eastoe, Latchford, McBride	20,156
3rd Sep	2 Leg 2	A	Blackpool	2-2	Latchford 2	10,579
24th Sep	3	H	WBA	1-2	Gidman	23,546
1981-82						
6th Oct	2 Leg 1	H	Coventry City	1-1	Ferguson	17,228
27th Oct	2 Leg 2	A	Coventry City	1-0	Ferguson	13,770
11th Nov	3	H	Oxford United	1-0	O'Keefe	14,910
15th Dec	4	H	Ipswich Town	2-3	McMahon 2	15,759
1982-83						
5th Oct	2 Leg 1	A	Newport County	2-0	McMahon, King	8,293
27th Oct	2 Leg 2	H	Newport County	2-2	King, Johnson	8,941
9th Nov	3	H	Arsenal	1-1	Stevens	13,089
23rd Nov	3 Replay	A	Arsenal	0-3		19,547
1983-84						
4th Oct	2 Leg 1	A	Chesterfield	1-0	Sharp	10,713
26th Oct	2 Leg 2	H	Chesterfield	2-2	Heath, Steven	8,067
9th Nov	3	H	Coventry City	2-1	Heath, Sharp	9,080
30th Nov	4	A	West Ham United	2-2	Reid, Sheedy	19,702
6th Dec	4 Replay	H	West Ham United	2-0	King, Sheedy	21,609
18th Jan	5	A	Oxford United	1-1	Heath	14,333
24th Jan	5 Replay	H	Oxford United	4-1	Richardson, Sheedy, Heath, Sharp	31,011
15th Feb	SF Leg 1	H	Aston Villa	2-0	Sheedy, Richardson	40,006
22nd Feb	SF Leg 2	A	Aston Villa	0-1		42,426
25th Mar	F	N	Liverpool	0-0 aet		100,000
28th Mar	F Replay	N	Liverpool	0-1		52,089

Date	Round	Venue	Opponents	Score	Scorers	Attendance
1984-85						
26th Sep	2 Leg 1	A	Sheffield United	2-2	Mountfield, Sharp	16,345
10th Oct	2 Leg 2	H	Sheffield United	4-0	Mountfield, Bracewell, Sharp, Heath	18,742
30th Oct	3	A	Manchester Utd	2-1	Sharp (pen), Gidman o.g.	50,918
20th Nov	4	H	Grimsby Town	0-1		26,298
1985-86						
25th Sep	2 Leg 1	H	Bournemouth	3-2	Lineker, Marshall, Hefferman o.g.	13,930
8th Oct	2 Leg 2	A	Bournemouth	2-0	Lineker, Richardson	8,081
29th Oct	3	A	Shrewsbury Town	4-1	Sharp, Hughes o.g., Sheedy, Heath	10,246
26th Nov	4	A	Chelsea	2-2	Sheedy, Bracewell	27,544
10th Dec	4 Replay	H	Chelsea	1-2	Lineker	26,373
1986-87						
24th Sep	2 Leg 1	H	Newport County	4-0	Langley, Heath, Wilkinson 2	11,957
7th Oct	2 Leg 2	A	Newport County	5-1	Wilkinson 3, Sharp, Mullen o.g.	7,172
28th Oct	3	H	Sheffield Wed.	4-0	Wilkinson 2, Heath, Mountfield	24,638
19th Nov	4	A	Norwich City	4-1	Steven, Sharp, Steven (pen), Heath	17,988
21st Jan	5	H	Liverpool	0-1		53,323
1987-88						
22nd Sep	2 Leg 1	H	Rotherham Utd	3-2	Snodin, Wilson, Clarke (pen)	15,369
6th Oct	2 Leg 2	A	Rotherham Utd	0-0		12,995
28th Oct	3	A	Liverpool	1-0	Stevens	44,071
17th Nov	4	H	Oldham Athletic	2-1	Watson, Adams	23,315
20th Jan	5	H	Manchester City	2-0	Heath, Sharp	40,014
7th Feb	SF Leg 1	H	Arsenal	0-1		25,476
24th Feb	SF Leg 2	A	Arsenal	1-3	Heath	51,148
1988-89						
27th Sep	2 Leg 1	H	Bury	3-0	Sharp, McDonald (pen), McCall	11,071
11th Oct	2 Leg 2	A	Bury	2-2	Steven (pen), Sharp	4,592
8th Nov	3	H	Oldham Athletic	1-1	Steven (pen)	17,230
29th Nov	3 Replay	A	Oldham Athletic	2-0	Cottee 2	14,573
14th Dec	4	A	Bradford City	1-3	Watson	15,055
1989-90						
19th Sep	2 Leg 1	A	Leyton Orient	2-0	Newell, Sheedy	8,214
3rd Oct	2 Leg 2	H	Leyton Orient	2-2	Whiteside, Sheedy	10,128
24th Oct	3	H	Luton Town	3-0	Newell 2, Nevin	18,428
22nd Nov	4	A	Nottingham Forest	0-1		21,324
1990-91						
25th Sep	2 Leg 1	A	Wrexham	5-0	Cottee 3, McDonald, Nevin	9,072
9th Oct	2 Leg 2	H	Wrexham	6-0	Sharp 3, Cottee, Ebbrell, McDonald	7,415
30th Oct	3	A	Sheffield United	1-2	Pemberton o.g.	15,045

Date	Round	Venue	Opponents	Score	Scorers	Attendance
1991-92						
24th Sep	2 Leg 1	H	Watford	1-0	Beardsley	8,264
8th Oct	2 Leg 2	A	Watford	2-1	Newell, Beardsley	11,561
30th Oct	3	H	Wolverhampton W.	4-1	Beagrie 2, Cottee, Beardsley	19,065
4th Dec	4	H	Leeds United	1-4	Atteveld	25,467
1992-93						
23rd Sep	2 Leg 1	A	Rotherham United	0-1		7,736
7th Oct	2 Leg 2	H	Rotherham United	3-0	Rideout 2, Cottee	10,302
28th Oct	3	H	Wimbledon	0-0		9,541
10th Nov	3 Replay	A	Wimbledon	1-0	Beardsley	3,686
2nd Dec	4	H	Chelsea	2-2	Barlow, Beardsley	14,457
16th Dec	4 Replay	A	Chelsea	0-1		19,496
1993-94						
21st Sep	2 Leg 1	A	Lincoln City	4-3	Rideout 3, Cottee	9,153
6th Oct	2 Leg 2	H	Lincoln City	4-2	Rideout, Snodin, Cottee 2	8,375
26th Oct	3	H	Crystal Palace	2-2	Beagrie, Watson	11,547
10th Nov	3 Replay	A	Crystal Palace	4-1	Watson 2, Ward (pen), Young o.g.	14,662
30th Nov	4	H	Manchester United	0-2		34,052
1994-95						
20th Sep	2 Leg 1	H	Portsmouth	2-3	Samways, Stuart (pen)	14,043
5th Oct	2 Leg 2	A	Portsmouth	1-1	Watson	13,605
1995-96						
20th Sep	2 Leg 1	A	Millwall	0-0		12,053
4th Oct	2 Leg 2	H	Millwall	2-4	Hinchcliffe (pen), Stuart	14,891
1996-97						
18th Sep	2 Leg 1	H	York City	1-1	Kanchelskis	11,527
24th Sep	2 Leg 2	A	York City	2-3	Rideout, Speed	7,854
1997-98						
16th Sep	2 Leg 1	A	Scunthorpe United	1-0	Farrelly	7,145
1st Oct	2 Leg 2	H	Scunthorpe United	5-0	Stuart, Oster , Barmby 2, Cadamarteri	11,562
15th Oct	3	A	Coventry City	1-4	Barmby	10,087
1998-99						
15th Sep	2 Leg 1	A	Huddersfield Town	1-1	Watson	15,395
23rd Sep	2 Leg 2	H	Huddersfield Town	2-1	Dacourt, Materazzi	18,718
28th Oct	3	A	Middlesbrough	3-2	Ferguson, Bakayoko, Hutchison	20,748
11th Nov	4	H	Sunderland	1-1	Collins	28,132
			(Sunderland won 5-4 on penalties)			
1999-2000						
14th Sep	2 Leg 1	A	Oxford United	1-1	Cadamarteri	7,345
22nd Sep	2 Leg 2	H	Oxford United	0-1		10,006
2000-01						
20th Sep	2 Leg 1	H	Bristol Rovers	1-1	Campbell	25,564
27th Sep	2 Leg 2	A	Bristol Rovers	1-1	Jeffers	11,045
			(Bristol Rovers won 4-2 on penalties)			

Date	Round	Venue	Opponents	Score	Scorers	Attendance
2001-02						
12th Sep	2	H	Crystal Palace	1-1	Ferguson (pen)	21,128
			(Crystal Palace won 5-4 penalties)			
2002-03						
1st Oct	2	A	Wrexham	3-0	Campbell, Rooney 2	10,073
6th Nov	3	A	Newcastle United	3-3	Campbell, Watson, Unsworth (pen)	26,950
			(Everton won 3-2 on penalties)			
4th Dec	4	A	Chelsea	1-4	Naysmith	21,128
2003-04						
24th Sep	2	H	Stockport County	3-0	Ferguson 2 (1 pen), Chadwick	19,807
29th Oct	3	H	Charlton Athletic	1-0	Linderoth	24,863
3rd Dec	4	A	Middlesbrough	0-0		18,568
			(Middlesbrough won 5-4 on penalties)			
2004-05						
22nd Sep	2	A	Bristol City	2-2	Ferguson (pen), Chadwick	15,264
			(Everton won 4-3 on penalties)			
27th Oct	3	H	Preston North End	2-0	Carsley, Bent	33,922
11th Nov	4	A	Arsenal	1-3	Gravesen	27,791
2005-06						
26th Oct	3	H	Middlesbrough	0-1		25,844
2006-07						
19th Sep	2	A	Peterborough	2-1	Stirling o.g., Cahill	10,756
24th Oct	3	H	Luton Town	4-0	Cahill, Keane o.g., McFadden, Anichebe	27,149
8th Nov	4	H	Arsenal	0-1		31,045

Everton and Liverpool players pose for a group picture after the 1984 League Cup final at Wembley ended goalless

EVERTON LEAGUE CUP RECORDS

Highest Home Attendance:

54,302 v Bolton Wanderers, 18th Jan 1977

Biggest Victories:

Date	Opponents	Venue	Score	Scorers	Attendance
29th Aug1978	Wimbledon	H	8-0	Latchford 5 (1 pen), Dobson 3	23,137
9th Oct 1990	Wrexham	H	6-0	Sharp 3, Cottee, Ebbrell, McDonald	7,415
13th Sept 1967	Bristol City	A	5-0	Kendall 2, Royle, Hurst, Brown	22,054
25th Sept 1990	Wrexham	A	5-0	Cottee 3, McDonald, Nevin	9,072
1st Oct 1997	Scunthorpe U	H	5-0	Stuart, Oster, Barmby 2, Cadamarteri	11,562

Biggest Defeats:

Date	Opponents	Venue	Score	Scorer	Attendance
18th Jan 1978	Leeds United	A	1-4	Thomas	35,020
4th Dec 1991	Leeds United	H	1-4	Atteveld	25,467
15th Oct 1997	Coventry City	A	1-4	Barmby	10,087
4th Dec 2002	Chelsea	A	1-4	Naysmith	21,128

Everton sendings-off:

Date	Player	Opponents	Venue	Mins
18th Jan 1978	Mark Higgins	Leeds United	A	45
26th Nov 1985	Kevin Sheedy	Chelsea	A	28
30th Oct 1990	Dave Watson	Sheffield United	A	60
23rd Sept 1998	Marco Materazzi	Huddersfield Town	H	70
27th Oct 2004	Lee Carsley	Preston North End	H	72
8th Nov 2006	James McFadden	Arsenal	H	19

Opponents' sendings-off:

Date	Player	For	Venue	Mins
28th Oct 1986	Lawrie Madden	Sheffield Wednesday	H	60
7th Oct 1992	Billy Mercer	Rotherham United	H	31
16th Dec 1992	Gareth Hall	Chelsea	A	64
6th Nov 2002	Stephen Caldwell	Newcastle United	A	110

THE CHARITY SHIELD RESULTS
(FA COMMUNITY SHIELD)

Date	Venue	Opponents	Score	Scorers	Attendance
1928					
24th Oct	Old Trafford	Blackburn Rovers	2-1	Dean 2	4,000
1932					
12th Oct	St. James' Park	Newcastle United	5-3	Dean 4, Johnson	10,000
1933					
18th Oct	Goodison Park	Arsenal	0-3		18,000
1963					
17th Aug	Goodison Park	Manchester United	4-0	Gabriel, Stevens, Temple, Vernon	54,844
1966					
13th Aug	Goodison Park	Liverpool	0-1		63,329
1970					
8th Aug	Stamford Bridge	Chelsea	2-1	Kendall, Whittle	43,547
1984					
18th Aug	Wembley Stadium	Liverpool	1-0	Grobbelaar o.g.	100,000
1985					
10th Aug	Wembley Stadium	Manchester United	2-0	Steven, Heath	82,000
1986					
16th Aug	Wembley Stadium	Liverpool	1-1	Heath	88,231
1987					
1st Aug	Wembley Stadium	Coventry City	1-0	Clarke	88,000
1995					
13th Aug	Wembley Stadium	Blackburn Rovers	1-0	Samways	40,149

Everton skipper Roy Vernon lifts the shield with a little help from chairman John Moores in 1963 following the 4-0 demolition of FA Cup holders Manchester United

151

THE OTHER COMPETITION RESULTS

Date	Round	Venue	Opponents	Score	Scorers	Attendance
1963-64 : BRITISH CHAMPIONSHIP						
27th Nov	Leg 1	A	Rangers	3-1	Scott, Temple, Young	64,006
2nd Dec	Leg 2	H	Rangers	1-1	Young	42,202
1970-71 : FA CUP 3RD/4TH PLACE PLAY-OFF						
7th May	-		Selhurst P. Stoke City	2-3	Whittle, Ball	5,031
1973-74 : TEXACO CUP						
18th Sep	1 Leg 1	H	Hearts	0-1		12,536
3rd Oct	1 Leg 2	A	Hearts	0-0		24,903
1985-86/1986-87 : SCREEN SPORT SUPER CUP						
18th Sep	Group	A	Manchester United	4-2	Lineker, Sharp, Sheedy 2	33,859
2nd Oct	Group	H	Norwich City	1-0	Lineker	10,329
23rd Oct	Group	A	Norwich City	0-1		12,196
4th Dec	Group	H	Manchester United	1-0	Stapleton o.g.	20,542
5th Feb	SF Leg 1	A	Tottenham Hotspur	0-0		7,548
19th Mar	SF Leg 2	H	Tottenham Hotspur	3-1	Mountfield, Heath, Sharp	12,008
16th Sep	F Leg 1	A	Liverpool	1-3	Sheedy	20,660
30th Sep	F Leg 2	H	Liverpool	1-4	Sharp (pen)	26,068
1986-87 : FULL MEMBERS CUP						
3rd Dec	3	H	Newcastle United	5-2	Sharp 3, Heath, Sheedy	7,530
3rd Mar	4	H	Charlton Athletic	2-2	Steven, Wilkinson	7,914
			(Charlton Athletic won 6-5 on penalties)			
1987-88 : MERCANTILE CREDIT FOOTBALL LEAGUE CENTENARY CHALLENGE						
25th Nov		H	Bayern Munich	3-1	Sharp 2, Heath	13,083
1987-88 : DUBAI CHAMPIONS CUP						
8th Dec		N	Rangers	2-2	Watson, Sheedy	8,000
			(Rangers won 8-7 on penalties)			
1987-88 : SIMOD CUP						
16th Feb	3	H	Luton Town	1-2	Power	5,207
1988-89 : MERCANTILE CREDIT FOOTBALL LEAGUE CENTENARY TROPHY						
29th Aug	1	A	Manchester United	0-1		16,439
1988-89 : SIMOD CUP						
20th Dec	3	H	Millwall	2-0	Cottee, Hurlock o.g.	3,703
18th Jan	4	A	Wimbledon	2-1	Clarke 2	2,477
28th Feb	SF	H	QPR	1-0	Nevin	7,072
30th Apr	F	N	Nottingham Forest	3-4 aet	Sharp, Cottee 2	46,604

Date	Round	Venue	Opponents	Score	Scorers	Attendance
1990-91 : ZENITH DATA SYSTEMS CUP						
18th Dec	2	A	Blackburn Rovers	4-1	Newell, Cottee, Watson 2	5,410
22nd Jan	3	H	Sunderland	4-1	Cottee 4	4,609
13th Mar	SF (Nrth)	A	Barnsley	1-0	Cottee	10,287
19th Mar	F Leg 1 (Nrth)	A	Leeds United	3-3	Beagrie, Warzycha, Milligan	13,387
21st Mar	F Leg 2 (Nrth)	H	Leeds United	3-1	Cottee 2, Ebbrell	12,603
7th Apr	F	N	Crystal Palace	1-4 aet	Warzycha	52,460
1991-92 : ZENITH DATA SYSTEMS CUP						
1st Oct	2	H	Oldham Athletic	3-2	Watson, Newell, Cottee	4,588
27th Nov	3	A	Leicester City	1-2	Beardsley	13,242

Everton manager Colin Harvey with his players ahead of extra time during the 1989 Simod Cup final against Nottingham Forest at Wembley

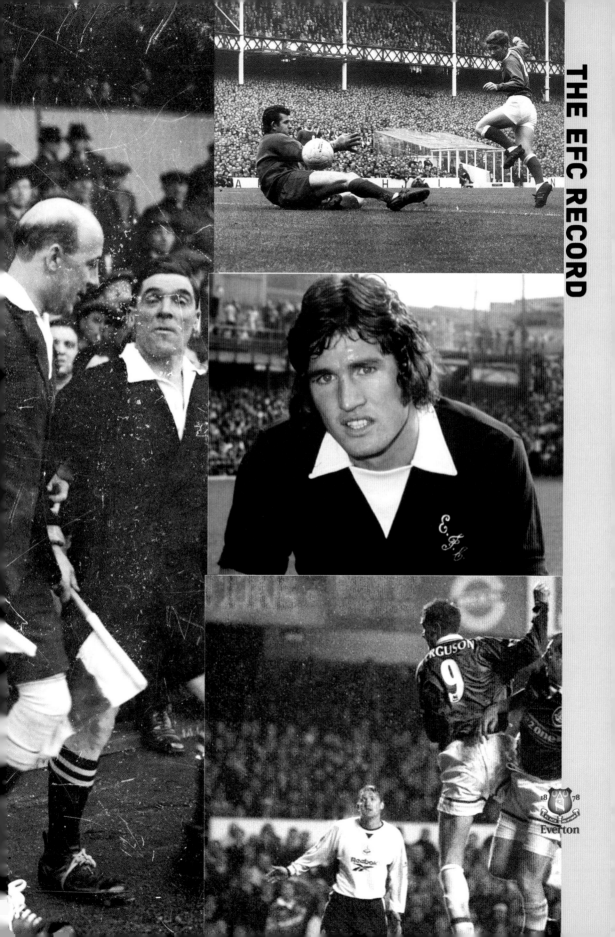

Everton

THE MARATHON MEN

OVERALL APPEARANCES

1	Neville Southall	750
2	Brian Labone	534
3	Dave Watson	528
4	Ted Sagar	497
5	Kevin Ratcliffe	493
6	Mick Lyons	473
7	Jack Taylor	456
8	Peter Farrell	453
9	Graeme Sharp	446
10	Dixie Dean	433

Mick Lyons, No. 6 in the all-time list

LEAGUE APPEARANCES

1	Neville Southall	578
2	Ted Sagar	463
3	Brian Labone	451
4	Dave Watson	423
5	Peter Farrell	422
6	Jack Taylor	400
7	Dixie Dean	399
8	Tommy Eglington	394
9	Mick Lyons	390
10	Tommy T.E. Jones	383

Peter Farrell, No. 5 in the league list

EUROPEAN APPEARANCES

1	Colin Harvey	19
=	Brian Labone	19
3	Johnny Morrissey	17
=	Tommy Wright	17
5	Derek Temple	16
6	Jimmy Gabriel	15
7	Neville Southall	13
=	Gordon West	13
=	Alex Young	13
10	Brian Harris	12
=	Andy Rankin	12
=	Dennis Stevens	12

**Brian Labone (top) and Gordon West,
prominent in the European list**

FA CUP APPEARANCES

1	Neville Southall	70
2	Kevin Ratcliffe	57
3	Jack Taylor	56
4	Graeme Sharp	54
5	Harry Makepeace	52
6	Dave Watson	48
7	Brian Labone	45
8	Jack Sharp	42
9	Gordon West	40
10	Alex "Sandy" Young	39

Neville Southall - FA Cup record holder

LEAGUE CUP APPEARANCES

1	Neville Southall	65
2	Graeme Sharp	48
3	Kevin Ratcliffe	46
4	Dave Watson	39
5	Mick Lyons	37
6	Adrian Heath	35
7	Kevin Sheedy	32
8	Andy King	30
=	Gary Stevens	30
10	Bob Latchford	28
11	Trevor Steven	27
12	Alan Harper	25
=	Peter Reid	25

Bob Latchford, No. 10 in the League Cup list

Trevor Steven – Below Latchford in the League Cup appearance list

THE RECORD GOALSCORERS

OVERALL

		TIME WITH CLUB	GAMES	GOALS
1	Dixie Dean	1925-1937	433	383
2	Graeme Sharp	1980-1991	446	159
3	Bob Latchford	1974-1981	289	138
4	Alex "Sandy" Young	1901-1911	314	125
5	Joe Royle	1966-1974	276	119
6	Roy Vernon	1960-1965	203	111
=	Dave Hickson	1951-1955 & 1957-59	243	111
8	Edgar Chadwick	1888-1899	300	110
9	Tony Cottee	1988-1994	240	99
10	Jimmy Settle	1898-1908	269	97
=	Kevin Sheedy	1982-1992	368	97
12	Alfred Milward	1888-1897	224	96
13	Adrian Heath	1981-1988	307	94
14	Alex Stevenson	1934-1949	271	90
15	John Willie Parker	1951-1956	176	89
=	Alex Young	1960-1968	275	89

LEAGUE

1	Dixie Dean	1925-1937	399	349
2	Graeme Sharp	1980-1991	322	111
3	Alex "Sandy" Young	1901-1911	275	110
4	Bob Latchford	1974-1981	236	106
5	Joe Royle	1966-1974	232	102
6	Roy Vernon	1960-1965	176	101
7	Edgar Chadwick	1888-1899	270	97
8	Dave Hickson	1951-1955 & 1957-59	225	95
9	Alfred Milward	1888-1897	201	85
10	Jimmy Settle	1898-1908	237	84

EUROPEAN (3+ GOALS)

1	Fred Pickering	1964-1967	9	6
2	Andy Gray	1983-1985	3	5
3	Andy King	1976-1980 & 1982-84	5	4
=	Joe Royle	1966-1974	6	4
=	Graeme Sharp	1980-1991	8	4
=	Alan Ball	1966-1971	10	4
7	Bob Latchford	1974-1981	7	3
=	Alex Young	1960-1968	13	3
=	Johnny Morrissey	1962-1971	17	3

FA CUP (10+ GOALS)

		TIME WITH CLUB	GAMES	GOALS
1	Dixie Dean	1925-1937	32	28
2	Graeme Sharp	1980-1991	54	20
3	Dave Hickson	1951-1955 & 1957-59	18	16
4	Kevin Sheedy	1982-1992	38	15
=	Alex "Sandy" Young	1901-1911	39	15
6	Jack Taylor	1896-1910	56	14
7	Edgar Chadwick	1888-1898	30	13
=	Jimmy Settle	1898-1908	32	13
9	Jack Sharp	1899-1910	42	12
10	Tommy Browell	1911-1913	10	11
=	Alfred Milward	1888-1897	23	11

LEAGUE CUP (7+ GOALS)

1	Bob Latchford	1974-1981	28	19
2	Graeme Sharp	1980-1991	48	15
3	Tony Cottee	1988-1994	23	11
=	Adrian Heath	1981-1988	35	11
5	Andy King	1976-1980 & 1982-84	30	10
6	Kevin Sheedy	1982-1992	32	9
7	Martin Dobson	1974-1979	22	8
8	Frank Wignall	1959-1962	3	7
=	Paul Wilkinson	1984-1987	4	7
=	Paul Rideout	1992-1997	13	7
=	Dave Watson	1986-1999	39	7

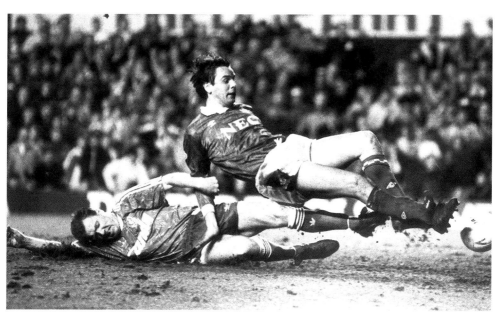

Graeme Sharp slides home his 20th and final FA Cup goal, against Liverpool in 1991

THE YOUNGEST/OLDEST

Youngest player

	Opposition	Date Of Debut	Age
James Vaughan	Crystal Palace	10th April 2005	16 years & 271 days
Joe Royle	Blackpool	15th January 1966	16 years & 282 days
Wayne Rooney	Tottenham Hotspur	17th August 2002	16 years & 297 days
Francis Jeffers	Manchester United	26th December 1997	16 years & 335 days
Alan Tyrer	Fulham	16th January 1960	17 years & 40 days
George Sharples	West Brom.	5th November 1960	17 years & 47 days
Alec Farrall	Lincoln City	22nd April 1953	17 years & 51 days
Roy Parnell	Wolves	21st January 1961	17 years & 105 days
Richard Dunne	Swindon Town	5th January 1997	17 years & 107 days
Michael Branch	Manchester United	21st February 1996	17 years & 127 days

Previous record holders for youngest player

Edgar Chadwick	Accrington Stanley	8th September 1888	19 years & 55 days
Alfred Milward	Blackburn Rovers	10th November 1888	18 years & 60 days
William Brown	Manchester City	12th December 1914	17 years & 215 days
Tommy Lawton	Wolves	13th February 1937	17 years & 130 days

Youngest player to score (* on debut)

James Vaughan	Crystal Palace	10th April 2005	16 years & 271 days*
Wayne Rooney	Wrexham	1st October 2002	16 years & 342 days
Tommy Lawton	Wolves	13th February 1937	17 years & 130 days*
Alan Tyrer	Leeds United	23rd April 1960	17 years & 137 days
Bert Llewellyn	Blackpool	22nd August 1956	17 years & 200 days

Previous record holders for youngest scorer

Edgar Chadwick	Accrington Stanley	15th September 1888	19 years & 62 days
Alfred Milward	Stoke City	12th January 1889	18 years & 123 days

Oldest player

	Opposition	Date Of Final Game	Age
Ted Sagar	Plymouth Argyle	15th November 1952	42 years & 281 days
Ted Taylor	Tottenham Hotspur	11th February 1928	40 years & 341 days
Nigel Martyn	Chelsea	28th January 2006	39 years & 170 days
Neville Southall	Tottenham Hotspur	29th November 1997	39 years & 74 days
Richard Gough	Bradford City	28th April 2001	39 years & 23 days
Wally Fielding	Tottenham Hotspur	11th October 1958	38 years & 319 days
Jack Taylor	Barnsley	31st March 1910	38 years & 63 days
Dave Watson	Tottenham Hotspur	15th January 2000	38 years & 56 days
Tom Fern	Sunderland	1st January 1924	37 years & 279 days
George Jackson	Portsmouth	24th April 1948	37 years & 101 days

Oldest player to score

Wally Fielding	West Brom.	27th September 1958	38 years & 305 days

MOST GOALS FOR EVERTON IN A LEAGUE SEASON

Name	Season	Division	Games	Goals	Goal average
Dixie Dean	1927/28	1	39	60	1.54
Dixie Dean	1931/32	1	38	45	1.18
Dixie Dean	1930/31	2	37	39	1.05
Bertie Freeman	1908/09	1	37	38	1.03
Bobby Parker	1914/15	1	35	36	1.03
Tommy Lawton	1938/39	1	38	34	0.89
Dixie Dean	1925/26	1	38	32	0.84
John Willie Parker	1953/54	2	38	31	0.82
Bob Latchford	1977/78	1	39	30	0.77
Gary Lineker	1985/86	1	41	30	0.73

MOST GOALS FOR EVERTON IN A SEASON
- ALL COMPETITIONS

Name	Season	Games	Goals	Goal average
Dixie Dean	1927/28	41	63	1.54
Dixie Dean	1930/31	42	48	1.14
Dixie Dean	1931/32	39	46	1.18
Gary Lineker	1985/86	57	40	0.70
Bertie Freeman	1908/09	38	38	1
Bobby Parker	1914/15	40	38	0.95
Tommy Lawton	1938/39	43	38	0.88
Fred Pickering	1964/65	51	37	0.73
Dixie Dean	1925/26	40	33	0.83
Dixie Dean	1932/33	46	33	0.72
John Willie Parker	1953/54	41	33	0.80
Bob Latchford	1977/78	46	32	0.70
Wilf Chadwick	1923/24	44	30	0.68
Graeme Sharp	1984/85	55	30	0.55

Gary Lineker and Graeme Sharp, 30-goal Everton strikers

HAT-TRICK HEROES

EVERTON LEAGUE HAT-TRICKS

Player	Goals	Opponents	Venue	Date	Goal Times			
Steve Watson	3	Leeds United	H	28/9/2003	27	37	52	
Nick Barmby	3	West Ham United	A	26/2/2000	7	64	67	
Kevin Campbell	3	West Ham United	H	8/5/1999	13	19	77	
Duncan Ferguson	3	Bolton Wanderers	H	28/12/1997	16	40	66	
Gary Speed	3	Southampton	H	16/11/1996	30	32	72	
A. Kanchelskis	3	Sheffield Wed.	A	27/4/1996	22	55	65	
Tony Cottee	3	Swindon Town	H	15/1/1994	42	82	89	
Tony Cottee	3	Sheffield United	H	21/8/1993	36	84	90	
Tony Cottee	3	Tottenham H.	H	5/10/1991	14	21	29	
Peter Beardsley	3	Coventry City	H	21/9/1991	40	61	75	
Tony Cottee	3	Newcastle United	H	27/8/1988	1	31	61	
Graeme Sharp	4	Southampton	A	3/10/1987	2	16	20	60
Wayne Clarke	3	Newcastle United	H	20/4/1987	49	82	90	
Gary Lineker	3	Southampton	H	3/5/1986	30	34	62	
Gary Lineker	3	Manchester City	H	11/2/1986	5	46	57	
Gary Lineker	3	Birmingham City	H	31/8/1985	11	22	86	
Adrian Heath	3	Notts County	H	4/2/1984	26	38	69	
Bob Latchford	3	Crystal Palace	H	20/9/1980	50	58	60	
Bob Latchford	3	Leeds United	H	13/11/1979	6	22	45	
Andy King	3	Bristol City	H	10/2/1979	33	66	69	
Bob Latchford	3	Coventry City	H	26/11/1977	42	44	90	
Bob Latchford	4	QPR	A	8/10/1977	8	18	48	68
Joe Royle	4	Southampton	H	20/11/1971	15	32	62	72
David Johnson	3	Southampton	H	20/11/1971	13	27	85	
Joe Royle	3	Southampton	H	27/9/1969	12	67	85	
Joe Royle	3	Leicester City	H	30/11/1968	16	60	69	
Alan Ball	3	West Brom	H	28/9/1968	2	59	73	
Alan Ball	4	West Brom	A	16/3/1968	23	26	52	78
John Morrissey	3	Sunderland	H	16/5/1967	41	42	72	
Alex Young	3	Sheffield Wed.	H	31/8/1965	40	57	85	
Fred Pickering	3	Tottenham H.	H	29/8/1964	25	72	80	
Fred Pickering	3	Nottingham Forest	H	14/3/1964	7	23	43	
Roy Vernon	3	Fulham	H	11/5/1963	5	8	85	
John Morrissey	3	West Brom	H	29/9/1962	20	43	51	
Roy Vernon	3	Cardiff City	H	28/4/1962	19	36	83	
Derek Temple	3	Ipswich Town	H	16/9/1961	18	30	84	
Roy Vernon	3	Arsenal	H	29/4/1961	21	24	89	
Bobby Collins	3	Cardiff City	H	15/4/1961	4	28	85	
Bobby Collins	3	Newcastle United	H	19/11/1960	35	49	53	
Edward Thomas	3	Nottingham Forest	H	23/1/1960	32	84	86	
Alan Shackleton	3	Birmingham City	H	14/11/1959	5	6	76	
Jimmy Harris	3	Tottenham H.	A	11/10/1958	10	49	83	
Edward Thomas	4	Preston North End	H	8/3/1958	15	43	53	82
John Parker	3	Rotherham United	H	13/3/1954	75	80	89	
John Parker	4	Plymouth Argyle	H	27/2/1954	16	55	75	83
Eddie Wainwright	3	Derby County	A	13/2/1954	60	81	87	
Dave Hickson	3	Stoke City	A	7/11/1953	3	35	75	
John Parker	3	Oldham Athletic	H	29/8/1953	55	60	80	
Dave Hickson	3	Brentford	H	7/2/1953	7	13	54	

HAT-TRICK HEROES

EVERTON LEAGUE HAT-TRICKS

Player	Goals	Opponents	Venue	Date	Goal Times				
Harold Potts	3	Bury	A	13/12/1952	61	62	88		
Tommy Eglington	5	Doncaster Rovers	H	27/9/1952	16	22	46	67	69
John Parker	3	Hull City	H	11/4/1952	20	60	81		
Harry Catterick	3	Fulham	A	7/10/1950	22	29	43		
Eddie Wainwright	3	Huddersfield Town	H	3/9/1949	6	16	88		
Eddie Wainwright	4	Blackpool	H	5/3/1949	12	25	32	80	
Jock Dodds	3	Preston North End	H	25/9/1948	26	44	59		
Jock Dodds	3	Huddersfield Town	A	28/4/1948	N/A				
Jock Dodds	3	Wolverhampton W.	A	21/2/1948	12	53	56		
Eddie Wainwright	3	Sunderland	H	15/2/1947	9	51	75		
Stanley Bentham	3	Sunderland	H	10/4/1939	12	36	80		
Tommy Lawton	4	Middlesbrough	A	11/3/1939	37	38	49	83	
Tommy Lawton	3	Middlesbrough	H	5/11/1938	5	21	87		
Robert Bell	3	Leeds United	H	22/10/1938	41	44	52		
Alex Stevenson	3	Portsmouth	H	30/4/1938	15	18	83		
Jimmy Cunliffe	3	Derby County	H	25/12/1936	N/A				
Dixie Dean	3	West Brom	H	7/11/1936	11	28	65		
Dixie Dean	3	Birmingham City	H	25/4/1936	8	24	53		
Jimmy Cunliffe	4	West Brom	H	11/4/1936	22	50	79	83	
Jimmy Cunliffe	4	Stoke City	H	2/11/1935	5	7	77	84	
Dixie Dean	3	Tottenham H.	H	29/12/1934	12	54	65		
Tommy White	3	Blackburn Rovers	H	14/10/1933	4	6	16		
Dixie Dean	3	Leicester City	H	8/3/1933	f/h	s/h	s/h		
Tommy Johnson	3	Blackburn Rovers	H	27/12/1932	38	40	88		
Dixie Dean	3	West Ham United	H	16/4/1932	3	66	75		
Dixie Dean	3	Huddersfield Town	H	19/3/1932	10	11	60		
Dixie Dean	3	Blackburn Rovers	H	26/12/1931	4	7	46		
Dixie Dean	4	Leicester City	H	28/11/1931	6	f/h	56	s/h	
Dixie Dean	5	Chelsea	H	14/11/1931	5	8	15	24	32
Dixie Dean	5	Sheffield Wed.	H	17/10/1931	42	47	65	73	75
Dixie Dean	3	Sheffield United	A	10/10/1931	40	s/h	s/h		
Dixie Dean	3	Liverpool	A	19/9/1931	1	15	21		
Tommy White	3	Portsmouth	A	2/9/1931	N/A				
Jimmy Dunn	3	Birmingham City	H	29/8/1931	N/A				
Dixie Dean	3	Charlton Athletic	A	7/2/1931	22	44	87		
Dixie Dean	4	Plymouth Argyle	H	27/12/1930	32	63	68	87	
Jimmy Stein	4	Plymouth Argyle	H	27/12/1930	1	5	69	71	
Dixie Dean	4	Oldham Athletic	H	6/12/1930	6	40	54	72	
Dixie Dean	3	Stoke City	H	22/11/1930	8	31	67		
Tommy White	3	Sunderland	H	3/5/1930	31	65	s/h		
Dixie Dean	3	Portsmouth	A	28/9/1929	21	44	63		
Dixie Dean	3	Derby County	H	1/1/1929	f/h	41	44		
Dixie Dean	3	Bolton Wanderers	A	29/12/1928	13	60	79		
Dixie Dean	3	Newcastle United	H	22/12/1928	10	55	82		
Dixie Dean	3	Portsmouth	H	1/9/1928	30	62	68		
Dixie Dean	3	Bolton Wanderers	H	25/8/1928	13	60	75		
Dixie Dean	3	Arsenal	H	5/5/1928	3	4	82		
Dixie Dean	4	Burnley	A	28/4/1928	1	23	28	62	
Dixie Dean	3	Liverpool	A	25/2/1928	17	40	53		

HAT-TRICK HEROES

Player	Goals	Opponents	Venue	Date	Goal Times				
Dixie Dean	3	Aston Villa	A	10/12/1927	16	19	83		
Dixie Dean	3	Leicester City	H	5/11/1927	24	65	80		
Dixie Dean	3	Portsmouth	A	29/10/1927	41	81	86		
Dixie Dean	5	Manchester Utd	H	8/10/1927	1	8	30	40	65
Dixie Dean	4	Sunderland	H	25/12/1926	N/A				
Dixie Dean	3	Newcastle United	H	24/4/1926	14	63	s/h		
Dixie Dean	3	Newcastle United	A	12/12/1925	9	63	70		
Dixie Dean	3	Leeds United	H	24/10/1925	3	s/h	55		
Dixie Dean	3	Burnley	A	17/10/1925	48	75	80		
Wilf Chadwick	3	Tottenham H.	H	19/4/1924	20	33	s/h		
Wilf Chadwick	4	Manchester City	H	22/12/1923	17	31	46	s/h	
Jack Cock	3	Middlesbrough	H	28/2/1923	18	19	41		
Wilf Chadwick	3	Middlesbrough	A	17/2/1923	N/A				
Bobby Irvine	3	Huddersfield Town	H	14/4/1922	N/A				
Sam Chedgzoy	3	Huddersfield Town	H	14/4/1922	N/A				
Bobby Irvine	3	Aston Villa	H	21/1/1922	62	65	67		
Stanley Davies	3	Manchester Utd	H	27/8/1921	17	35	74		
S. Fazackerley	3	Chelsea	H	6/4/1921	10	f/h	s/h		
Joe Peacock	3	Derby County	H	11/9/1920	N/A				
Joe Clennell	3	Bradford City	H	8/11/1919	10	20	80		
Bobby Parker	3	Bolton Wanderers	H	22/3/1915	3	50	80		
Bobby Parker	3	Aston Villa	A	10/2/1915	23	34	80		
Bobby Parker	3	Manchester City	H	12/12/1914	19	s/h	s/h		
Bobby Parker	4	Sheffield Wed.	A	28/11/1914	N/A				
Bobby Parker	3	Sunderland	H	21/11/1914	17	32	73		
Bobby Parker	3	Liverpool	A	3/10/1914	10	17	88		
Joe Clennell	3	Tottenham H.	A	2/9/1914	57	60	80		
Bobby Parker	3	Manchester Utd	H	26/12/1913	35	s/h	s/h		
William Lacey	3	Notts County	H	21/1/1911	f/h	s/h	s/h		
Alex Young	3	Blackburn Rovers	H	19/11/1910	47	54	71		
Bertie Freeman	3	Bolton Wanderers	H	30/10/1909	44	65	67		
Bertie Freeman	3	Sheffield Wed.	A	20/9/1909	25	28	s/h		
Bertie Freeman	3	Chelsea	H	20/3/1909	N/A				
Bertie Freeman	3	Sheffield United	H	20/2/1909	15	s/h	s/h		
Bertie Freeman	3	Sunderland	H	7/11/1908	44	s/h	87		
Bertie Freeman	3	Sheffield United	A	17/10/1908	11	41	88		
Alex Young	3	Manchester City	H	26/9/1908	10	20	25		
Hugh Bolton	3	Middlesbrough	H	29/12/1906	50	s/h	s/h		
Alex Young	4	Manchester City	H	3/9/1906	30	s/h	s/h	90	
Jack Sharp	3	Sheffield United	H	10/2/1906	40	s/h	s/h		
Frank Oliver	3	Notts County	H	14/10/1905	18	s/h	s/h		
Alex Young	4	Nottingham Forest	H	5/11/1904	f/h	f/h	s/h	s/h	
Alex Young	4	Liverpool	H	1/4/1904	f/h	40	42	52	
John Brearley	3	Middlesbrough	H	3/1/1903	51	54	85		
Jack Taylor	3	Wolverhampton W.	H	7/9/1901	s/h	75	86		
Jimmy Settle	3	Wolverhampton W.	H	7/9/1901	11	22	40		
Andrew Hartley	3	Wolverhampton W.	H	18/9/1897	30	s/h	s/h		
John Bell	3	West Brom	H	17/4/1897	1	5	s/h		
Jack Taylor	3	West Brom	A	16/1/1897	55	56	s/h		

HAT-TRICK HEROES

EVERTON LEAGUE HAT-TRICKS

Player	Goals	Opponents	Venue	Date	Goal Times			
John Cameron	3	Burnley	H	28/11/1896	5	29	s/h	
Thomas McInnes	3	Stoke City	H	14/12/1895	50	s/h	88	
Alfred Milward	3	Birmingham City	A	07/12/ 1895	35	s/h	s/h	
Edgar Chadwick	3	Sheffield United	H	5/10/1895	f/h	s/h	s/h	
John Bell	3	Aston Villa	A	30/9/1895	f/h	s/h	s/h	
Alex Latta	3	Birmingham City	A	3/11/1894	1	23	s/h	
Jack Southworth	3	Nottingham Forest	H	15/9/1894	5	9	f/h	
Jack Southworth	3	Birmingham City	H	3/9/1894	N/A			
Jack Southworth	6	West Brom	H	30/12/1893	N/A			
Jack Southworth	4	Sheffield Wed.	H	23/12/1893	5	f/h	f/h	s/h
Edgar Chadwick	3	Sunderland	H	30/09/1893	f/h	s/h	s/h	
Alex Latta	3	Derby County	A	5/11/1892	44	s/h	s/h	
Fred Geary	3	Derby County	A	5/11/1892	8	f/h	s/h	
Alex Latta	4	Manchester Utd	A	19/10/1892	N/A			
Alex Latta	3	Notts County	H	6/4/1892	N/A			
Alex Latta	3	West Brom	H	7/11/1891	N/A			
Edgar Chadwick	3	Burnley	H	27/12/1890	N/A			
Thomas Wylie	4	Derby County	H	13/12/1890	16	41	71	89
Alex Latta	3	Notts County	H	7/12/1889	N/A			
Fred Geary	3	Stoke City	H	2/11/1889	N/A			
Alex McKinnon	3	Derby County	H	27/10/1888	N/A			

Steve Watson is mobbed after scoring one of his three goals against Leeds United in September 2003 – the last player to achieve the feat

HAT-TRICK HEROES

EVERTON FA CUP HAT-TRICKS

Player	Goals	Opponents	Venue	Date	Goal Times
Graeme Sharp	3	Sheffield Wed.	A	27/1/1988	6 39 43
Tommy Lawton	4	Doncaster Rovers	H	21/1/1939	44 49 75 87
Jackie Coulter	3	Sunderland	H	30/1/1935	14 30 92
Albert Geldard	3	Grimsby Town	H	12/1/1935	29 31 66
Dixie Dean	4	Southport	H	28/2/1931	1 30 35 62
Dixie Dean	4	Crystal Palace	A	24/1/1931	30 54 67 85
Thomas Browell	3	Stockport County	H	15/1/1913	30 57 70
Thomas Browell	4	Bury	H	8/2/1912	3 51 60 83
Hugh Bolton	4	Oldham Athletic	H	5/2/1908	f/h 41 69 89
Jimmy Settle	3	Southampton	H	4/3/1905	32 s/h 89
John Bell	3	Southport	A	2/2/1895	15 18 89
Fred Geary	3	Derby County	H	18/1/1890	n/a
Alexander Brady	3	Derby County	H	18/1/1890	n/a
Alfred Milward	3	Derby County	H	18/1/1890	n/a

EVERTON LEAGUE CUP HAT-TRICKS

Player	Goals	Opponents	Venue	Date	Goal Times
Paul Rideout	3	Lincoln City	A	21/9/1993	25 64 85
Graeme Sharp	3	Wrexham	H	9/10/1990	9 21 89
Tony Cottee	3	Wrexham	A	25/9/1990	2 35 69
Paul Wilkinson	3	Newport County	A	7/10/1986	2 45 88
Bob Latchford	5	Wimbledon	H	29/8/1978	9 18 64 83 85
Martin Dobson	3	Wimbledon	H	29/8/1978	45 49 80
Frank Wignall	3	Tranmere Rovers	A	21/12/1960	10 55 88

EVERTON EUROPEAN HAT-TRICKS

Player	Goals	Opponents	Venue	Date	Goal Times	Competition
Andy Gray	3	Fortuna Sittard	H	6/3/1985	48 74 76	ECWC
Alan Ball	3	IBK Keflavik	H	16/9/1970	39 59 67	European Cup

EVERTON HAT-TRICKS (OTHER MATCHES)

Player	Goals	Opponents	Venue	Date	Goal Times	Competition
Tony Cottee	4	Sunderland	H	22/01/1991	27 72 75 87	ZDS Cup
Graeme Sharp	3	Newcastle United	H	3/12/1986	5 21 39	F. Members Cup
Dixie Dean	4	Newcastle United	A	12/10/1932	f/h 45 47 s/h	C.Shield

Hat-trick king – the legendary William Ralph Dean

BIGGEST-EVER VICTORIES

Date	Opponents	Venue	Competition	Score
18th Jan 1890	Derby County	Home	FA Cup	Won 11-2
3rd Sept 1906	Manchester City	Home	League	Won 9-1
27th Dec 1930	Plymouth Argyle	Home	League	Won 9-1
28th Feb 1931	Southport	Home	FA Cup	Won 9-1
2nd Nov 1889	Stoke City	Home	League	Won 8-0
21st Jan 1939	Doncaster Rovers	Home	FA Cup	Won 8-0
20th Nov 1971	Southampton	Home	League	Won 8-0
29th Aug 1978	Wimbledon	Home	League Cup	Won 8-0
28th Nov 1931	Leicester City	Home	League	Won 9-2
21st Oct 1893	Darwen	Home	League	Won 8-1
23rd Dec 1893	Sheffield Wed.	Home	League	Won 8-1
31st Oct 1931	Newcastle United	Home	League	Won 8-1
4th Jan 1890	Aston Villa	Home	League	Won 7-0
4th Oct 1890	Derby County	Home	League	Won 7-0
22nd Oct 1927	West Ham United	Home	League	Won 7-0
7th Feb 1931	Charlton Athletic	Away	League	Won 7-0
25th Dec 1936	Derby County	Home	League	Won 7-0
17th Oct 1931	Sheffield Wed.	Home	League	Won 9-3
30th Sept 1893	Sunderland	Home	League	Won 7-1
30th Dec 1893	West Bromwich A.	Home	League	Won 7-1
21st Nov 1914	Sunderland	Home	League	Won 7-1
5th Nov 1927	Leicester City	Home	League	Won 7-1
4th Oct 1930	Charlton Athletic	Home	League	Won 7-1
14th Oct 1933	Blackburn Rovers	Home	League	Won 7-1
3rd Mar 1937	Leeds United	Home	League	Won 7-1
27th Sept 1952	Doncaster Rovers	Home	League	Won 7-1
30th Nov 1968	Leicester City	Home	League	Won 7-1
16th Nov 1996	Southampton	Home	League	Won 7-1

BIGGEST-EVER DEFEATS

Date	Opponents	Venue	Competition	Score
26th Dec 1934	Sunderland	Away	League	Lost 7-0
22nd Feb 1939	Wolverhampton W.	Away	League	Lost 7-0
10th Sept 1949	Portsmouth	Away	League	Lost 7-0
11th May 2005	Arsenal	Away	League	Lost 7-0
11th Oct 1958	Tottenham H.	Away	League	Lost 10-4
7th Apr 1953	Huddersfield Town	Away	League	Lost 8-2
7th Nov 1959	Newcastle United	Away	League	Lost 8-2
26th Oct 1912	Newcastle United	Home	League	Lost 6-0
8th Nov 1913	Blackburn Rovers	Away	League	Lost 6-0
7th Jan 1922	Crystal Palace	Home	FA Cup	Lost 6-0
7th Sept 1935	Liverpool	Away	League	Lost 6-0
11th Sept 1948	Chelsea	Away	League	Lost 6-0
5th May 1951	Sheffield Wed.	Away	League	Lost 6-0
25th Dec 1956	Tottenham H.	Away	League	Lost 6-0
10th Dec 1963	Arsenal	Away	League	Lost 6-0

THE INDIVIDUAL HONOURS

Honours won (that season)

1985	Neville Southall	First Division, European Cup Winners' Cup, Charity Shield
1986	Gary Lineker	

PFA PLAYER OF THE YEAR

1985	Peter Reid	First Division, European Cup Winners' Cup, Charity Shield
1986	Gary Lineker	

MANAGER OF THE YEAR

1985	Howard Kendall	First Division, European Cup Winners' Cup, Charity Shield
1987	Howard Kendall	First Division, Charity Shield (shared)
2003	David Moyes	
2005	David Moyes	

PLAYER WITH MOST MEDALS (MAJOR COMPETITIONS ONLY)

5	Neville Southall (2 League, 2 FA Cup, 1 European Cup Winners' Cup)
4	Alan Harper (2 League, 1 FA Cup, 1 European Cup Winners' Cup)
=	Derek Mountfield (2 League, 1 FA Cup, 1 European Cup Winners' Cup)
=	Kevin Ratcliffe (2 League, 1 FA Cup, 1 European Cup Winners' Cup)
=	Peter Reid (2 League, 1 FA Cup, 1 European Cup Winners' Cup)
=	Graeme Sharp (2 League, 1 FA Cup, 1 European Cup Winners' Cup)
=	Trevor Steven (2 League, 1 FA Cup, 1 European Cup Winners' Cup)
=	Gary Stevens (2 League, 1 FA Cup, 1 European Cup Winners' Cup)

Kevin Ratcliffe - Decorated Everton player

NATIONALITIES

A total of 45 players (set to rise with the addition of Steven Pienaar, Stefan Wessels and Ayegbeni Yakubu for the 2007/08 season) from countries outside of the British Isles have represented Everton since the South African, David Murray, played three times for the club during the mid-1920s. There was a substantial gap for the next overseas player – Stefan Rehn of Sweden in 1989 – but since the early 1990s there has been a great rise in players from countries outside of the British Isles.

Scandinavia has been a particularly fertile area for recruits with nine players from Sweden and Denmark. The list below gives all the details, with each player listed alongside the country they are aligned to for international football, with their country of birth shown if different. Those players who have appeared for one of the home countries or the Republic of Ireland, but were born overseas, have been excluded.

COUNTRIES REPRESENTED	PLAYERS
Australia	Jason Kearton, Tim Cahill
Brazil	Juliano Rodrigo, Anderson Silva de Franca
Canada	Tomasz Radzinski (born in Poland)
China	Li Tie, Li Weifeng
Croatia	Slaven Bilic (born in Yugoslavia)
Denmark	Claus Thomsen, Thomas Gravesen, Peter Degn, Per Kroldrup
France	Mickael Madar, Olivier Dacourt, David Ginola
Ghana	Alex Nyarko
Holland	Ray Atteveld, Andy Van der Meyde, Sander Westerveld
Israel	Idan Tal
Italy	Marco Materazzi, Alessandro Pistone, Matteo Ferrari
Ivory Cost	Ibrahima Bakayoko
Nigeria	Daniel Amokachi, Joseph Yobo, Victor Anichebe
Norway	Thomas Myhre, Espen Baardsen (born in the USA)
Poland	Robert Warzycha
Portugal	Abel Xavier (born in Mozambique), Nuno Valente, Manuel Fernandes
Russia	Andrei Kanchelskis (born in Ukraine)
South Africa	David Murray
Spain	Mikel Arteta
Sweden	Stefan Rehn, Anders Limpar, Niclas Alexandersson, Tobias Linderoth (born in France), Jesper Blomqvist
Switzerland	Marc Hottiger
USA	Predrag Radosavijevic (born in Yugoslavia), Joe-Max Moore, Brian McBride, Tim Howard

Home nation-capped Everton players (August 1, 2007)

England

39	Alan Ball
33	Ray Wilson
26	Brian Labone, Gary Stevens
25	Trevor Steven
17	Wayne Rooney
16	Dixie Dean
13	Peter Reid
12	Bob Latchford
11	Gary Lineker, Tommy Wright
9	Cliff Britton, Johnny Holt, Martin Keown
8	Sam Chedgzoy, Tommy Lawton, Keith Newton
7	Edgar Chadwick
6	Dave Watson
5	Nick Barmby, **ANDY JOHNSON**, Joe Mercer
4	Tony Cottee, Albert Geldard, Harry Hardman, Andy Hinchcliffe, Harry Makepeace, Alf Milward, **PHIL NEVILLE** Ted Sagar
3	Paul Bracewell, Charlie Gee, Tommy Johnson, Fred Pickering, Jimmy Settle, Gordon West
2	Tom Booth, Wally Boyes, Bert Freeman, Fred Geary, George Harrison, Frank Jefferis, Joe Royle, Jack Sharp,
1	Walter Abbott, Benjamin Baker, Michael Ball, William Balmer, Warney Cresswell, Jimmy Cunliffe, Martin Dobson, Dicky Downs, Colin Harvey, Bob Howarth, Tony Kay, Derek Temple, David Unsworth, Tommy White, Sam Wolstenholme

Trevor Steven (top), capped 25 times for England while at Everton and current international Phil Neville (below)

171

Home nation-capped Everton players (August 1, 2007)
Scotland

43	David Weir
32	Gary Naysmith
27	**JAMES McFADDEN**
13	Scot Gemmill
12	Graeme Sharp
11	Stuart McCall
10	Don Hutchison
8	Asa Hartford, Pat Nevin
6	Bobby Collins, John Collins, Bruce Rioch
5	Torry Gillick, Alex Scott
3	Jack Bell, Duncan Ferguson, Ian Wilson, George Wood
2	Jimmy Gabriel, Neil McBain, Alex Young, Alex 'Sandy' Young
1	George Brewster, John Connolly, Jimmy Dunn, Andy Gray, Alex Parker, Jack Robertson, Jock Thomson, Alec Troup, George Wilson

David Weir and James McFadden line up for Scotland (top), while (below) Neville Southall in action during one of his 92 games for Wales while at Everton, a club record

Wales

92	Neville Southall
58	Kevin Ratcliffe
23	Barry Horne
17	T.G. Jones
16	Dai Davies, Mark Pembridge
13	Pat Van den Hauwe, Roy Vernon
12	Simon Davies
9	Gary Speed
8	Tom Griffiths
6	Charlie Parry, Ben Williams
4	Dave Smallman
3	Smart Arridge, Stanley Davies, John Oster
2	Joe Davies, Ll. Davies, Ted Hughes, Aubrey Powell, Leigh Roose
1	Phil Griffiths, Jack Humphreys, Rob Jones, Mickey Thomas

Home nation-capped Everton players (August 1, 2007)
Northern Ireland

16	Billy Scott
14	Val Harris,
	Alex Stevenson
12	Billy Bingham,
	Dave Clements,
	Billy Cook
11	Bryan Hamilton,
	Bobby Irvine
10	Bill Lacey
7	Peter Farrell
6	Tommy Eglington,
	Tommy Jackson
5	Jackie Coulter,
	Jimmy Sheridan
3	Jimmy Hill,
	John Houston
2	A. McCartney,
	Peter Scott,
	Norman Whiteside

Norman Whiteside, the last full Northern Ireland international at Everton (top), and current Republic of Ireland midfielder Lee Carsley in action (below)

Republic of Ireland

42	Kevin Sheedy
26	Peter Farrell
24	Kevin Kilbane
22	Tommy Eglington
17	Jimmy O'Neill
15	**LEE CARSLEY**
6	Alex Stevenson
5	Don Donovan,
	Richard Dunne
4	Peter Corr,
	Jim McDonagh,
	Mick Meagan,
	Gerry Peyton,
	Mike Walsh (1981-83)
3	Tommy Clinton,
	Terry Phelan
2	Gareth Farrelly
1	James Kendrick,
	Eamonn O'Keefe,
	Mick Walsh (1978-79)

Everton's most capped overseas player is Thomas Gravesen, with 44 matches for Denmark.

ARSENAL
FIXTURE 03/05/08

FINAL STANDINGS 06/07

		W	D	L	PTS
3	Liverpool	20	8	10	68
4	**Arsenal**	**19**	**11**	**8**	**68**
5	Tottenham	17	9	12	60

LEAGUE RECORD

	PL	W	D	L
Home:	86	38	23	25
Away:	86	16	13	57
Overall:	172	54	36	82

LAST 2 LEAGUE MEETINGS

18/03/2007

Everton	1-0	Arsenal
Johnson 90		

28/10/2006

Arsenal	1-1	Everton
Van Persie 71		Cahill 11

CLUB DETAILS

Nickname:	The Gunners
Ground:	Emirates Stadium, capacity 60,432 (away allocation 3,000)
Manager:	Arsene Wenger (app. 30/09/96)
Assistant:	Pat Rice
Year formed:	1886

USEFUL INFORMATION

Website:	www.arsenal.com
Address:	Emirates Stadium, Highbury House, 75 Drayton Park N5 1BU
Switchboard:	0207 704 4000

TRAVEL INFORMATION

By Tube: The nearest station is Arsenal (Piccadilly Line), around three minutes walk from the ground. Finsbury Park and Highbury & Islington are also within a 10-minute walking distance.

By Bus: Main bus stops are located on Holloway Road, Nag's Head, Seven Sisters Road, Blackstock Road and Highbury Corner. Regular services will take you to within 10 minutes walk of the ground.

ASTON VILLA
FIXTURE 22/09/07

FINAL STANDINGS 06/07

		W	D	L	PTS
10	Blackburn	15	7	16	52
11	**Aston Villa**	**11**	**17**	**10**	**50**
12	Middlesbro	12	10	16	46

LEAGUE RECORD

	PL	W	D	L
Home:	92	45	23	24
Away:	92	25	22	45
Overall:	184	70	45	69

LAST 2 LEAGUE MEETINGS

02/04/2007

Aston Villa	1-1	Everton
Agbonlahor 83		Lescott 15

11/11/2006

Everton	0-1	Aston Villa
		Sutton 42

CLUB DETAILS

Nickname:	The Villans
Ground:	Villa Park, capacity 42,573 (away allocation 3,000)
Manager:	Martin O'Neill (app. 05/08/06)
Coaches:	Steve Walford, John Robertson
Year formed:	1874

USEFUL INFORMATION

Website:	www.avfc.co.uk
Address:	Villa Park, Trinity Road, Birmingham B6 6HE
Switchboard:	0871 423 8100

TRAVEL INFORMATION

By Train: Witton station is a 5-minute walk from the ground, while Aston is 15 minutes away. From New Street Station, a taxi should take 15 minutes.

By Bus: The number 7 West Midlands Travel Bus runs from Birmingham City Centre directly to the ground (Witton). To check services check at: www.travelwm.co.uk .

BIRMINGHAM CITY
FIXTURE 12/04/08

FINAL C'SHIP STANDINGS 06/07

		W	D	L	PTS
1	Sunderland	27	7	12	88
2	**Birmingham**	**26**	**8**	**12**	**86**
3	Derby	25	9	12	84

LEAGUE RECORD

	PL	W	D	L
Home:	56	35	15	6
Away:	56	22	16	18
Overall:	112	57	31	24

LAST 2 LEAGUE MEETINGS

22/04/2006

Everton	0-0	Birmingham

29/10/2005

Birmingham	0-1	Everton
		Davies 43

CLUB DETAILS

Nickname: Blues
Ground: St. Andrew's, capacity 30,009 (away allocation 2,500-4,500)
Manager: Steve Bruce (app. 12/12/01)
First-team coach: Eric Black
Year formed: 1875

USEFUL INFORMATION

Website: www.bcfc.co.uk
Address: St. Andrew's Stadium, Birmingham B9 4NH
Switchboard: 0844 557 1875

TRAVEL INFORMATION

By Train: The nearest local railway station is Bordesley, which is a 10-minute walk. Mainline station Birmingham New Street will cost around £6 in a taxi.
By Bus: Numerous routes serve the ground from the city centre, including numbers 96, 97, 58 and 60 - details can be found at www.networkwestmidlands. com .

BLACKBURN ROVERS
FIXTURE 02/02/08

FINAL STANDINGS 06/07

		W	D	L	PTS
9	Portsmouth	14	12	12	54
10	**Blackburn**	**15**	**7**	**16**	**52**
11	Aston Villa	11	17	10	50

LEAGUE RECORD

	PL	W	D	L
Home:	69	38	14	17
Away:	69	17	15	37
Overall:	138	55	29	54

LAST 2 LEAGUE MEETINGS

10/02/2007

Everton	1-0	Blackburn Rovers
Johnson 10		

23/08/2006

Blackburn Rovers 1-1	Everton
McCarthy 50	Cahill 84

CLUB DETAILS

Nickname: Rovers
Ground: Ewood Park, capacity 31,367 (away allocation 4,000)
Manager: Mark Hughes (app. 15/09/04)
Assistant: Mark Bowen
Year formed: 1875

USEFUL INFORMATION

Website: www.rovers.co.uk
Address: Ewood Park, Bolton Road, Blackburn, Lancashire BB2 4JF
Switchboard: 08701 113232

TRAVEL INFORMATION

By Train: Blackburn station is a mile and a half away, while Mill Hill is 1 mile from the stadium. Direct trains run from Manchester Victoria, Salford Crescent and Preston.
By Bus: The central bus station is next to the railway station. Services 3, 3A, 3B, 46, and 346 all go from Blackburn to Darwen. Ewood Park is a mile and a half along the journey.

BOLTON WANDERERS
FIXTURE 01/09/07

FINAL STANDINGS 06/07

		W	D	L	PTS
6	Everton	15	13	10	58
7	**Bolton**	**16**	**8**	**14**	**56**
8	Reading	16	7	15	55

LEAGUE RECORD

	PL	W	D	L
Home:	64	38	17	9
Away:	64	26	13	25
Overall:	128	64	30	34

LAST 2 LEAGUE MEETINGS

09/04/2007

Bolton Wanderers	1-1	Everton
Davies 18		Vaughan 33

18/11/2006

Everton	1-0	Bolton Wanderers
Arteta 60		

CLUB DETAILS

Nickname: The Trotters
Ground: Reebok Stadium, capacity 28,000 (away allocation 3-5,000)
Manager: Sammy Lee (app. 30/04/07)
Coach: Ricky Sbragia
Year formed: 1874

USEFUL INFORMATION

Website: www.bwfc.co.uk
Address: Reebok Stadium, Burnden Way, Lostock, Bolton BL6 6JW
Switchboard: 01204 673673

TRAVEL INFORMATION

By Train: Horwich Parkway station is 100 yards from the stadium, which is on the Manchester Airport to Preston and Blackpool North/Blackpool North and Preston to Manchester Airport line.
By Bus: The club operate regular buses to and from Bolton town centre.

CHELSEA
FIXTURE 10/11/07

FINAL STANDINGS 06/07

		W	D	L	PTS
1	Man Utd	28	5	5	89
2	**Chelsea**	**24**	**11**	**3**	**83**
3	Liverpool	20	8	10	68

LEAGUE RECORD

	PL	W	D	L
Home:	68	33	21	14
Away:	68	12	21	35
Overall:	136	45	42	49

LAST 2 LEAGUE MEETINGS

13/05/2007

Chelsea	1-1	Everton
Drogba 57		Vaughan 50

17/12/2006

Everton	2-3	Chelsea
Arteta (pen) 38, Yobo 64		Howard (o.g.) 49, Lampard 81, Drogba 87

CLUB DETAILS

Nickname: The Blues
Ground: Stamford Bridge, capacity 42,360 (away allocation 3,000)
Manager: Avram Grant (app. 20/09/07)
Assistant: Steve Clarke
Year formed: 1905

USEFUL INFORMATION

Website: www.chelseafc.com
Address: Stamford Bridge, Fulham Road, London SW6 1HS
Switchboard: 0870 300 2322

TRAVEL INFORMATION

By Tube: Fulham Broadway is on the District Line, around 5 minutes walk. Take a train to Earl's Court and change for Wimbledon-bound trains. West Brompton is a new railway station accessible from Clapham Junction.
By Bus: Numbers 14, 211 and 414 go along Fulham Road from central London via West Brompton train station.

DERBY COUNTY
FIXTURE 27/10/07

FINAL C'SHIP STANDINGS 06/07

		W	D	L	PTS
2	Birmingham 26	8	12	86
3	**Derby**	**25**	**9**	**12**	**84**
4	West Brom	22	10	14	76

LEAGUE RECORD

	PL	W	D	L
Home:	62	38	12	12
Away:	62	23	9	30
Overall:	124	61	21	42

LAST 2 LEAGUE MEETINGS

23/03/2002

Derby County	3-4	Everton
Strupar 57, 81,		Unsworth 38, Stubbs 52,
Morris 76		Alexandersson 54,
		Ferguson 71

15/12/2001

Everton	1-0	Derby County
Moore 76		

CLUB DETAILS

Nickname: The Rams
Ground: Pride Park, capacity 33,600 (away allocation 3,000)
Manager: Billy Davies (app. 02/06/06)
Assistant: David Kelly
Year formed: 1884

USEFUL INFORMATION

Website: www.dcfc.co.uk
Address: Pride Park, Derby DE24 8XL
Switchboard: 0870 444 1884

TRAVEL INFORMATION

By Train: Derby Midland station is a 15-minute walk from Pride Park. When leaving the station use the footbridge directly into Pride Park.
By Bus: A regular shuttle service operates from the city centre.

FULHAM
FIXTURE 15/03/08

FINAL STANDINGS 06/07

		W	D	L	PTS
15	West Ham	12	5	21	41
16	**Fulham**	**8**	**15**	**15**	**39**
17	Wigan	10	8	20	38

LEAGUE RECORD

	PL	W	D	L
Home:	19	15	4	0
Away:	19	3	4	12
Overall:	38	18	8	12

LAST 2 LEAGUE MEETINGS

06/04/2007

Everton	4-1	Fulham
Carsley 25, Stubbs 34		Bocanegra 22
Vaughan 45,		
Anichebe 80		

04/11/2006

Fulham	1-0	Everton
Jensen 66		

CLUB DETAILS

Nickname: Cottagers
Ground: Craven Cottage, capacity 22,000 (away allocation 3,000)
Manager: Lawrie Sanchez (app. 11/04/07)
Assistant: Les Reed
Year formed: 1879

USEFUL INFORMATION

Website: www.fulhamfc.com
Address: Craven Cottage, Stevenage Road, Fulham, London SW6 6HH
Switchboard: 0870 442 1222

TRAVEL INFORMATION

By Tube: Alight at Putney Bridge (District line) from Central London. Turn left out of station and right down Ranleigh Gardens. At the end of the road (before the Eight Bells pub) turn left into Willow Bank and right through the underpass into Bishops Park. Walk along river to ground (note park is closed after evening games).
By Bus: The numbers 74 and 220 both run along Fulham Palace Road.

LIVERPOOL
FIXTURE 29/03/08

FINAL STANDINGS 06/07

		W	D	L	PTS
2	Chelsea	24	11	3	83
3	**Liverpool**	**20**	**8**	**10**	**68**
4	Arsenal	19	11	8	68

LEAGUE RECORD

	PL	W	D	L
Home:	88	33	27	28
Away:	88	23	28	37
Overall:	176	56	55	65

LAST 2 LEAGUE MEETINGS

03/02/2007

Liverpool	0-0	Everton

09/09/2006

Everton	3-0	Liverpool

Cahill 24,
Johnson 36, 90

CLUB DETAILS

Nickname: Reds/Pool
Ground: Anfield, capacity 45,522
(away allocation 2,000)
Manager: Rafael Benitez (app. 16/06/04)
Assistant: Pako Ayesteran
Year formed: 1892

USEFUL INFORMATION

Website: www.liverpoolfc.tv
Address: Anfield Road, Liverpool
L4 0TH
Switchboard: 0151 263 2361

TRAVEL INFORMATION

By Train: The nearest Merseyrail station is Kirkdale, which is accessible from Liverpool Central (take any train heading for Ormskirk or Kirkby) - from there it is a 20-25 minute walk. Alternatively, take a taxi or bus from Liverpool Lime Street Station (2 miles away).
By Bus: Numbers 26 or 27 from Paradise Street Interchange, or a 17 or 217 from Queen Square bus station run directly to the ground.

MANCHESTER CITY
FIXTURE 23/02/08

FINAL STANDINGS 06/07

		W	D	L	PTS
13	Newcastle	11	10	17	43
14	**Man City**	**11**	**9**	**18**	**42**
15	West Ham	12	5	21	41

LEAGUE RECORD

	PL	W	D	L
Home:	74	37	22	15
Away:	74	15	17	42
Overall:	148	52	39	57

LAST 2 LEAGUE MEETINGS

01/01/2007

Manchester City	2-1	Everton

Samaras 50, 72 (p)   Osman 84

30/09/2006

Everton	1-1	Manchester City

Johnson 44   Richards 90

CLUB DETAILS

Nickname: Blues/The Citizens
Ground: City of Manchester Stadium, capacity 48,000
(away allocation 4,800)
Manager: Sven-Goran Eriksson
(app. 06/07/07)
Assistant: Hans Backe
Year formed: 1887

USEFUL INFORMATION

Website: www.mcfc.co.uk
Address: City of Manchester Stadium, SportCity, Rowsley Street, Manchester M11 3FF
Switchboard: 0870 062 1894

TRAVEL INFORMATION

By Train: The nearest station is Ashburys (a 10-minute walk), which is a five-minute train ride from Manchester Piccadilly (which itself is a 20-25 minute walk).
By Bus: Numbers 216 and 217 are the main services from the city centre, but 53, 54, 185, 186, 230, 231, 232, 233, 234, 235, 236, 237, X36 and X37 also run to SportCity.

MANCHESTER UNITED
FIXTURE 22/12/07

FINAL STANDINGS 06/07

		W	D	L	PTS
1	**Man Utd**	**28**	**5**	**5**	**89**
2	Chelsea	24	11	3	83
3	Liverpool	20	8	10	68

LEAGUE RECORD

	PL	W	D	L
Home:	78	37	17	24
Away:	78	15	20	43
Overall:	156	52	37	67

LAST 2 LEAGUE MEETINGS

28/04/2007

Everton	2-4	Manchester Utd
Stubbs 12,		O'Shea 61,
Fernandes 50		Neville 68 (og),
		Rooney 79, Eagles 90

29/11/2006

Manchester Utd	3-0	Everton
Ronaldo 39, Evra 63,		
O'Shea 89		

CLUB DETAILS

Nickname:	Red Devils
Ground:	Old Trafford, capacity 76,312 (away allocation 3,000)
Manager:	Sir Alex Ferguson (app. 06/11/86)
Assistant:	Carlos Queiroz
Year formed:	1878

USEFUL INFORMATION

Website:	www.manutd.com
Address:	Sir Matt Busby Way, Old Trafford, Manchester M16 0RA
Switchboard:	0870 442 1994

TRAVEL INFORMATION

By Train: Special services run from Manchester Piccadilly to the clubs own railway station. There is also a Metrolink service, with the station located next to Lancashire County Cricket Club on Warwick Road, which leads up to Sir Matt Busby Way.

By Bus: Numbers 114, 230, 252 and 253 all run from the city centre to the ground.

MIDDLESBROUGH
FIXTURE 06/10/07

FINAL STANDINGS 06/07

		W	D	L	PTS
11	Aston Villa	11	17	10	50
12	**Middlesbro**	**12**	**10**	**16**	**46**
13	Newcastle	11	10	17	43

LEAGUE RECORD

	PL	W	D	L
Home:	54	37	12	5
Away:	54	14	15	25
Overall:	108	51	27	30

LAST 2 LEAGUE MEETINGS

26/12/2006

Everton	0-0	Middlesbrough

14/10/2006

Middlesbrough	2-1	Everton
Yakubu 27 (p),		Cahill 77
Viduka 71		

CLUB DETAILS

Nickname:	Boro
Ground:	Riverside Stadium, capacity 35,100 (away allocation 4,000)
Manager:	Gareth Southgate (app. 07/06/06)
Coach:	Colin Cooper
Year formed:	1876

USEFUL INFORMATION

Website:	www.mfc.co.uk
Address:	Riverside Stadium, Middlesbrough, Cleveland TS3 6RS
Switchboard:	0844 499 6789

TRAVEL INFORMATION

By Train: Middlesbrough station is about 15 minutes walk from the stadium, served by trains from Darlington. Take the back exit from the station, turn right then after a couple of minutes right again into Wynward Way for the ground.

By Bus: Numbers 36, 37 and 38 go from the town centre close to the ground.

NEWCASTLE UNITED
FIXTURE 01/01/08

FINAL STANDINGS 06/07

		W	D	L	PTS
12	Middlesbro	12	10	16	46
13	**Newcastle**	**11**	**10**	**17**	**43**
14	Man City	11	9	18	42

LEAGUE RECORD

	PL	W	D	L
Home:	73	40	14	19
Away:	73	16	17	40
Overall:	146	56	31	59

LAST 2 LEAGUE MEETINGS

30/12/2006
Everton 3-0 Newcastle
Anichebe 9, 58,
Neville 62

24/09/2006
Newcastle 1-1 Everton
Ameobi 14 Cahill 41

CLUB DETAILS

Nickname: Magpies
Ground: St James' Park, capacity 52,387 (away allocation 3,000)
Manager: Sam Allardyce (app. 15/05/07)
Coaches: Steve Round, Terry McDermott Nigel Pearson
Year formed: 1881

USEFUL INFORMATION

Website: www.nufc.co.uk
Address: St. James' Park, Newcastle-upon-Tyne NE1 4ST
Switchboard: 0191 201 8400

TRAVEL INFORMATION

By Train: St James' Park is a 10-minute walk from Newcastle Central Station. The stadium is also served by its own Metro station (St James' Metro).
By Bus: Any bus from the town centre heading towards Gallowgate takes you past the stadium.

PORTSMOUTH
FIXTURE 01/12/07

FINAL STANDINGS 06/07

		W	D	L	PTS
8	Reading	16	7	15	55
9	**Portsmouth**	**14**	**12**	**12**	**54**
10	Blackburn	15	7	16	52

LEAGUE RECORD

	PL	W	D	L
Home:	26	13	5	8
Away:	26	9	3	14
Overall:	52	22	8	22

LAST 2 LEAGUE MEETINGS

05/05/2007
Everton 3-0 Portsmouth
Arteta (p) 59,
Yobo 62, Naysmith 90

09/12/2006
Portsmouth 2-0 Everton
Taylor 14, Kanu 26

CLUB DETAILS

Nickname: Pompey
Ground: Fratton Park, capacity 20,200 (away allocation 2,000)
Manager: Harry Redknapp (app. 07/12/05)
Assistant: Tony Adams
Year formed: 1898

USEFUL INFORMATION

Website: www.pompeyfc.co.uk
Address: Fratton Park, Frogmore Road, Portsmouth, Hants PO4 8RA
Switchboard: 0239 273 1204

TRAVEL INFORMATION

By Train: Fratton Bridge Station is a 10-minute walk from the ground - on arrival by train you pass the ground on your left. Portsmouth mainline station is at least a 25-minute walk.
By Bus: 13, 17 and 18 all run to the ground, while other services that stop close to Fratton Park are the 3, 16, 16A, 24, 27 (all Fratton Bridge); 4, 4A, 6 (all Milton Road).

READING

FIXTURE 18/08/07

FINAL STANDINGS 06/07

		W	D	L	PTS
7	Bolton	16	8	14	56
8	**Reading**	**16**	**7**	**15**	**55**
9	Portsmouth	14	12	12	54

LEAGUE RECORD

	PL	W	D	L
Home:	2	1	1	0
Away:	2	2	0	0
Overall:	4	3	1	0

LAST 2 LEAGUE MEETINGS

14/01/2007

Everton	1-1	Reading
Johnson 81		Lescott (o.g.) 28

23/12/2006

Reading	0-2	Everton
Johnson 14,		
McFadden 47		

CLUB DETAILS

Nickname:	The Royals
Ground:	Madejski Stadium, capacity 24,161 (away allocation 2,327)
Manager:	Steve Coppell (app. 09/10/03)
Coaches:	Kevin Dillon, Wally Downes
Year formed:	1871

USEFUL INFORMATION

Website:	www.readingfc.co.uk
Address:	Madejski Stadium, Junction 11, M4, Reading, Berkshire RG2 0FL
Switchboard:	0118 968 1100

TRAVEL INFORMATION

By Train: Reading Central is 3 miles away - but could take over an hour on foot. From the station a Fastrack Park & Ride is available - outside the main entrance turn right and they are 200 yards down the road.
By Bus: The shuttle bus services (Number 79) are provided between the stadium and the station, running from 1pm on a Saturday (for 3pm kick-offs).

SUNDERLAND

FIXTURE 08/03/08

FINAL C'SHIP STANDINGS 06/07

		W	D	L	PTS
1	**Sunderland**	**27**	**7**	**12**	**88**
2	Watford	26	8	12	86
3	Preston	25	9	12	84

LEAGUE RECORD

	PL	W	D	L
Home:	72	44	11	17
Away:	72	17	11	44
Overall:	144	61	22	61

LAST 2 LEAGUE MEETINGS

01/04/2006

Everton	2-2	Sunderland
Osman 5,		Stead 16, Delap 80
McFadden 26		

31/12/2005

Sunderland	0-1	Everton
		Cahill 90

CLUB DETAILS

Nickname:	The Black Cats
Ground:	Stadium of Light, capacity 49,000 (away allocation 3,600)
Manager:	Roy Keane (app. 30/08/06)
Head coach:	Tony Loughlin
Year formed:	1879

USEFUL INFORMATION

Website:	www.safc.com
Address:	The Sunderland Stadium of Light, Sunderland SR5 1SU
Switchboard:	0191 551 5000

TRAVEL INFORMATION

By Train: Sunderland mainline station is a 10-15 minute walk. The Metro service also runs from here, with St. Peter's or the Stadium of Light stations nearest the stadium.
By Bus: Numbers 2, 3, 4, 12, 13, 15 and 16 all stop within a few minutes walk of the ground. All routes connect to the central bus station, Park Lane Interchange.

TOTTENHAM HOTSPUR
FIXTURE 14/08/07

FINAL STANDINGS 06/07

		W	D	L	PTS
4	Arsenal	19	11	8	68
5	Tottenham	17	9	12	60
6	Everton	15	13	10	58

LEAGUE RECORD

	PL	W	D	L
Home:	70	30	23	17
Away:	70	14	20	36
Overall:	140	44	43	53

LAST 2 LEAGUE MEETINGS

21/02/2007

Everton	1-2	Tottenham H.
Arteta 42		Berbatov 35, Jenas 89

26/08/2006

Tottenham H.	0-2	Everton
		Davenport (o.g.) 53, Johnson 66

CLUB DETAILS

Nickname:	Spurs
Ground:	White Hart Lane, capacity 36,240 (away allocation 3,500)
Manager:	Martin Jol (app. 05/11/04)
Assistant:	Chris Hughton
Year formed:	1882

USEFUL INFORMATION

Website:	www.spurs.co.uk
Address:	Bill Nicholson Way, 748 High Road, Tottenham, London N17 0AP
Switchboard:	0208 365 5000

TRAVEL INFORMATION

By Tube: The nearest tube station is Seven Sisters (Victoria - a 25-minute walk), with trains running to Liverpool Street. The nearest mainline station is White Hart Lane, approx 5 minutes walk, on the Liverpool Street-Enfield Town line.

By Bus: A regular service runs from Seven Sisters past the stadium entrance (numbers 259, 279, 149).

WEST HAM UNITED
FIXTURE 15/12/07

FINAL STANDINGS 06/07

		W	D	L	PTS
14	Man City	11	9	18	42
15	West Ham	12	5	21	41
16	Fulham	8	15	15	39

LEAGUE RECORD

	PL	W	D	L
Home:	52	34	8	10
Away:	52	17	13	22
Overall:	104	51	21	32

LAST 2 LEAGUE MEETINGS

21/04/2007

West Ham	1-0	Everton
Zamora 13		

03/12/2006

Everton	2-0	West Ham
Osman 51,		
Vaughan 90		

CLUB DETAILS

Nickname:	The Hammers
Ground:	Upton Park, capacity 35,647 (away allocation 2,000)
Manager:	Alan Curbishley (app. 13/12/06)
Assistant:	Mervyn Day
Year formed:	1895

USEFUL INFORMATION

Website:	www.whufc.com
Address:	Boleyn Ground, Green Street, Upton Park, London E13 9AZ
Switchboard:	0208 548 2748

TRAVEL INFORMATION

By Tube: Upton Park is the closest tube station, around 45 minutes from Central London on the District (and also Hammersmith & City) line. When you exit the station turn right, the stadium is then a two-minute walk. East Ham and Plaistow Stations, which are further away, may also be worth using to avoid congestion after the match.

By Bus: Routes 5, 15, 58, 104, 115, 147, 330 and 376 all serve The Boleyn Ground.

WIGAN ATHLETIC
FIXTURE 19/01/08

FINAL STANDINGS 06/07

		W	D	L	PTS
16	Fulham	8	15	15	39
17	**Wigan**	**10**	**8**	**20**	**38**
18	Sheff Utd	10	8	20	38

LEAGUE RECORD

	PL	W	D	L
Home:	2	0	1	1
Away:	2	1	1	0
Overall:	4	1	2	1

LAST 2 LEAGUE MEETINGS

21/01/2007

Wigan	0-2	Everton
		Arteta 65 (p), 90

16/09/2006

Everton	2-2	Wigan
Johnson 49,		Scharner 62, 68
Beattie 60 (p)		

CLUB DETAILS

Nickname: The Latics
Ground: JJB Stadium, capacity 25,023 (away allocation 5,000+)
Manager: Chris Hutchings (app. 14/05/07)
Assistant: Frank Barlow
Year formed: 1932

USEFUL INFORMATION

Website: www.wiganlatics.co.uk
Address: JJB Stadium, Robin Park, Newtown, Wigan WN5 0UZ
Switchboard: 01942 774000

TRAVEL INFORMATION

By Train: Wigan Wallgate and Wigan North Western are a 15-minute walk from the stadium. From either station head under the railway bridge and keep to the right - following the road (A49) for 10 minutes. The complex should soon be visible.
By Bus: No particular route, as the venue is within easy distance of the station.

Mikel Arteta celebrates one of his goals at Wigan – he will be looking for a repeat in January

TICKETS

Address	Ticket Office, Goodison Park, Goodison Road, Liverpool L4 4EL

Telephone Numbers   Ticket Office   0870 442 1878

Email   boxoffice@evertonfc.com

Ticket Office Hours

Monday-Friday 8am-6pm
Saturday (non-matchdays) 10am to 4pm
Sunday closed
Matchdays (Saturday) 9am to kick-off and after the game
Matchdays (Sunday) 9am to kick-off and after the game
Matchdays (midweek) 8am to kick-off and after the game

Prices

Top Balcony	£31
Under 16	£17
Main Stand	£33
Under 16	£19
OAPs (over 65)	£23
Upper Gwladys	£31
Under 16	£17
Lower Gwladys	£28
Under 16	£17
OAPs (over 65)	£21
Upper Bullens	£33
Under 16	£19
Lower Bullens	£28
Under 16	£17
OAPs (over 65)	£21
Paddock	£31
Under 16	£17
Park End	£34
Under 16	£19
Family Enclosure	£31
Under 16	£15

Everton E-Ticketing

Before you register to order your tickets, please note that you must have a valid email address and an international Visa or Mastercard. No other credit cards will be accepted.

EVERTONIA

The Official Members' Club for Evertonians of all ages, everywhere.

With membership fees still at £19.99 for adults and £9.99 for juniors, Evertonia is great value.

There are three ways to join:

Call 0870 442 1878;
Visit the Goodison Park Box Office;
Buy online.

Adult benefits for Evertonia (£19.99):

* 1 week ticket priority period to ensure you are first in line to purchase home Barclays Premier League tickets.
* Free entry to Everton reserves and ladies home fixtures.
* Free membership to our Away Travel Club (worth £5).
* £5 voucher off Everton v Fulham and Everton v Reading.
* Free access to the Evertonia members' only section here on evertonfc.com.
* Regular exclusive Evertonia email updates.
* The chance to attend an exclusive fans' forum where you can listen to the opinions of first-team players, have your say and hear fellow Evertonians air their views.
* Exclusive invitation to an open training day to give you an insight into match preparation and what's happening behind the scenes.

Junior benefits for Evertonia (£9.99):

* 1 week ticket priority period to ensure you are first in line to purchase home Barclays Premier League tickets.
* Free entry to Everton reserves and ladies home fixtures.
* Free membership to our Away Travel Club (worth £5) – please note U16s must be accompanied by an adult.
* 1 x £5 vouchers off selected Barclays Premier League fixtures (value £5.00).
* 10 per cent off our exclusive soccer camps.
* Your chance to attend our exciting Christmas Party to meet the players and much more.
* Exclusive invitation to an open training day to watch David Moyes put the players through their paces.
* Free access to the Evertonia members' only section on evertonfc.com.
* You could win tickets to watch Everton at Barclays Premier League away games.

GETTING TO GOODISON

How to get there - by car
(From the north and south) take the M6 exit at junction 26 onto the M58 and continue until the end
At the gyratory, go left to join the M57 Junction 7. Exit the M57 at Junction 4 to turn right into East
Lancashire Road (A580). Follow the road, across Queen's Drive, into Walton Lane. Goodison Road is
less than a mile along, on the right.
From the East:
From the M62, exit Junction 6 onto the M57, go to the end of the motorway and then left onto the
A59 Ormskirk Road. Then follow the same route for north.
From the West:
From the M53, continue to Wallasey and follow Liverpool via the Kingsway Mersey Tunnel. Turn left
at the end into Scotland Road, taking the right fork to the A58 Kirkdale Road. Follow the road round
for two miles and Goodison will appear in front of you.

How to get there - by train
Kirkdale Station is the closest to Goodison on the Northern Line (about a mile away), although
Sandhills Station the stop before has the benefit of a bus service to the ground (Soccerbus). Both
stations can be reached by first getting a train from Liverpool Lime Street (which is over 3 miles
from the ground) to Liverpool Central (Merseyrail Northern Line), and then changing there for
trains to Sandhills (2 stops away) or Kirkdale (3 stops). Note: only trains to Ormskirk or Kirkby go
to Kirkdale station. A taxi from Liverpool Lime Street should cost between £5 and £7.

How to get there - Soccerbus
There are frequent shuttle buses from Sandhills Station, to Goodison Park for all Everton home
Premiership and Cup matches. Soccerbus will run for two hours before each match (last bus from
Sandhills Station is approximately 15 minutes before kick-off) and for 50 minutes after the final
whistle (subject to availability). You can pay as you board the bus. Soccerbus is FREE for those who
hold a valid TRIO, SOLO or SAVEAWAY ticket or Merseytravel Free Travel Pass.

How to get there - by bus
Take a 102 (daytime only) or 130 (evenings/Sunday) from Paradise Street Bus Station or a 19/19A,
20, 21, 130 (evenings/Sunday), 311, 345 or 350/351 from Queen Square bus station directly to the
ground.
Other services which serve Goodison Park (not from the city centre) include 68/168 (Bootle-
Aigburth Vale) and 62/162 (Crosby/Bootle-Penny Lane).

How to get there - by air
Liverpool John Lennon Airport is around 11 miles from the ground, and taxis should be easily
obtainable. Alternatively, you can catch the 80A or 86A bus to Liverpool South Parkway Station, and
take a Northern Line train to Sandhills to connect for the Soccerbus service.

To check bus and train times (8am-8pm, 7 days a week):

Traveline Merseyside   0870 608 2 608
Soccerbus   0151 330 1066

EVERTON STADIUM TOUR

Have you ever wondered just what goes on behind the scenes at Goodison Park?
Have you dreamed of walking down the tunnel to the roar of 40,000 fans?
Do you want to know where exactly in the dressing room your favourite players get changed or where the players relax after the game?
If so then Everton Football Club is offering you the chance to experience Goodison Park at first hand!

A chance of a lifetime awaits you, as you experience the magic of our Goodison Park Stadium Tour. A warm welcome awaits all of our visitors to Goodison Park, particularly those with special needs, notification is required on booking, thus enabling us to cater fully for your groups needs.

Tours do not operate on a matchday or on the afternoon before a first-team home fixture.

All tours are non-smoking and last approximately one and a quarter hours. We can accommodate individuals, small parties or large groups. We also offer discounts for group bookings or people with disabilities.

Prices:

Adults	- £8.50
Children U16/Senior Citizens	- £5.00
Family Ticket	- £20.00 (2 Adults and 2 U16s)
U5s	- Free

To book call 0151 330 2212 or email stadiumtour@evertonfc.com

Everton legend Dave Hickson is a regular guide on the Everton stadium tour

EVERTON TV

The club's official online television channel, **evertonTV,** was launched in June 2006 with the aim of enhancing the Everton experience for supporters of all ages.

The service offers unprecedented access to the manager and the first-team squad, as well as unrivaled coverage of the academy and reserve side.

We also have an extensive web-based online video service, including match action from the most recent games, as well as archive footage from past matches.

There is live streaming of radio commentary from every Everton game, along with live video streaming of friendly matches where possible.

Also available is a channel devoted solely to the voice of the fans, with supporters able to send in their own video as well as video clips filmed by the evertonTV camera crew, in and around Goodison Park, as well as the other Premier League grounds when Everton are on their travels.

Other content includes community-based clips, highlighting the club's commitment to the local area while free-to-view content is also available as a taster for people considering the service.

evertonTV is sure to continue to grow and grow. Make sure you don't miss out.

Subscriptions cost £4.99 per month or just £40 for the whole year.
For more details visit evertonfc.com.

evertonTV home page via the official club website

EVERTON WEBSITE

One of the first clubs to establish an official club website, evertonfc.com is one of the most popular football club websites in the country offering news updated daily, regular exclusive interviews with players, managers and coaching staff as well as information about all things Everton.
The website also offers a number of interactive features, such as:

Desktop Messenger:	Provides news updates direct to your desktop.
Everton Chat Live:	Gives registered users the opportunity to take part in web chats with members of the first-team squad on a number of occasions every season.
Screensaves:	We offer a range of personalised Everton screensavers exclusive to the club available for fans to download for free.
Desktop Wallpapers:	A choice of Everton wallpapers is available for fans to download for free.
The Blue Room:	This is a chat forum where fans can go to discuss the current issues at the club. They can create their own forum topic and reply to others. This whole process is monitored by administrators who delete inappropriate messages.
Interactive article features:	We give fans the option of posting a comment in reply to any news article. A user can also click a 'thumbs up' button if they liked the article.
eAuction:	We regularly have signed shirts, photos and balls up for auction but are also unique items that will never be made available ever again, such as match-worn jerseys and boots.
Everton Mobile:	Offers features such as downloadable ringtones, wallpapers, games and icons for your mobile phone, as well as the oppprtunity to receive text and audio alerts.
Lotteries:	You can find information on Toffee Lotto - the Everton FC lottery game, as well as the matchday game - Grab-A-Grand.

Mikel Arteta being interviewed for evertonTV

CLUB STORES

There are currently two dedicated Everton stores, one at Goodison and one in Pyramids Centre, Unit 30, Birkenhead, selling the full range of Everton merchandise. This is also available at the club website or via Mail Order on 0870 442 1878 (select the merchandise option).

Everton FC Official Club Store
Goodison Road, Liverpool, L4 4EL
United Kingdom
Opening times: Mon-Sat 9.00am - 6.00pm
Sundays 11.00am - 3.00pm
Longer opening times on matchdays/nights

Birkenhead Official Club Store
Unit 30, Pyramids Centre, Birkenhead
United Kingdom
Opening times: Mon-Sat 9.00am - 6.00pm
Closed Wednesday and Sunday

Selected JJB Stores also stock Everton products, check jjbsports.com for store details near you. Addresses and contact details are as follows:

Online Store
evertonfc.com

New new home shirt, available at the club shop

EVERTON PUBLICATIONS

EFC

The official Everton matchday programme is published for every home fixture. This includes exclusive interviews with players, managers and coaching staff as well as in-depth club information.

How to subscribe

Phone: 0845 143 0001 (Monday-Friday 9am-5pm)

Website: www.merseyshop.com
(Click 'Subscriptions', 'Everton FC Subscriptions')

The Evertonian

Published on a monthly basis, 'The Evertonian' offers a more in-depth look at Everton in comparison to the programme. The publication contains a number of features with players, managers and coaching staff, as well as superb colour posters.

How to subscribe

Phone: 0845 143 0001 (Monday-Friday 9am-5pm)

Website: www.merseyshop.com
(Click 'Subscriptions', 'Everton FC Subscriptions')

BLUES

Official Everton bi-monthly magazine for youngsters, which includes features for the junior generation such as: Skills tips from Bellefield, cartoons, quizzes and competitions, along with large pull-out posters. p

How to order

Phone: 0845 143 0001 (Monday-Friday 9am-5pm)

Website: www.merseyshop.com
(Click 'Everton FC Publications', 'Everton Magazine Specials' or for subscriptions, click 'Subscriptions, 'Everton FC Subscriptions')

THE EVERTON COLLECTION CHARITABLE TRUST

About:

For over 25 years, Dr. David France has been assembling what has been quoted as the most comprehensive collection of football memorabilia in the world.

A collection of artefacts, letters and other club history, the David France Collection is a timeline of Everton Football Club stemming from the very roots of the club's existence to the present day. Containing items which crystallised and created a nation of blue-blooded Evertonians, the Collection traces the club's heritage back to 1878 and Everton's formation.

Further to this, the Collection is also of the utmost historical importance in illustrating and chronicling the formation of the oldest League system in the world. Featuring some of football's rarest artefacts, of the 10,000 collated items, many pre-date the formative years of the Football League. Boasting an anthology of programmes dating back to 1886, the Collection contains 6,065 programmes covering the club's participation in league, cup competitions, friendly games and reserve-team fixtures between 1886-2001. The programmes provided the starting block for David France's Collection when he first started assembling programmes as a young boy in 1953. Added to his first programme are now all the home and most of the away programmes for every game in which Dixie Dean played for Everton, along with 30 home issues and one away edition from the pre-League era and many more since.

A rare signed club picture from 1952-1953 is part of Dr. David France's extensive collection

THE EVERTON COLLECTION CHARITABLE TRUST

About:

Added to the programmes, season tickets, ticket stubs, medals, photographs, contracts, cash books, handbooks, financial statements and much more, every item amassed assists in mapping out the club's distinguished past and its unparalleled heritage. Other items include cigarette cards, postcards and international caps from the turn of the century. Each piece of memorabilia is unique and special in its own right. Some pieces date back to the pioneering days at Stanley Park, Priory Road and Anfield with the Everton Ledgers shedding much light and insight into the club's history from 1886 through to 1964, including diverse issues such as the choice of colours, selection of team line-ups and the acrimonious split which resulted in the formation of Liverpool Football Club.

With this in mind, the Collection not only documents the history and pedigree of Everton Football Club, but also the history of football in the city of Liverpool, Merseyside, and the world. Its contents provide an ideal tool to educate people in the history of the beautiful game and life in Liverpool itself, however it is also a box of memories opening a wealth of opportunity to look back and reminisce about the past and the glory of Everton Football Club.

Plans:

In September the Trust, which was established in 2005 in an attempt to raise the money to secure the Collection, took a huge step in acquiring it after being granted Heritage Lottery funding.

Once secured, it is due to be housed in the Liverpool Record Office where it will be joined by Everton's own archive, enhancing its unique status.

Lord Grandchester, chairman of the Trust, said: "We are delighted to be able to announce the success of our lottery application, this means that the history of Everton Football Club and indeed the history of football on Merseyside has been safeguarded for future generations."

Left to right: Graeme Sharp, Howard Kendall, Kevin Ratcliffe and Dave Watson were all involved in the Barcelona Cup game in March 2007 organised to raise funds for the collection

EVERTON FORMER PLAYERS' FOUNDATION

The Everton Former Players' Foundation is a charitable organisation that raises funds through public awareness and special events.

For example, the Foundation holds periodic evenings with the players where fans can come and meet their heroes as well as other similar events.

We also offer auction items for sale which are a great way for fans to get their hands on Everton memorabilia and for the Foundation to raise precious funds for the club's former players.

EFPF also benefits from events held by Everton Football Club and supporters associations, like the annual dinners.

The money raised by the Foundation goes towards the financial and medical assistance of former Everton players who did not have the luxury of today's inflated wages. Many players of the past still work today despite being due well-earned retirement.

Some players bear the physical scars of giving their all in the Royal Blue jersey, and the Foundation contributes where it can towards medical assistance that improves the lives of these heroes of days gone by.

The people behind the Everton Former Players' Foundation:

Bill Kenwright - Patron
Alex Young - Patron
Graeme Sharp - Patron
Barry Horne - Patron
Duncan McKenzie - Patron
Laurence Lee - Trustee and Chairman
Richard Lewis - Trustee
Darren Griffiths - Trustee
Len Capeling - Trustee
Gerry Moore - Trustee
Patrick Gaul - Trustee
Barry Joseph - Trustee
David Prentice - Trustee
Rev. Harry Ross - Trustee
Pat Labone - Secretary

New secretary Pat Labone, wife of the late, great Brian, and the Rev. Harry Ross

Website: http://www.efpf.co.uk/

Contact the Everton Former Players' Foundation at:

PO Box 354
Liverpool
L69 4QS
United Kingdom

The Foundation is a registered charity (#1080101) accountable to the Charities Commission.

Every penny is gratefully received and put to very good use.

EVERTON INTERNATIONAL

In line with the Club's objective to continually improve and further develop, a new department was established in September 2005. The International Department was created to grow the Club outside the UK by utilising the existing expertise from all areas of the business.
The objective of the department is to create long-term and mutually beneficial partnerships with other clubs, sporting organisations, governments and commercial partners, where Everton can create a permanent presence in the particular market. Everton believe the only way to have a successful international strategy is to give something back to the community in which you operate and the club utilises, amongst other things, its renowned Football in the Community programmes for this purpose.

The department has already established a strong partnership with the Ontario Soccer Association in Canada, developing a unique community venture called Play Soccer. The purpose of this programme is to encourage youth to 'play soccer' and thereby increase participation levels in football and sport in general.

The club is also working on many projects to assist football development throughout the globe utilising the expertise of our Academy staff to leave a lasting impression on the game overseas.

For more information regarding the international initiatives undertaken by Everton you can also contact International Development Manager, David Cook:

david.cook@evertonfc.com or
+44 (0)151 286 6866.

The work of Everton In The Community is a key driver for the club's work overseas

EVERTON AGAINST RACISM

Club Policy

The policy at Everton Football Club is to help keep racism and hooliganism out of football. As far as we are concerned, racial abuse directed towards any player or supporter will not be tolerated inside Goodison Park. Any offenders of such abuse could be subjected to a ban from our stadium. At Everton, we are committed to providing a football club that is truly accessible to supporters from all sections of the community as we strongly believe that there is no place for racism at Goodison Park or in society as a whole.

Over the years, we have worked hard in implementing this fundamental policy and we are dedicated more than ever to actively eradicating any such behaviour and we urge all our supporters to embrace this ideal.

We also actively support football's national anti-racism campaigns, Kick It Out and Show Racism the Red Card and the principles they stand for.

As a professional football club, we are commited, wherever practicable, to achieving and maintaining a workforce which broadly reflects the communities within which we operate and are conscious that we are in an industry with a very high profile. At Everton, we wish to uphold the principles of anti-racism and equal opportunities in all our dealings, both public and private.

Alan Johnson
Race & Diversity Manager

Tel: 0870 442 1878
email: alan.johnson@evertonfc.com

EDSA

The Everton Disabled Supporters' Association (EDSA) was formed in July 1995 and has a fast growing membership of Everton supporters with disabilities.

The main aim of the association is to represent and promote the interests of disabled Evertonians. EDSA has forged strong links with Everton Football Club, who totally support all the aims and objectives of the association.

There are now over 100 disabled spaces in the stadium, with tickets offered to EDSA members on a rota system, with toilet facilities, souvenir stalls, programme sellers, food and betting kiosks, plus multiple television sets to watch evertonTV.

Membership of the Association is open to any disabled person or anyone representing disabled people.

Applications may be accepted or rejected by the committee at its discretion and the committee shall have no obligation to state reasons for any rejection.

Each member shall pay an annual subscription of £10.00.

Membership of EDSA is also open to any individual or organisation interested in furthering the work of EDSA.

How to join

Telephone: 0151 286 9666 and speak to our chairman Steve Heneghan
Write to: EDSA at 22, Sandon Street, Waterloo, Liverpool L22 5NW
Email: steve@edsa.freeserve.co.uk

EXTRA TIME STUDY CENTRE

THE EVERTON FC STUDY SUPPORT CENTRE

Having opened in May 2001, the Extra Time Study Centre has helped to raise the achievement of children and young people in Liverpool.

The partnership between Liverpool Children's Services, the DfES and Everton Football Club has proved successful, with the club showing tremendous commitment to ensuring the success of Extra Time. Not only have they created an ideal inspirational setting for learning, they are exceptional in providing rewards, access to the grounds including tours and use of club facilities, and involving club staff in learning events.

Current and former players including Joseph Yobo, Victor Anichebe and Richard Wright have visited the centre to help and inspire some 8,000 children from over 200 schools.

With a diverse range of community teaching and learning programmes, which provide unique basic skills and ICT learning experiences, the centre aims to support the educational needs of children in the area and beyond.

Extra Time has undergone transformation and has introduced a range of new multimedia technologies, which establishes Extra Time as a cutting-edge centre for digital creativity through filmmaking, animation, digital photography, video conferencing and music production.

Extra Time's partnership with Liverpool Hope University has also grown significantly and over 250 undergraduates have attended Extra Time since 2004 to work as volunteer Study Supporters.

The centre continues to be supported by Warburtons the Bakers through the provision of healthy eating workshops and a walking bus and Merseyside Fire Service through raising awareness of fire safety amongst young people.

The centre achieved the Quality in Study Support Established status in May 2005.

Address: Extra Time Study Support Centre
                                  Everton Football Club
                                  Goodison Park
                                  Liverpool
                                  L4 4EL

Telephone: 0151 284 0625
Fax: 0151 330 0544

General Enquiry Email: extratime@evertonfc.com

EVERTON CHARITIES

The charity department, established in 1995, accepts requests by email, telephone and letter. We receive requests from schools, major charities and individuals. We also respond to birthdays, weddings and we issue condolence letters when requested.

To send in a request, please email:

charity@evertonfc.com or call 0151 282 9896

Everton Football Club nominates three major charities each year that are strongly supported throughout the year – Alder Hey Childrens Hospital, The Roy Castle Lung Cancer Foundation and Claire House Childrens Hospice.

Alder Hey Children's Hospital

Alder Hey is a world famous hospital that has helped youngsters from all over the globe and whose vision is to continually provide world-class healthcare for children and young people.
Their Imagine appeal is the name of the Alder Hey charity – a fundraising initiative that helps continue their pioneering work, caring for over 200,000 children and young people per year.
Each donation received helps to achieve a little bit more, from researching medical conditions, to buying vital equipment.

To donate to the Imagine appeal please visit:

http://www.imagineappeal.com/

The Roy Castle Lung Cancer Foundation

The Roy Castle Lung Cancer Foundation is the only charity in the UK wholly dedicated to defeating lung cancer, the biggest cancer killer in the world. Established as the Lung Cancer Fund in 1990, two years later entertainer Roy Castle – who was diagnosed with lung cancer – courageously devoted much of the last year of his life to promoting the work of the charity, to which he gave his name. With the money raised, the Roy Castle International Centre for Lung Cancer Research was built. The ultimate vision of the Foundation is to defeat lung cancer.

To donate to the Foundation please visit:

http://www.roycastle.org

Claire House

Claire House is a children's hospice based in Wirral, Merseyside who care for youngsters 0-18 years with life threatening or life limiting conditions.
The hospice serves children and their families from Merseyside, Cheshire and North Wales and is dedicated to enhancing the quality of life, providing specialist respite, palliative, terminal and bereavement care.
To donate to Claire House visit:

http://www.claire-house.org.uk/

The Everton players also choose a charity of their choice, which they will visit throughout the season and help to raise awareness of the campaign they are being associated with.

EFC IN THE COMMUNITY

From the June 2004 Everton Football In The Community (EFITC) has operated as a financially independent, registered charitable company (No. 1099366).

The charity is completely financially independent of Everton Football Club, who is our main sponsor and provides substantial non-financial support.

The charity is governed by a board of trustees that is made up of a balance between Everton Football Club officials and local independent non-Everton staff.

Our vision:

"To motivate, educate and inspire by harnessing the power of football and sport, improving the quality of the lives of all within our community, locally and regionally."

Main Activity Areas:

Schools-Based Development Activities
We offer many services to all schools within and around the Merseyside area (Liverpool, Sefton, Knowsley, St Helens, Halton, Wirral & West Lancs). Activities include practical football, literacy, numeracy, ICT and health education.

Disability Awareness and Empowerment
EFITC are already THE example of best practice for delivering football opportunities for disabled people, but it's not just about football!

Socially Inclusive Activities
EFITC aims to help those who are affected by homelessness, old age, drug and alcohol misuse, as well as providing socially inclusive activities for asylum seekers and refugees towards a goal of crime prevention and reducing anti-social behaviour.

Women and Girls Development
We aim to develop females' participation in the game of football at all ages and levels, and have a dedicated development officer in this area.

If you would like to contact us you can call:

0151 330 2307 or email: community@evertonfc.com

EVERTON TIGERS

Everton became only the sixth football club in the history of British basketball to field a team in 2007. Based around the club's community work and existing community basketball club Toxteth Tigers, the 13th member of the British Basketball League have specifically targeted youth development as one of the main goals.

The senior team will be headed by Toxteth coach Henry Mooney, and the Tigers will be using Greenbank Sports Academy in Sefton Park as their home venue.

YOUNG EVERTON

2007 was the year of youth at Goodison Park with the club officially launching 'Young Everton' in January, 2007.

Much work was done on a series of new initiatives specifically aimed at the next generation of Evertonians.

Under the umbrella of 'Young Everton' the club is hoping to attract more and more young people to support the Blues and help build a long-term future for Everton to support its illustrious past.

Each month there will be something new for young Toffees to get their teeth into and projects will include working within the local community and schools, promoting a healthy and active lifestyle as well as enhancing the matchday experience at Goodison.

Everton chief executive Keith Wyness said:

"Young people are the future of this football club and we only felt it was right and proper to give them their own focus as they play an absolutely massive part in what we do here everyday.

"Perhaps sometimes there has been too much directed at the older Evertonians and whilst all supporters are a priority for us, we hope the youngsters will get something out of what we have planned over the next 12 months and beyond."

To kick off 'Young Everton' the club gave away 1,000 free tickets for the home game with Reading on January 14, 2007.

Further initiatives are set to be launched and unveiled during the course of 2008.

EVERTON IN THE MEDIA

LOCAL MEDIA

Liverpool Echo
Local evening daily, Monday-Saturday.
Saturday edition contains the 'Football Echo'.
Price: 45p

Liverpool Daily Post
Local morning daily, Monday-Saturday.
Price: 50p

LOCAL RADIO

BBC Radio Merseyside
Former Blues winger Ronnie Goodlass provides expert analysis as part of the full coverage of all Everton first-team games. Post-match fans' debate is a regular feature, while football is covered throughout the week, with Fridays Bluewatch programme (8pm) previewing the weekend action.
Frequency: 95.8FM/1485AM

Radio City/Magic
Ian Snodin is a prominent figure of a Saturday during the football season, while full commentary on all Everton matches is provided with guest summarisers including Barry Horne and Graham Stuart, who also contribute to the station's post-match debate.
Frequency: 96.7FM/1548AM

Century FM
Coverage of all first-team games is available, with a daily football phone-in Monday-Friday (known as the 'Legends' phone-in), including Graeme Sharp.
Frequency: 105.4FM

NATIONAL RADIO

BBC Radio Five Live
Coverage of all first-team games is available, with weekend games covered mainly via bulletins from commentators including Stuart Hall, as well as a 606 phone-in of a Saturday and Sunday.
Frequency: 909/693AM

Talk Sport
Regular updates on all league and cup games involving Premiership clubs, plus a regular phone-in 505 show.
Frequency: 1053/1089/1107AM

2008	Jan	Feb	March	April	May	June
Monday						
Tuesday	1			1		
Wednesday	2			2		
Thursday	3			3	1	
Friday	4	1		4	2	
Saturday	5	2	1	5	3	
Sunday	6	3	2	6	4	1
Monday	7	4	3	7	5	2
Tuesday	8	5	4	8	6	3
Wednesday	9	6	5	9	7	4
Thursday	10	7	6	10	8	5
Friday	11	8	7	11	9	6
Saturday	12	9	8	12	10	7
Sunday	13	10	9	13	11	8
Monday	14	11	10	14	12	9
Tuesday	15	12	11	15	13	10
Wednesday	16	13	12	16	14	11
Thursday	17	14	13	17	15	12
Friday	18	15	14	18	16	13
Saturday	18	16	15	18	17	14
Sunday	20	17	16	20	18	15
Monday	21	18	17	21	18	16
Tuesday	22	18	18	22	20	17
Wednesday	23	20	18	23	21	18
Thursday	24	21	20	24	22	18
Friday	25	22	21	25	23	20
Saturday	26	23	22	26	24	21
Sunday	27	24	23	27	25	22
Monday	28	25	24	28	26	23
Tuesday	29	26	25	29	27	24
Wednesday	30	27	26	30	28	25
Thursday	31	28	27		29	26
Friday		29	28		30	27
Saturday			29		31	28
Sunday			30			29
Monday			31			30

July	Aug	Sept	Oct	Nov	Dec	
		1			1	Monday
		2			2	Tuesday
		3	1		3	Wednesday
		4	2		4	Thursday
	1	5	3		5	Friday
	2	6	4	1	6	Saturday
	3	7	5	2	7	Sunday
	4	8	6	3	8	Monday
	5	9	7	4	9	Tuesday
	6	10	8	5	10	Wednesday
	7	11	9	6	11	Thursday
	8	12	10	7	12	Friday
	9	13	11	8	13	Saturday
	10	14	12	9	14	Sunday
	11	15	13	10	15	Monday
	12	16	14	11	16	Tuesday
	13	17	15	12	17	Wednesday
	14	18	16	13	18	Thursday
	15	18	17	14	18	Friday
	16	20	18	15	20	Saturday
	17	21	18	16	21	Sunday
	18	22	20	17	22	Monday
	18	23	21	18	23	Tuesday
	20	24	22	18	24	Wednesday
	21	25	23	20	25	Thursday
	22	26	24	21	26	Friday
	23	27	25	22	27	Saturday
	24	28	26	23	28	Sunday
	25	29	27	24	29	Monday
	26	30	28	25	30	Tuesday
	27		29	26	31	Wednesday
	28		30	27		Thursday
	29		31	28		Friday
	30			29		Saturday
	31			30		Sunday
						Monday

OTHER USEFUL CONTACTS

The Premier League
11, Connaught Place, London W2 2ET
Phone: 0207 298 1600

The Football Association
25 Soho Square, London W1D 4FA
Phone: 0207 745 4545

The Football League
Edward VII Quay, Navigation Way,
Preston, Lancashire
PR2 2YF
Phone: 01772 325800/
0870 442 0 1888
Fax: 01772 325801
Email: fl@football-league.co.uk

Professional Footballers' Association
2, Oxford Court,
Bishopsgate,
Off Lower Mosley Street,
Manchester
M2 3WQ
Phone: 0161 236 0575

Everton Former Players' Foundation
PO Box 354
Liverpool
L69 4QS
Donations can be made by cheque, made
payable to Everton Former Players' Association

Published in Great Britain in 2007 by: Trinity Mirror Sport Media, PO Box 48, Old Hall Street, Liverpool L69 3EB

ISBN: 1 9052 6643 2
978 1 9052 6643 2

Printed and finished by Scotprint, Haddington, Scotland